EMILY HALL TREMAINE

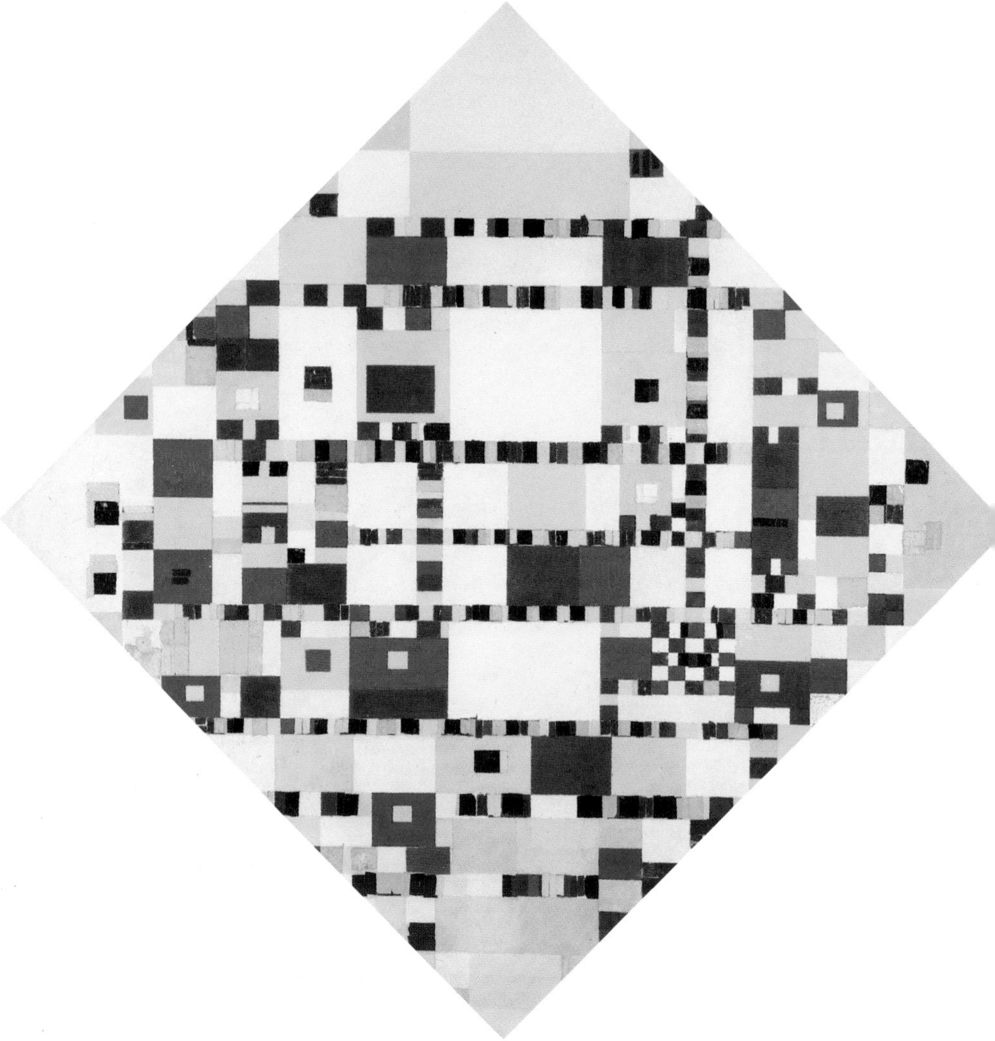

EMILY HALL TREMAINE

COLLECTOR ON THE CUSP

KATHLEEN L. HOUSLEY

THE EMILY HALL TREMAINE FOUNDATION

FIRST EDITION

Frontispiece: Piet Mondrian. *Victory Boogie-Woogie* (1942–44).
Oil and tape on canvas, 50″ × 50″. Permission granted by the Gemeentemuseum den Haag.

Library of Congress Cataloging-in-Publication Data
Housley, Kathleen L.
Emily Hall Tremaine: Collector on the Cusp / Kathleen L. Housley. —
1st ed.
    p.   cm.
Includes index
ISBN 0-9705011-0-2
Library of Congress Control Number: 00-093291

Published in the United States by the Emily Hall Tremaine Foundation,
290 Pratt Street, Meriden, CT, 06450

Distributed by University Press of New England, Hanover and London

Designed by Richard Hendel. Set in Minion type by Tseng Information Systems.

CONTENTS

ACKNOWLEDGMENTS

This book would not have been possible without the support of the Tremaine family who have graciously shared both memories and memorabilia. Cognizant that their own love of art was nurtured by Emily Hall Tremaine, they encouraged me to seek behind the surface facts of her life to comprehend the nature of her artistic vision. Burton G. Tremaine, Jr., and Dorothy Tremaine Hildt, Emily's stepchildren, supplied much-needed information about the 1940s and 1950s. Burton G. Tremaine, III, John M. Tremaine, Janet Tremaine Stanley, and Sarah C. Tremaine provided a clear picture of what it was like to be Emily's step-grandchildren growing up in the turbulent 1960s. Catherine Tremaine's recollections increased the scope of the chapters dealing with the 1970s and 1980s.

Sally Bowles, president of the Emily Hall Tremaine Foundation in Meriden, Connecticut, was a source of encouragement throughout the long process. Nor could I have completed the task without the help of Kathleen Mitchell, administrator at the foundation. She started to work for the Miller Company in 1963, becoming secretary to the Tremaines in 1966. Among her responsibilities from then until Burton's death in 1991 was the administration of the art collection.

I want to thank Nicholas Fox Weber, director of the Josef and Anni Albers Foundation in Bethany, Connecticut, and Gregory Hedberg, curator at the Wadsworth Atheneum at the time of the Tremaine exhibition, for their scrupulous review of an early draft. I am also indebted to Eugene Gaddis, archivist, and Ann Brandwein, assistant archivist, at the Wadsworth Atheneum in Hartford, Connecticut. Staff members at the Museum of Modern Art were supportive, especially Michelle Elligott, assistant archivist.

Three foundations were forthcoming with information: Brenda Danilo-witz, curator at the Josef and Anni Albers Foundation, provided insight into the problematic relationship between the Albers and the Tremaines. Gary Milligan at the Buckminster Fuller Institute in Santa Barbara, California, un-earthed a letter from Emily to Fuller about his Dymaxion house. Margo Stipe at the Frank Lloyd Wright Foundation in Scottsdale, Arizona, provided me with the lively correspondence between the Tremaines and Wright.

In Butte, Ellen Crain, director of the Butte–Silver Bow Public Archives, was tireless in locating articles about the Hall family. Erin Sigl, owner of the Cop-per King Mansion, originally the home of William Andrews Clark and now a bed-and-breakfast, went out of her way to help me gain an understanding of what Butte was like in the first two decades of the twentieth century. Both her knowledge and her hospitality were most appreciated.

In Santa Barbara, the job of locating old articles fell to Michael Redmon, librarian of the Santa Barbara Historical Society. Christina Carbone, architec-tural historian and Architectural Drawings Collection assistant at the Univer-sity of California at Santa Barbara, provided me with access to Lutah Maria Riggs's drawings, photographs, and models of the mansion that Emily named "Brunninghausen."

I would also like to thank Mr. and Mrs. S. Robert Weltz, Jr., present owners of Brunninghausen (although it is no longer called by that name), and Mr. and Mrs. Arthur Baer, present owners of the house in Madison, Connecticut, for being gracious hosts.

Although acknowledgments are usually for the individuals who have made a project possible, I would like to conclude by thanking an institution — Olin Library, Wesleyan University, in Middletown, Connecticut. People may tout computer technology all they want, but it was of little use on this project. The bits of information I needed could only be found the hard way: by scanning indexes in the backs of books, sorting through endnotes, checking citations. Without access to a superior collection of books and articles about art, I would have missed several vital references. Art Librarian Susanne Javorski and As-sistant Art Librarian Marie Keeys were tireless in providing guidance when I was unsure where to turn. There is no substitute for a fine library with open stacks. Nor is there a substitute for a knowledgeable librarian.

EMILY HALL TREMAINE

Do not look for obscure formulas or mysteries. I give you pure joy. Look at my works until you see them. Those who are closest to God have seen them.—Constantin Brancusi

EYES LIKE GIMLETS

Emily Hall Tremaine had "eyes like gimlets," exclaimed Philip Johnson, who was her friend, her architect of choice, and occasionally her rival collector. Tremaine's ability to punch through the turbulence of contemporary art—distinguishing between foolishness and genius, hoax and honest endeavor—filled Johnson with amazement and envy. "I remember the most acute sense of jealousy I had was when the Tremaines discovered Claes Oldenburg and they went down to his store, which is now so famous. I never went. It never crossed my mind. I never heard of it. And I was supposed to know about modern art. That was my business. But it was their business a lot more than it was mine. They bought [Oldenburg's] great *7-UP* right off the bat when the paint was still fresh. They walked right off with it. They did the same thing with Rothko. They had better Klees than I ever had. Better everything. It's a shocker."[1]

Johnson was not the only expert who had deep respect for Emily Tremaine's collecting prowess. To art historian Robert Rosenblum, the Tremaine collection was "so museum-worthy that it alone could recount to future generations the better part of the story of twentieth-century art."[2] Among its more than four hundred works were paintings by Pollock, de Kooning, Warhol, Stella, Johns, and Rauschenberg. However, at the time that the Tremaines began to purchase their works, these innovative artists were, for the most part, not yet recognized by the art world. When people asked her why she was so interested in collecting new works, Emily explained, "You see a prophetic vision, especially if you train yourself to see it. You almost see what's coming through the artist. That's why I haven't been interested very much in reaching back. I'd rather keep looking at what is going on today."[3]

Many other great collectors of modern and contemporary art belonged to the Tremaines' generation, among them Peggy Guggenheim, several members of the Rockefeller family, Raymond and Patsy Nasher, John and Dominique de Menil, Herbert and Dorothy Vogel, Stanley Marsh, Edgar Kaufman, Victor and Sally Ganz, and Robert and Ethel Scull. The quality that set Emily apart was the singularity of her vision. Grounded intellectually in Modern Art, Emily was able to spot developing trends in contemporary art and to assess how they reinforced, rejected, or reinterpreted tradition. This was one of the aspects of the collection that most impressed Robert Rosenblum:

> Confronted here with both the Old and the New Testaments of our century's art (the dividing line falling roughly around the apocalyptic year 1945), we may be surprised to see how intricate the dialogues between these two epochs can become. For me, at least, there are four key works—one hesitates to say paintings, so radical are their breaks with the conventions of the easel picture—that rise to special altitudes over the Tremaine Collection and that provide, in the title metaphor of Baudelaire's "Les Phares," lighthouses of art that can illuminate a vast territory. They are in chronological order, Delaunay's *Premier Disque*, 1913–1914; Mondrian's *Victory Boogie-Woogie*, 1942–44; Johns's *Three Flags*, 1958; and Stella's *Luis Miguel Domínguin*, 1960. So grouped they become a triumphant quartet of canvases that redefine, separately and together, our ideas of what a painting can be. It must have been a rare toughness and consistency of vision that permitted the Tremaines to single out these four disturbing iconic images which assail our preconceptions about a painting as an illusion occurring within a framed rectangular field. For every one of these paintings flouts that tradition.[4]

Born in Butte, Montana, on January 31, 1908, Emily inherited a love of art from her mother and an analytical mind from her father. She began collecting in the 1930s when she was married to Baron Maximilian von Romberg. Her first purchase was the painting *The Black Rose* by Georges Braque. Shortly thereafter, she began to get requests from museums to borrow it. "To me, there was never any joy in anything I could not share, and with this awakening—

that the world was asking that it be shared—I think I became a collector," Emily explained to an interviewer.

Following the baron's untimely death in a plane crash in 1938, Emily's life swerved in a dangerous direction. Precipitately marrying Adolph Spreckels, she was dismayed to discover that he was a Nazi-sympathizer and was prone to violence. Only after their acrimonious and much publicized divorce, and her subsequent marriage to Burton Gad Tremaine, Sr., did she begin again to concentrate on collecting art.

Burton Tremaine was president of the Miller Company in Meriden, Connecticut, which produced lighting fixtures and specialty copper-based alloys. He enjoyed painting as a hobby and had a fine eye for color, form, and industrial design. A newspaper reporter described Burton in later life as "a tall, commanding figure built in the American mold, a man of action with the look we associate with the comradeship and open-handedness of our wide-open spaces." The same reporter described Emily as "small beside him, simply but elegantly groomed, intensely feminine under a matter-of-fact manner. Her deep voice is enriched by a marvelous chuckle like thunder too distant to be threatening. She has the subtlest of smiles."[5] They were totally different in personality as well. He was outgoing and impetuous, she was reserved and calculating, yet their approach to art was complementary. Risk-takers, they loved the thrill of the hunt and the notoriety that came from purchasing the work of young artists before it was scrutinized and categorized by art critics. They reveled in the eventual satisfaction of having their judgment proved correct. They did not buy for speculation, but they were pleased when their purchases appreciated in value. Years later, Gregory Hedberg, curator at the Wadsworth Atheneum in Hartford, Connecticut, during the 1970s and 1980s, evaluated the crucial role that Burton played in the process: "While there would not have been a Tremaine collection without Emily, in my opinion it would have been far smaller and less adventurous without Burton. Working with them on the Tremaine exhibition in 1984, with the hundreds of decisions that had to be made, and remembering my gallery visits with them, it was Burton who often pushed Emily to 'go for it.' In their collecting, while Emily was like a Greek intellectual seeing every side of the question, Burton was like a 'do it now' Roman who acted. He had little tolerance for details."

Beyond the initial pleasure of the hunt and the gratification of ownership, there was the satisfaction that Emily took in displaying the art in ways that were aesthetically pleasing yet thought-provoking. In their New York City apartment and at their home in Madison, Connecticut, she skillfully juxtaposed modern and contemporary art, frequently changing the positions of paintings and sculptures to make intriguing visual connections. Not far from her sculptures by Jean Arp and Giacometti, she carefully balanced an angular and brooding work by Alexander Liberman. Picasso's *New Hebrides Mask* shared wall space with a cartoon titled *I Can See the Whole Room and There's Nobody In it!* by Roy Lichtenstein. Barnett Newman's anguished black-and-white painting *Outcry,* inspired by Christ's last words, "Why have you forsaken me?" hung beside Robert Irwin's tranquil golden orb, transcendently unnamed. When asked about what it was like to live surrounded by such works of art, she liked to quote Brancusi: "I give you pure joy."

How could anyone come to know such a complex and private person with a closely guarded inner life? During Emily's lifetime it was a major dilemma for her family and friends. Some people perceived a single aspect of her personality but were aware there were many other aspects that were hidden. Some saw her as friendly and encouraging; others saw her as cold and controlling. Some considered her deep belief in Christian Science as foolishness that had nothing to do with her art; others viewed it as wisdom that helped define her vision of perfection.

For all her efforts to overcome what she saw as the false materiality of the world, Emily was a sensualist who longed to experience life physically. As a young woman walking the wing of a plane buzzing the polo fields in Montecito, California, and later as a matron exploring transcendental meditation, she wanted to sense the wind—of the Pacific, or of the divine—herself. An illustrative story is told by the artist Richard Tuttle about Emily when she was in her late sixties:

> It was probably in the mid-1970s. She had already had a serious operation, and everybody knew she wasn't in the best of health. I remember a Saturday afternoon in February when the weather was terrible; there was snow and slush everywhere, and it was so cold. For collectors, Saturday was usually gallery-hopping day, but nobody, nobody was out that day. I was at the Betty Parsons Gallery—I don't remember why—when we heard a noise out in the gallery. We went out, and there was Emily. The snow was puddling off her little plastic boots. The day is lost in poetic haze, but somehow I connected this puddling with her feelings for art. More faint-hearted people were at home, but here was Emily. She didn't care that she was making a mess out of the gallery floor. She was out there with a total concern for art. It's a fascinating thing to understand people who live with

art. If you have art in your life, it is a powerful force, a force that can be too much for some people. But Emily had learned how to live with art, how to live with that force. She was a person who could be thrilled by the things that came into her life.[6]

By the time of Emily's death in 1987, the collection that had cost at most $500,000 to acquire was worth more than $84 million, and many of the artists whose early works she and her husband Burton had collected now were members in good standing of the art world, with numerous one-man shows and museum retrospectives to their credit. The enormous escalation in value had led to internecine warfare among museums hoping to be willed the collection and among dealers hoping to handle its sale. The financial appreciation also had led to disillusionment and bitterness on Emily's part. She longed to be esteemed for her perspicacity in buying the great works of unknown artists before the rest of the world became aware of them, but the value of the collection had come to be defined not by inherent aesthetic worth but by the sum the works would bring in the market — and that could only be determined by sale. The Tremaines sold Jasper Johns's *Three Flags* to the Whitney Museum of American Art in 1980 for $1,000,000, which was at that time the highest amount ever paid for the work of a living American artist. Having purchased it in 1961 for approximately $1000, the Tremaines had seen a 1000-fold increase in its value. The irony is that by selling it, Emily got the recognition for which she longed at the same time that she helped fuel the very market that she detested.

Emily attempted to follow Piet Mondrian's aphorism, "If we cannot free ourselves, we can free our vision." Because she considered art collecting "a quest for the sublime," every aspect of life touching on it mattered.[7] She wanted the paint on the walls, the lighting, the color of the upholstery, the cut of her hair, the shape of the breakfast plates, the tint of her glass frames, the slant of sun, even the angle of the earth to be perfect. She wanted in the final analysis to make her entire life a work of art, to merge perceiver and perceived.

"Emily was an original eye," recalled Philip Johnson. "People with an original eye and all the money in the world — it never happens. But she was also highly whimsical in her twists and turns. She was both ornery and generous. She had tunnel vision. It was art. That was her universe. She not only knew about it but she put her money where her mouth was." Johnson paused, then added reflectively, "I want her back."[8]

Butte and its immediate vicinity present as ugly an outlook as one could wish to see. It is so ugly indeed that it is near the perfection of ugliness. And anything perfect, or nearly so, is not to be despised. I have reached some astonishing subtleties of conception as I have walked for miles over the sand and barrenness among the little hills and gulches.
—Mary MacLane

CHAPTER ONE

BUTTE

Emily Hall, the woman who would devote her life to surrounding herself with beauty, was born in Butte, Montana, the city that author Mary MacLane asserted was "near to the perfection of ugliness." It was a description in which Butte took perverse pride, in the same way that a battered prizefighter is proud of his misshapen face, paid for with his own blood.

In 1908, the year that Emily was born, Butte also liked to boast that it was the "richest hill on earth," and the "biggest mining camp in the world," and it could prove both claims. The city was a mile high, just west of the Continental Divide, and its mining shafts were sunk nearly a mile deep, with approximately 3,000 miles of tunnels. In 1864, men had discovered gold and silver along the beautiful meandering stream they named the Silver Bow. Then they found copper in a place a few miles to the east called Baboon Gulch. They renamed that place Butte, after one of its principal geographical features, and set to digging. With the spiraling need for copper, driven by Thomas Alva Edison's discovery of how to harness the power of electricity, the fortunes made in this metal dwarfed the fortunes previously made in gold and silver. By the 1890s, the "Copper Kings," as the three principal mine owners in Butte were called, were making millions of dollars a month.

Butte was a strange, dangerous, hell-roaring town that swaggered with pride in being one of the roughest and richest places around. Although Butte had stone and brick commercial buildings in Gothic and Beaux Arts styles that looked as if they had been transplanted from a prosperous eastern city, it also had a red-light district, called "the Line," that cast its glow far and wide. There was a well-known verse that went, "First came the men to work in the mine, then came the ladies to live on the line." Alcohol-induced violence in and around the saloons was as common as fatalities in the mines. The police called the city "an island of easy money entirely surrounded by whiskey." Butte had the reputation of a good-time town; but for many — especially miners and prostitutes — the good times were too short.

None of these characteristics were unique to Butte. Other western towns were equally infamous. What set Butte apart was a feeling of compression. Millionaires who were in the same league as the Vanderbilts and the Morgans lived in ornate mansions just blocks away from the hovels of Chinese laborers and the "cribs" of prostitutes. The standard building lot was only twenty-five feet wide because the land that really mattered was not on the surface: it was below ground, went straight down, and was seamed with gold, silver and copper. As a result, Butte was a place of bitter paradox, where what once had been naturally beautiful had been either blasted or poisoned. Joseph Pennell, an artist who visited the city in 1916, described it as a mountain "crowned not with trees but with chimneys. Low black villages of miners' houses straggle toward the foot of the mountain. The barren plain is covered with gray, slimy masses of refuse which crawl down to it — glaciers of work — from the hills. The plain is seared and scorched and cracked with tiny canyons, all their lines leading to the mountain."[1] There were no trees because all the timber for fifty miles around Butte had been cut to provide support beams in the mines. The tree trunks, shorn of bark, cross-braced and pegged, now rose in the darkness underground, holding up the earth into which their roots had once sunk. Smaller trees and branches were fed into the huge open-hearth copper smelters that cast a heavy pall of sulfurous smoke over the city and the surrounding land. That which was not cut simply died. On the "richest hill on earth" not even a blade of grass grew. The once pure stream with the lovely name of Silver Bow Creek now ran with arsenic leached from the copper tailings. Any animal unfortunate enough to quench its thirst in the Silver Bow died within hours.

In the strange world of Butte, into which Emily would be born, the abstract was beautiful and the real was ugly. If Butte ever offered beauty to young eyes, it was reduced to color and angular geometry. Under the brooding black hoist houses, the main shafts dropped out of sight thousands of feet down into mines with names such as Orphan Girl, Never Sweat, Sun Dog, Vulcan, Wake-up Jim, and Free-for-all. Only the town amusement park, called Columbia Gardens, offered flowers and grass, although even there the real fascination for the young was the graceful curve of its roller coaster.

What prompted Emily's father to move to Butte in 1888 is uncertain. William Hubbard Hall was born in Tallahassee, Florida, on April 27, 1856. During his childhood, his family moved from place to place. They lived for a few years in Mississippi, then Ohio, and finally settled in Charleston, Illinois, where William's father, Dr. Jesse C. Hall, set up his dental practice and also worked as a jeweler, a common ancillary business for dentists because of their ability to work with gold. William's older brother Horace recalled that, following the Civil War, the Hall family struggled with hard times when corn meal and molasses were the mainstays of the family diet. Because they had little money, to Horace, "a dollar looked as big as a cartwheel." However, by the time William was a teenager, the family had settled down and its fortunes had improved. There were four children: Horace, William, Clarence, and Sylvia. At the age of eighteen, Horace decided to leave the cornfields of Illinois and seek adventure as a cattle hand in Texas. In 1872, full of the bravado of a young man new to the West, he wrote to his younger brother William, whom he called Billie: "Well I am still out in the mountains running wild beeves [sic] and ripping around generally. . . . I am going to join the Texas Rangers, will be out a year, going right out where the Comanche dwells, not to make a war treaty neither." The next year he wrote from Willow Creek, Texas, to encourage his brother to join him; but William was not yet ready to seek his fortune out West, regardless of Horace's enticing descriptions of galloping with the Texas Rangers after Comanche.[2] Choosing a more prosaic career route, William headed east and attended the Pennsylvania College of Dental Surgery, from which he graduated in 1877. He set up a practice in Terre Haute, Indiana. It was not until eleven years later that he finally decided to take his brother's persistent advice about going West. His destination was not Willow Creek, Texas, however, but Butte. By that time, the town was already the world's greatest copper producer, and its population was soaring. The railroad brought in immigrants looking for jobs—especially men who had worked in the mines in Ireland and Cornwall—and it hauled out millions of tons of ore.

Besides street names such as Granite, Mercury, and Copper, Butte also had street names that commemorated the place where fortunes were made and lost

William Hubbard Hall was a dentist as well as a businessman in Butte, Montana.

in the trading of copper stock—New York City. That is why William's dental office stood on the corner of Broadway and Columbia Streets, one block uphill (everything in Butte was either uphill or downhill) from Park. The unassuming story-and-a-half clapboard building was large enough to house William's dental office in the front and his residence in the back, which was an ideal arrangement for a thirty-two-year-old bachelor. By all accounts, William's practice grew rapidly, and he soon was highly respected. According to a history of the area published in 1899, "He has a large office, employs several assistants, and avails himself of all the latest improvements. He has also established a dental supply house—the only one in Montana. . . . He has also been the owner of ranching interests at Butte. . . . Dr. Hall is an accomplished gentleman, a splendid dentist, and the people of Butte know it and have accorded him a large and remunerative practice."[3]

There is a story that William became wealthy by being paid for his dental services in Amalgamated Copper stock in lieu of cash. Although it is intriguing to envision a grateful miner (just relieved of the throbbing pain caused by an impacted molar) plunking down a share of stock instead of cash on his way out the office door, the truth is that Hall was a prudent businessman who owned stock in many companies, who was the vice president of the first telephone company in Butte, and who started a successful mining supply business. In fact, his financial dealings became so extensive, that, when he died in 1931, his obituary in the *New York Times* did not even mention the fact that he had been a dentist, identifying him instead as a "mining engineer." An indication of his reputation is his inclusion in the *Butte Blue Book of 1901,* which was "a complete list of the prominent people of the community, with special reference to those who figure conspicuously in the social world."[4]

William's social prominence is confirmed by his close friendship with J. Ross Clark, president of the W. A. Clark and Brother Bank in Butte. Clark's Italianate mansion, with its elaborate front gate, wrap-around porches, and stained glass window, was only a few doors away from William's combination office and house. William was also a friend of Clark's brother, William Andrews Clark, whose mansion made J. Ross's house look like servants' quarters. William Andrews Clark had built the imposing structure on the steep corner of Idaho and Granite Streets in 1884 for $260,000, an enormous sum for the era. It was filled with frescos, paintings, Tiffany stained-glass windows, and intricate woodwork of rosewood, oak and mahogany.[5]

In 1904, William was forty-eight years old, which meant that he fell into the dubious category of "confirmed bachelor," so it was a surprise to Butte society when he announced that he had proposed to a wealthy young widow named Purdon Smith Miller while on a visit to Southern California, and that they planned to be married at her sister's home in Los Angeles before going to Europe for an extended honeymoon. Although she was always called Purdon, her full maiden name was Sarah Purdon Smith, a name she had inherited from her grandmother. She was the daughter of Emma Fahs and Stephen Morgan

Purdon Smith Hall was the daughter of a wealthy industrialist who founded the S. Morgan Smith Company, manufacturer of water turbines in York, Pennsylvania.

Smith, an industrialist from York, Pennsylvania, whose company made water turbines.

William was well established and highly regarded in Butte, even though he was a dentist (not a career that gave one immediate access to society's front parlors), and Purdon's family considered him an acceptable match for their daughter. In a letter to her mother, Purdon tried to overcome any reservations her family might have. "Really the people from Montana carry on so about Dr. Hall being caught and how girls in Montana, heiresses of all degrees have tried for years and years to land him and how grand a character he is, popular and loved until I feel I am marrying a prince."[6]

Purdon's father had moved to California in 1902 with his wife and daughters in an attempt to fight a recurrence of the tuberculosis that he had contracted years earlier. Ironically, this was the second time that the onset of tuberculosis had changed the course of his life and the lives of his children and grandchildren to come, including Emily. In 1870, while serving as a Moravian minister in Canal Dover, Ohio, Stephen Smith suffered his first bout of tuberculosis, which damaged his vocal cords. This calamity forced a change in careers, thereby catapulting the family from an austere to a sumptuous lifestyle, to which they readily adapted.[7]

Prior to his illness, Smith, who liked to tinker, had invented a washing machine. Years later his son Beauchamp ruminated on his motivation: "He had six children and living on a clergyman's salary, I wouldn't be surprised if he had to help with the laundry." The machine consisted of a wooden box inside which were two rubber-covered boards that imitated the action of a washboard when powered by a hand-operated crank. After he could no longer preach, he disconsolately packed up his family and moved to York, Pennsylvania, where he approached the York Manufacturing Company to see if they would be interested in producing his invention. When their response was affirmative, he named the washer the "Success." Mechanically inclined, he went on to design milling machinery and water turbines and established his own manufacturing firm, the S. Morgan Smith Company. Eventually, he became president of the Atlanta Water and Electrical Company, the Delta Power and Light Company, and several mills, and also had part ownership in a gold mine in Arizona. Following his death, the S. Morgan Smith Company would become one of the leading producers of water turbines in the twentieth century, and provided the turbines for Hoover Dam among other large projects, before merging with Allis-Chalmers.

With the rapid influx of wealth came an equally rapid change of class.

Daughters of poorly paid Moravian ministers who designed washing machines on the side did not go to finishing schools, but daughters of industrialists did. Purdon graduated from Miss Ann Brown's Finishing School and attended the Art Students' League in New York City. While there, she developed a lifelong love of art that she would eventually inculcate in her daughters. She also formed an abiding friendship with Edith Dimock, who married William Glackens, a highly regarded American painter of the Ashcan school (named for their frequent choice of gritty urban environments as subjects).

Tuberculosis is an insidious disease, killing by slow degrees. It was in the hope that plentiful sunlight and dry warmth would stem the disease's advance that Smith, his daughters, and his wife had gone to Southern California, but nothing helped. On Easter Sunday 1903, Smith died at the age of sixty four, leaving his children a fortune. His funeral in York, Pennsylvania, was a major event. More than ten thousand people filed by his casket to pay their respects. Because he had served as a chaplain during the Civil War, an honor guard of aging veterans stood at the head and foot of the casket. Five ministers participated in the service, which was so packed the crowds overflowed into the church vestibule and stairways.[8]

After her father's death, Purdon remained in California where she was introduced to William Hall who was there on vacation. From that meeting eventually came their betrothal, and on March 22, 1905, their marriage, at which J. Ross Clark was the best man. An article in the *Butte Miner* trumpeted the event with the headline "Doctor W. H. Hall Takes Bride At Los Angeles, Prominent Butte Dentist Weds Mrs. Purdon Smith Miller — Society Function — Will go Abroad."[9]

Following their three-month honeymoon throughout Europe, they returned to Butte and settled in the house that William had recently purchased for his new bride. It was located on the corner of Broadway and Columbia, directly across the street from his dental office. Built of red brick, with a bay window and a front porch with gingerbread trim, it was a good, solid house, not showy but socially acceptable. Other than a few square feet between the front door and the sidewalk, there was no yard, which was typical of Butte, where buildings were packed tightly together on land far too valuable to waste on lawns.

It was here that the following year on July 30, 1906, Purdon gave birth to twins, Adeline Jane (usually called Jane) and William Hubbard Hall. Young William died shortly after birth.[10] A year and a half later on January 31, 1908, a second daughter was born: Emily Purdon Hall.

It was one of the coldest days of the winter. The daily newspaper, the *Butte Inter-Mountain,* noted that "the minimum temperature as reported by Weather Observer J. R. Wharton's self-recording thermometer was 15° below zero."[11] That was not an unusual temperature for Butte, where winter could be brutally cold, made more so by the winds sweeping across the treeless landscape around the city and whistling forlornly through the head frames that rose high above the shafts. If it were possible for Butte to be uglier than usual, January was surely the month to achieve it. The snow, which in other places in the state was a pure scintillating expanse of white, was in Butte a sulfurous yellow, settling on the houses that hunkered against the hill. With the temperature so low, the smoke from the smelters, furnaces, and cookstoves hugged the ground instead of rising up into the sky over the Continental Divide. But regardless of the frigid temperature outside, in the Hall house there was warmth. As the society page of the *Butte Miner* reported, "Dr. and Mrs. W. H. Hall were made happy on Friday by the arrival of a little daughter, who came to be company for the little sister, who came to gladden their home nearly two years ago. It goes without saying that the Hall household is a happy one." Emily Purdon Hall had blond hair, which darkened to brown as she grew up, a pert mouth, and a serious expression that stayed with her throughout her life. Even in her earliest photos, she furrowed her brows and did not smile, giving her face an attitude of shy thoughtfulness.

Besides Emily's birth, the year 1908 brought another major change to the family. William gave up his dental practice, at least on a full-time basis, so that the family could spend six months each year in Southern California. They left Butte annually in November and returned in June. Other than the year in which she was born, Emily never lived in Butte through one of its infamous winters. Instead of pulling teeth and filling cavities, William became more deeply involved in business and finance, becoming president of the Western Mining Supply Company. In addition to selling mining equipment, the company was an engineering firm that designed power plants.

On November 25, 1909, the Halls traveled back to York, Pennsylvania, where Emily was baptized in the home of her grandmother. Although her mother and grandmother were Christian Scientists, Emily was baptized by the minister of the Moravian Church in which her grandfather had served as minister forty years earlier.[12] Christian Science, founded in 1879 by Mary Baker Eddy, was a new theological graft onto the Smith tree. Its main tenet was maintenance of health and the overcoming of sickness via spiritual purity

Emily Hall at five years old in Butte.

and unity with God. Purdon was an ardent believer and instilled that belief so deeply in Emily that eventually it became pivotal to her comprehension of modern and contemporary art.

However, that linkage between religion and art lay far in the future. First came the years of growing up in Butte. What was it like to be a child in such a strange, crowded place? When nineteen-year-old Mary MacLane wrote her best-selling book about Butte seven years before Emily was born, she spoke of its "deadly thrall," which was one of the reasons she chose to live in New York City when she reached adulthood, a choice Emily also would make. As MacLane wrote, "My hope when I went [to New York] was that I might get local color — not to write with, but to swath myself in — I wanted to gather up great lumps of it and throw it into my unquiet life, to make it of vermilion and indigo."[13] Although Emily never knew MacLane, she shared this senti-ment, as well as the sense of thralldom that pulled them both back to Butte — Emily for visits, Mary for good. Emily only spent the first nine years of her life in Butte, and, of that, only half of each year, yet the place left its mark on her and helped shape her artistic perceptions. For example, more than forty years later, Emily came to own the overpowering canvas by Franz Kline called *Lehigh* (1956). Starkly black and white, it depicted the equally devastated coal mining fields of Pennsylvania by means of jagged, raw brush strokes.

Along with the singular environment came a singular outlook on life. When a siren at one of the mines began piercing the gritty air with an upward wail, a communal shudder seized Butte. People dropped what they were doing and raced to the mine frame from which the sound came. Banker, dentist, society matron, and prostitute waited together to see if anyone would emerge alive from the shaft, his face darkened with smoke and dirt, and fear glinting in his eyes. It made no difference if a person did not work in the mines and had no relative down below. The mines affected everyone in Butte. The mines were Butte. Even when they were asleep at night, the townspeople listened for the wailing siren that signaled disaster far below their beds. This sense of forebod-ing made a strange, strong bond between economic classes and ethnic groups, such as Cornish and Irish miners, that was hard for visitors to fathom. Even when people left Butte for good, this attitude tended to cling to them like flecks of copper. For Emily, just as the painting by Franz Kline evoked Butte externally, the *Moon Garden Reflections* (1957) by Louise Nevelson evoked it internally. To anyone born in Butte, these dark and shadowy sculptures sum-mon up powerful images of abandoned mine shafts, derelict equipment, and figures in coffin-like boxes.

Perhaps because William was in his fifties when Emily was born, or perhaps because he had lived in Butte's surrealistic atmosphere for twenty years, he did not act like a young, ebullient father. Like many men of his era, William was self-made. He did not come out of a wealthy, privileged background, so he was at a loss as to how to relate to his two daughters, born into very different circumstances. Years later, Emily recalled that although he loved her and Jane, he did not know how to play with them or what to give them as gifts. One Christmas he shot a rabbit for her and hung it on the Christmas tree. She also remembered pulling her little wagon through the city streets in the morning, collecting discarded whiskey bottles and redeeming them for two cents. However, these incidents may have stuck in Emily's memory because they revealed the importance her father placed on being parsimonious, even when he was rich. She learned the lesson well; throughout her life, Emily was known for her propensity to count pennies at the same time that she spent heavily.

Aside from the ugliness of their surroundings and their father's tendency to be aloof, the Hall girls had a normal, albeit privileged, childhood. There were school work, music lessons, horseback riding, and taking turns on the swings at Columbia Gardens. There were baby dolls, bicycles, dollhouses, and china tea sets. There were books; Emily's favorite was *Beautiful Children from British Museums,* which was in her mother's library. And there were friendships. Emily was a close friend of Huguette Clark, William Clark's youngest daughter. It was probably through Huguette that Emily first saw a major private art collection. William Clark's collection, amassed over a twenty-year period, included works by Corot, Daumier, Degas, Gainsborough, Rembrandt, Reynolds, Turner and Van Dyke.[14]

Although it was Purdon's desire to take her daughters on long trips through Europe, by the time Emily was old enough to go, World War I had already broken out. Instead they traveled throughout the United States, visiting all forty-eight states, and motoring back to Pennsylvania often to visit Purdon's family. Every autumn, as soon as the temperature began to plummet in Butte and the snow began to fall, the Halls packed up their automobile and headed to the warmth of California. There they would rent a place for the winter, often in Santa Barbara where in January the temperature was usually in the sixties or seventies. It could be rainy from October through February, but the showers were followed by warm bursts of full sun that made the droplets glisten on the palm trees and the cacti. In the spring, the weather was dry and sunny with a breeze off the Pacific. Looking south from the adobe steeple of the Santa Barbara Mission, one could see straight across the boat-filled water to the Channel Islands rising abruptly from the Pacific Ocean. Turning around one could look north across the terra cotta roof tiles and the inner courtyards of the Mission to the steep Santa Ynez Mountains, glinting yellow, with dusty-green splotches of chaparral. Whereas a stunted geranium attempting to bloom in a Butte kitchen window was a prize possession, in Santa Barbara waist-high geraniums grew wild. In Butte, a little patch of grass was much admired, in Santa Barbara the showy bird of paradise, with its eye-catching contrast of orange and blue, was so ubiquitous that rarely did anyone stop to notice. Like the French Riviera, to which it often was compared, Santa Barbara already was becoming a playground for the rich, having attracted the attention of several silent-screen stars, including Charlie Chaplin. Only ninety miles north of Los Angeles, it was an ideal retreat for the Hollywood set. Santa Barbara was not a city where one made money; it was a place where one spent it, having made it elsewhere.

In 1917 the Halls finally left Butte for good, although for many years they continued to own property there and often returned to visit, staying either at the exclusive Silver Bow Club or the Hotel Finlen, which was designed as a copy of the Hotel Astor in New York City. They moved to Portland, Oregon, because William still had business interests in Butte and did not want to be too far away.

In the fall of 1918 Purdon wrote from Portland to her sister Sue Etnier about her fear of the influenza epidemic that was sweeping around the world during the final days of World War I and that would eventually kill approximately 500,000 people in the United States alone by the end of December. "I am in perfect dread these days of telegrams. With all the family exposed to the influenza in different parts of the Earth, I am fearing one or more of them may get a bad dose." In Portland, as in many other cities and towns, the schools were closed, and twelve-year-old Jane and ten-year-old Emily were kept at home, where they tried to keep themselves amused by building intricate doll houses. Purdon wrote:

> The children have been getting orange boxes together, standing them on end and making the most attractive doll houses and it has kept them busy for weeks. It seems to me all the neighboring children have been camping here and bringing all their trash with them, but they have all had a wonderful time. Now that they are completely furnished and decorated (10 and 12-room houses comprising each as many as 6 and 8 orange boxes adorning the boudoir and back bedrooms), I do not know what they will do

if school keeps closed until Xmas. There are a great many deaths from it here and I have been staying away from stores and elevators and keeping the children out of danger. . . . It has been a gorgeous autumn here. Two days ago I walked over 8 miles. I enjoy the tramps around these mountains. Emily and Jane go with me sometimes. Emily doesn't like walking at all, but when she sees me starting off alone, although her 'leg or knee or foot hurts' when I suggest a walk to Council Crest or somewhere equally as difficult, she invariably comes running after me because she doesn't like me to go alone. She thinks it is dangerous and lonely for me and she cannot stand me to take the chance alone. I never go more than a two-hour tramp with her. She leads me on some of their horseback trails and is so delightfully entertaining that I adore having her with me. She reads and remembers what she reads and tells me so many events of interest that she seems more like a grownup companion than a child. Her adorable affectionate nature, always ready to help me or give me a little caress of some sort, makes me tremble for fear she might marry some brute who would not appreciate her fine nature. I don't mean that she is a saint by any means for she can fight to a finish almost any child in the neighborhood and does it when she doesn't get fair play but it takes very little to lead her to letting her higher self rule her.[15]

Fortunately the Halls weathered the influenza epidemic, and with World War I finally over and peace returning, they got the long-awaited chance to take the girls on a tour of all of Europe and Northern Africa, giving special attention to museums from London to Cairo. Their early education had been relatively straightforward, partially because the war had kept them from traveling extensively, but from here on they were taught by a long string of tutors with interludes spent in boarding schools. Although rich in foreign languages and the history of art, their education lacked consistency, as Emily recalled: "My mother decided that we could learn French more quickly if we didn't go to school but had tutors and in choosing tutors, she would also choose art teachers. They'd take us around Paris and teach us about art as well as the language. We had one woman from the Beaux Arts who was wonderful. We'd spend every afternoon with her either at the Gallery Luxembourg or the Louvre or smaller galleries. She was a very intelligent woman, and I think in that year or two I probably picked up more than I would have in a regular course. I got a fairly good sense of quality and history. I really had very little formal education. My mother liked to travel and we just went to school when we lit someplace. I think I went to twenty schools probably. If

Emily Hall on a hunting trip.

my parents wanted to spend their winter in Egypt, we'd go to Egypt, and if there was a school in Egypt, okay. If there wasn't a school, they would get a tutor for us."

For Emily, one of the most positive aspects of such an artistically peripatetic lifestyle was the fact that she came to see art as not only exalted but also commonplace, a normal part of each day. Looking back on her early years, she expressed a regret that her mother had not availed herself of the opportunity of buying for each daughter a painting by Monet, as had been suggested by a friend. "I could have been a Monet collector at twelve," Emily recalled.[16] She regretted even more missing out on the chance of visiting the artist's studio. Instead, she had to settle for collecting postcards of artwork from Botticelli to Van Gogh. She mounted them carefully in a scrapbook that she created herself from hand-crafted Italian paper. She considered it her first collection and it went with her on the family's frequent trips. It would be years before she would have the wherewithal to begin collecting original art, but the impulse—first to understand and appreciate, then to own and assemble in an ordered manner—was already there in her teens.[17]

Whenever they returned to Santa Barbara, the Hall girls attended various private schools and encountered the normal social hurdles of being teenagers. When she was fifteen, Emily complained to her father by letter that the school she was attending would not allow her to have a phonograph in her room because it would detract from studying. She also complained about Jane's being allowed to use the car more than she. She considered the car to be an important means of impressing her friends. In his reply her father, who was in Butte at the time on business, upbraided her gently, "I am afraid, my dear little girl, that you over-estimate Jane's advantage over you in having the use of the auto. . . . After school begins she will not have the car and until then it is my wish that you have as much command of it as she. Your mother is the one to say when it should be used and the use it is put to. The mere fact of having things to attract people does not make friends. It is quite as likely to make people envious and spiteful. Friends, the kind that one wants to have and keep, can not be bought.[18]

In 1924, when William was sixty-eight years old, the Halls decided to settle down permanently in the Montecito section of Santa Barbara, although they still spent six months a year in Europe, Washington, D.C., New York City, or wherever else the spirit of travel moved them. They purchased the magnificent Glen Oaks mansion from the estate of James Hobart Moore. The purchase price was $175,000 for the forty-acre tract. Initially called Field Place, it had been built in the 1890s for a relative of Stanford White, the renowned architect. Even by Montecito standards, it was unabashedly grand. Because Moore, an avid four-in-hand driver, owned fourteen horses, numerous carriages, and three cars, it had a vast stable and garage. There were also rustic bridges that crossed scenic gullies, a reservoir, sloping lawns across which live oaks sprawled, and an ornate main gate. Not content with what was there already, the Halls converted one of the buildings into a school for Jane and

Emily and constructed a recreation building complete with a bowling alley. Eventually there would be a swimming pool. Emily's bedroom on the second floor was filled with an assortment of objects acquired in Europe: a foot-tall bronze statue called Dancing Satyr, a pair of bronze faun vases, an English flintlock pistol, an antique sixteenth century Roundhead helmet, a seventeenth century engraved helmet, a pair of steel gauntlets, and a coat of chain mail. There were also artworks in the house, the most valuable being the *Duchesse de Dreux Breze* by Nicolas de Largilliere, painted in the late 1600s or early 1700s, but although Purdon appreciated art, she and William were not collectors.[19]

Despite the new schoolroom, Emily's education continued to be a hodge-podge of different schools and tutors, but inconsistency in classroom instruction does not necessarily mean insufficiency of learning. Although over-wrought with a teenager's sense of the dramatic, a piece entitled "Philae" that sixteen-year-old Emily wrote for the *Silver Quill,* the literary journal at Miss Ransom's and Miss Bridge's School in Piedmont, California (yet another school that she attended briefly), reflects her worldly perspective and presages her interest in form and color. The essay is about an Arab saying his prayers to Allah on the top of a temple "dedicated to an earlier creed."

> A mass of perfect architecture, cold and silent as a tomb, awe-inspiring in its majestic splendor, the temple cast a saturnine cloud about those who sailed through the vast portals or walked atop its mighty walls. The palm trees, now black against the flaming sky, were like sinister shadows which slowly, as the light decreased, changed their forms and became hovering genii guarding their sacred charge. The light waned, and the feathery clouds changed from brilliant crimson to soft rose and then to violet.[20]

In 1927 at a coming-out party given by her parents, the beautiful nineteen-year-old debutante with dark, curly hair and soulful eyes was introduced to a German baron named Maximilian Edmund Hugo Wilhelm von Romberg. They recognized each other at once, for they had met several years earlier as young children when they were both touring through Egypt with their families. Now sixteen years old, the young baron was already extremely handsome with brown hair that he wore slicked back, blue eyes, and a chiseled profile that deserved to be minted into a coin. He was trained in the sports of European nobility—riding and fencing—yet was thoroughly American in his love of everything fast and dangerous, which would in time include cars, planes, Hollywood-style parties, big-game hunting, and generally living on the edge.

A newspaper article written a few years after the marriage of Emily and Max gave the following account of their instant infatuation:

> It was the culmination of the fairy tale romance that began in 1922 in Cairo, Egypt. There Baron von Romberg, traveling with his tutor and the Baroness-to-be with her governess were introduced by Gali-Gali, the world famous magician, on the porch of Shepherd's. It was not exactly a formal introduction as Gali-Gali simply chose the two youngsters to help with one of his tricks. It was a trick in which he gave a shilling to the little boy on one side of the porch and a half crown to the little girl on the other side. When the trick was over the little girl had the shilling and the little boy the half crown, but they were still on opposite sides of the porch. Although they saw one another from time to time at European resorts, they didn't get any nearer than they were on the porch of Shepherd's until five years later on the other side of the world in Santa Barbara, California. There they met at the debut party given for Emily by her parents, Mr. and Mrs. Hall of Montecito. They remembered one another at once and six months later their engagement was announced. So naturally everyone said it was fate, but the little girl said she just wanted to get her half crown back.[21]

Absolutely smitten with each other, Max and Emily wanted to get married immediately. On February 4, 1928, Max wrote to Emily: "Please excuse any scrawls in this letter but I have today received some of the nearly best news in the world. To wit: Your honorable father has to my honorable mother consented to our union in (un)holy matrimony the minute I reach 18. What could be sweeter darling except that we could get married right away. . . . With all my love, your little Heidelberg." To reach 18 faster than the natural flow of time would allow, Max had added a year to his age, telling William Hall that he was born in 1910. On March 7, the sixteen-year-old baron planned to celebrate his eighteenth birthday.

Why should one spend the hours of life on formulae, semi-colons, and our crazy English spelling? I don't believe God made man to fiddle with pencil marks on paper. He gave him earth and air to feel. And now even wings with which to fly. — Charles A. Lindbergh

CHAPTER TWO

THE GERMAN BARON

Baron Maximilian Edmund Hugo Wilhelm von Romberg carried a heritage as long and heavy as his name. He was the only son of one of the first German officers to be killed in World War I — Baron Maximilian Conrad Joseph Gustave Felix Edward von Romberg. He was the grandson of Baron Wilhelm von Romberg, First General of the southern troops in the Franco-Prussian War. Max's mother was Antoinette MacDonough Converse, daughter of a wealthy, old-line Massachusetts banking family. Her wedding to the baron in July 1907 had been a major society event, linking European nobility with Boston Brahmins.[1]

Little Max was born on March 7, 1911, in Wiesbaden, a famous spa in southern Germany dating back to Roman times. Its many hot springs and flower-filled parks attracted visitors from all over the world. Since the unification of the German states in 1871 under Otto von Bismarck, Wiesbaden had served as a Prussian district capital. Max's father, a captain in the Eightieth Prussian Fusiliers, was killed on September 23, 1914, at the age of thirty-seven, only fifty-one days after Germany declared war on France. In the First Battle of the Marne, which took place throughout September, German troops attempted to sweep through Alsace Lorraine toward Paris but were forced to retreat short of their goal. Captain von Romberg fell at Cerny, which came under intense artillery bombardment on September 23. Suddenly a widow, Antoinette tried to re-order her life and that of her son. To attempt a trans-Atlantic trip back to her own family was risky, in spite of the fact that the United States was at that point a neutral nation, but to stay in Wiesbaden was also risky, because of its location in the southwest corner of the German Empire near Alsace Lorraine, which France was determined to reclaim. Antoinette made the uneasy decision to stay in Wiesbaden with her little son.[2]

Only three years old at the time of his father's death, Max was the nineteenth in his family to hold the title of baron, which extended back more than one thousand years. This was a heavy heritage for a fatherless young boy to carry, especially after the Great War came to an exhausted end. In the United States at that time, the title of baron would have caused him to be branded as a "Hun" or a "Bosch." On the other hand, in Germany he would have been suspect because his mother was a Yankee, notwithstanding his father's death in battle, which made him a hero. It is not surprising that Max and his mother chose to travel during the 1920s, never settling anywhere, though Max always called Wiesbaden his home. Several times they visited Santa Barbara, where Antoinette had relatives. Eventually she married Richard Wayne, a star of silent films, and moved to Nice on the French Riviera. As for Max, by the time he met Emily Hall, he was already dashing, passionate, and reckless. His love for her immediately took on all the elements of high romance. When she went with her parents to New York City early in 1928 to shop in preparation for the wedding, there were red roses waiting for her at the Hotel Gotham. Max sent a steady flow of telegrams ending "Lyric Love and How," and signed "Heidelberg," one of the secret nicknames the two teenagers used between themselves. He was so young that, before he was allowed to come to New York, he had to make arrangements with his tutor to send him his lessons by mail. Emily's letters to him were awash not only in love but in witty humor. "We've been shopping madly all day—it's just as well you're not here because I seem to anchor myself permanently to each and every shop window till Mother's left arm is exhausted dragging me on. . . . Get ready to tie yourself in small knots of wonder. Mother actually is having someone design a wedding gown for me." She described the various dresses she had already tried on and had not liked, and resorted to sketching one gown, appending a caption. "Note safety skirt, can't execute rear-kick, damn. The only favorable idea advanced for this outfit is the veil over the face. One look at my face and they decided to use the veil double. It's supposed to be a Juliet effect, but I keep remembering Romeo died of sorrow."[3]

The marriage of Emily Hall and Baron Maximilian von Romberg, April 14, 1928, in New York City. She was twenty years old and he was seventeen.

At 4:00 in the afternoon on April 14, 1928, before a congregation that comprised ambassadors, millionaires, family from York, and friends from Montecito and Butte, Emily Purdon Hall married Maximilian von Romberg at the Episcopal Church of the Transfiguration in New York City, known affectionately by New Yorkers as "The Little Church Around the Corner." Max was then pretending to be eighteen and Emily was twenty. Coiffed in a Juliet cap with a tulle veil and carrying a sheaf of calla lilies, she wore a medieval-style princess gown designed by de Long. It was of cream-colored satin that swept back into a train draped with tulle. Her sister Jane, her maid of honor, wore a gown of spring green taffeta with a natural-colored straw picture hat trimmed with green and pink ribbon. The bridesmaids in pink taffeta frocks included Huguette Clark, William Andrews Clark's daughter, and Margaret Alexander, another close friend. A reception followed at Sherry's, which had long been one of New York City's most swank establishments. An article on the society page of the *New York Times* said that after a wedding trip to Washington, D.C., the couple would divide their time between Wiesbaden and Boston.[4] Max was planning to attend Harvard the following fall.

From April until September, when classes were to begin, the couple settled into Glen Oaks and whiled away their time attending parties and learning how to fly airplanes. Flying had become a national craze. Only a year before, after several pilots had been killed in the attempt, a tall, handsome mail pilot named Charles Lindbergh had riveted the nation with his solo flight across the Atlantic. As all the newspapers proclaimed, it was a daring exploit for the young man previously nicknamed "Slim" but henceforth called "Lucky Lindy." From the moment he set the wheels of the *Spirit of St. Louis* down in Paris, Lucky Lindy could not go anywhere without reporters waiting to snap his picture and get details of his flight. So it was in Santa Barbara. Two weeks before the von Romberg wedding, Earle Ovington, the owner of a small air-field in Santa Barbara, observed a plane circling overhead. Because few planes used the field, children had taken over the expanse of grass to fly kites, whose long white tails fluttered beneath bright patches of color against a blue sky. Ovington dashed out to tell the children to reel in their yards and yards of string, then hustled them to the side of the field. Since there was no windsock, he held a handkerchief above his head so that the unknown pilot could determine the wind's direction and land without mishap. When the plane set down and taxied to a stop, and the pilot stepped out, Ovington was overwhelmed to find it was Lindbergh. As it happened at every place he landed, reporters soon got word of his arrival and raced to get photos and interviews, but Ovington managed to shepherd him away to safety.

Just as had the rest of the nation, Santa Barbara caught the flying fever, and no one had a worse case than Max. If a young man felt the need to test himself against the elements, flying was the way to do it. Max liked to tell reporters that he came from a warrior family. Without any battlefields on which to prove his mettle, Max chose the sky, soon taking on the playful epithet of "a son of a Beech" for his devotion to a series of Beechcraft airplanes. In June 1928, having completed their training, including the crucial solo flight,

Emily and Max traveled to the East Coast, picked up their first plane, donned leather flying helmets, goggles, and flying suits, and headed cross-country. They hopped from airfield to airfield, finally reaching Los Angeles, where their names were engraved on a gold plate at the Ambassador Hotel as one of the first twenty-five air arrivals. From there it was only a short hop up the coast to Santa Barbara.[5]

Max had hardly settled back down to life on the ground before he lost his driver's license for reckless driving and was fined $75.00.[6] The pattern of their marriage was set: Max sought danger at high speed or great height. He would play polo as if the opposing team were an attacking army. He would come so near to being killed — in planes, cars, trains and on horseback — that friends were convinced he possessed some kind of powerful good-luck charm.

Lindbergh himself best explained the attraction that people like Max felt to flying: "I began to feel that I lived on a higher plane than the skeptics of the ground; one that was richer because of its very association with the element of danger they dreaded, because it was freer of the earth to which they were bound. In flying, I tasted a wine of the gods of which they could know nothing. Who valued life more highly, the aviators who spent it on the art they loved, or these misers who doled it out like pennies through their antlike days? I decided that if I could fly for ten years before I was killed in a crash, it would be a worthwhile trade for an ordinary lifetime."[7] Max died precisely ten years after he began to fly. Perhaps he too felt that it was a worthwhile trade.

Max's first brush with death occurred in September 1928, just five months after his wedding. He had flown his newly acquired plane to Mines Field in Los Angeles, the terminus for the great cross-country air races that had begun at Roosevelt Field in New York. Such air races were truly aeronautic fairs. While the participants were racing, other pilots and would-be pilots gathered at the terminus to look at each other's planes, trade tales of dangerous exploits, take part in shorter races, and watch daredevils do nosedives and barrel rolls. In Los Angeles, forty thousand spectators were invited to taste "the horrors of war," when nine army airships from Fort Crockett, Texas, "strafed" an imaginary enemy in front of the grandstand. Anyone who got a stiff neck from looking up at the skies for too long could wander through the exhibition building, in which he would see the newest developments in aircraft design, study the details of the powerful Wright engines, and contemplate instrumentation such as the earth-inductor compass, designed to aid pilots flying blind in dense fog or snow.

The excitement of the races was heightened by the ever-present possibility of death. On September 8, the first day of the event, an older type of airplane, called a Jenny, nose-dived into a crash. No one on the ground was hurt, but the passenger was killed and the pilot seriously injured. The next day there were two crashes. The first, from an altitude of two thousand feet, resulted in the death of the pilot and the mechanic. The second crash seriously injured a lieutenant from the aircraft carrier *U.S.S. Langley*, when his plane sideslipped out of a steep bank. But none of these accidents impeded the airshow in any way; quite to the contrary, crack-ups brought out more spectators. Although there was no winner of the nonstop race from New York—every pilot having been forced down en route—the airshow itself was judged a success.[8] On his way home, while attempting to land in Santa Barbara, Max almost became one of the casualty statistics when his engine exploded and the cockpit began to fill with smoke and flame. Emily watched in distress from the ground as the sound of the engine died and the skies became ominously silent. Max narrowly escaped death by making what was known as a "dead-stick" landing (meaning there was no power to the propeller). He set the plane down without injury to himself and with only minor damage to the fuselage.[9]

Max and Emily made an effort to settle down in Cambridge, but, after such excitement, student life proved to be too sedentary. It soon became clear that Max needed to be outside where he could feel the rush of wind on his face and the rush of adrenaline through his veins. Their stay in Boston was brief, but it would have a deep influence on Emily, not apparent at the time. In December, 1928, three students named John Walker, Lincoln Kirstein, and Edward Warburg, fascinated with modern art and troubled by the lack of attention it was receiving, formed the Harvard Society for Contemporary Art. During its brief lifetime, the society was very influential in introducing Americans to this new form of artistic expression just making its way across the Atlantic. Everyone in the art world was well aware of the International Exhibition of Modern Art held at the Sixty-ninth Regiment Armory in New York City in 1914, at which the notorious painting *Nude Descending a Staircase* by Marcel Duchamp had been shown, along with Constantin Brancusi's *The Kiss* and paintings by Picasso and Matisse. The director of the Societé Anonyme in New York City, Katherine Dreier, was doing her utmost to bring attention to modern art. Boston, on the other hand, seemed particularly resistant to anything new in art, and the Harvard Society wanted to change that.

How Emily came to know the three students is unclear, but she may have been introduced by her aunt's nephew A. Everett Austin, Jr. (nicknamed

Chick), who knew them all well. Only twenty-nine years old, Chick was already director of the venerable Wadsworth Atheneum in Hartford, Connecticut. Under his guidance, the Wadsworth was becoming the most avant-garde museum in the country, exhibiting works by many modern artists, including Picasso, Matisse, Derain, and de Chirico. But Chick's fascination with new forms of art went far beyond paintings, and under his guidance the Wadsworth presented modern ballet, theater, and music. Suave, urbane, and utterly charming, Chick seemed to know everyone in the world of the arts and was delighted to be able to introduce them to one another.

During the year that Max and Emily spent in Boston, the Harvard Society presented groundbreaking shows that included works by Georges Braque and Giorgio de Chirico. The art of these two men was the first that Emily found tantalizing enough to collect. When she and Max returned to Montecito, her mind began to bend toward art, but several years would pass before she concentrated on collecting.

Released from the onerous necessity of attending classes, Max began to travel with Emily. They visited his mother in France and other relatives in Germany, stopping in Paris to purchase clothes, and they stayed for long stretches in New York City, the place they both considered their second home. Wearing the high boots and jodhpurs that pilots of the era favored as flight attire, even though the costume was a fashion holdover from the days of cavalry, they flew to wherever they could set their plane down. Sporty automobiles were another attraction. They drove a Lincoln Sport Phaeton to Montana, where they went hunting. With Max behind the wheel of a Bugatti, they sped in winter over the snow-covered roads of Nice. When cars and planes wouldn't suffice to get them where they wanted to go, they went by ship.

No matter where they went, they tried to return to Montecito for the start of the polo season. Max soon earned the reputation of being one of the toughest polo players on the coast. A reporter wrote:

> It is said that a polo player must have something more than skill and horsemanship to be able to play the game for all it is worth. That certain something is a combination of fearlessness and instinct. There is no doubt but what the young baron possesses all these attributes. If you have never watched him tearing down the field full speed ahead after the elusive ball, there is a great treat in store for you. I saw the baron climb into his car one day. It was one of those great big rakish-looking vehicles powered with oodles of horsepower. He stepped on the starter, threw her in gear, gave her the gun and in about two seconds he was lost in a cloud of dust. If he

handles his polo mounts like he can a gasoline chariot, no wonder he is pointed out on every field as one of the hardest riding players on the coast today.[10]

In many ways Max seemed more like an amiable child than a responsible man. In profile he looked like Rudolph Valentino. He had a boyish charm that women found irresistible and the titillating reputation of a man who openly courted danger. In the world of Southern California filled with glamour couples, Emily and Max were the glamour couple par excellence. They were so photogenic that a photographer did not have to worry about camera angle or light; all he had to do was point and click. In group shots they were always the center of focus, even if they stood to one side; they had that movie-star quality that drew the camera lens toward them and held it there. But it is rare for such couples to achieve long-term happiness. Max and Emily were no exception. They loved each other to the point of obsession, yet their marriage was threatened from within: "the other woman" was Max's incessant need to live dangerously.

The stability in Emily's life was provided by her father, William Hubbard Hall, who was Max's opposite. William had built his career in a hard and ugly place; aristocratic Max wanted only to play. William had come to wealth in his middle years; Max had never known a day without it. In his seventies, William continued to work. In fact, it was to negotiate a business deal that he and Purdon traveled to New York City in the winter of 1930. While staying at the Hotel Gotham, he became seriously ill. He hung on long enough for his daughters to travel to New York. On March 19, with his wife and daughters by his bedside, William died, just shy of his seventy-fourth birthday. There had been about him an air of steadiness and practicality. In a family of women prone to extravagance, his was the voice of moderation and gentle encouragement. He had written to Emily when she was fifteen years old, "Do not wait for friends to come to you. Go to them first. Go with a smile on your face and love of humanity in your heart and try to spread happiness and you will find you will not want for friends."

In her marriage to Max, Emily did not lack for friends, but she did lack steadiness, especially as he became more and more obsessed with polo. He played every chance he got and to the limits of his (and his horses') ability, charging down the 300-yard field, swinging his mallet as if it were a weapon. On April 1, 1933, Emily filed for divorce in New York, charging Max with neglect and "discourtesy" for making her a "polo widow." Five weeks later, the two reconciled, and the divorce did not become final. Emily called the divorce petition an April Fool's joke. Max gave Emily a diamond pin from Cartier in the shape of a polo player, and she wore it pinned to the brim of her hat.

Emily was not without a spirit of derring-do herself. Once she even wing-walked. Later in the day Emily's mother remarked that she had seen a daring young lady wing-walking, whereupon Emily was only too happy to blurt out, "That was me, Mother!"[11] But, clearly, Emily's need for danger was no match for Max's and as a result their marriage continued to be strained. They loved each other but had a difficult time living with each other. Finally, at the beginning of 1935, having once again become fed up with Max's flying, polo, big-game hunting, and driving cars at excessive speed, Emily left her husband for a second time.

On a stormy night in February, Max was driving his $9,000 Cadillac (painted the von Romberg colors of maroon and gray) to Palm Springs when the car skidded out of control, spun off the road, plunged thirty feet down an embankment, and overturned in White Water Creek. The car was totally wrecked ("telescoped" was the word the newspapers used), but Max escaped with minor cuts and bruises. However, his next accident just ten days later, this time on the polo field, was far more serious. The newspaper reported: "In a furious melee during the fifth chukker of the game, the horse ridden by the nobleman collided with that on which Will Andrews, 18, of the Pacific Military Academy, was mounted. The impact hurled the Baron head-first from his mount. He struck the ground with terrific force."[12] Although his skull was not fractured, he was in a deep coma, and at first the doctors were not certain he would live. For the next eighteen days, Emily stayed by his side, all thoughts of divorce gone. When Max finally returned to consciousness, he promised Emily from his hospital bed that he would never play again. The headline of an article in the *Los Angeles Examiner* shouted "No More Polo!" over a photo of Max (pale and unsmiling) and Emily walking arm-in-arm out of the hospital. " 'Never again' vowed the crack mallet-wielder and sportsman as he left Good Samaritan Hospital yesterday, convalescent from a serious skull injury. 'My doctor tells me I could take the saddle again next year, but my wife tells me something a lot different. I've quit the game for her sake.' "[13] To show that he was serious about quitting and about their reconciliation, he sold his string of polo ponies. But unfortunately, his resolve lasted only six months, after which time he received in the mail a new "crashproof" helmet from England, specially designed with a sponge-rubber lining. He begged Emily to allow him to go back on his word, she relented, and he immediately returned to the game. According to one reporter, "sports enthusiasts throughout the

Emily was editor and Max was photography editor of their short-lived magazine Apéritif.

country heralded his return to chukker festivities and it was not long before he was playing harder and faster than ever, but not hitting so well as he once did due to his injury, so after a few months he sold his new string and retired from polo again. However, upon his re-retirement from polo, the Baron was not content to sit idly in the sunshine of his Montecito terrace. With several other well known sportsmen, he organized a series of hunting expeditions that took them to Mexico, Canada, and finally Alaska." [14]

Perhaps to take her mind off Max's dangerous exploits and their troubled marriage, Emily decided to try her hand at publishing a monthly magazine, which she named *Apéritif*.[15] The first issue appeared in 1935. Basically a society magazine, *Apéritif* could also be politically provocative. For the only time in her life, Emily unsheathed her rapier wit in print, proving definitively that she could be as incorrigible and unpredictable as Max. On one page would be an advertisement for a swank restaurant and a photo of a tennis player; on the next page would be a tongue-in-cheek editorial, written by Emily, making fun of the nation's paranoia about Communists:

From an exhaustive two hour study of the Red Menace we are rather be-
wildered to find that any political opponent is a Red. As every candidate is
someone's opponent, a rather alarming state of affairs is here made public for the first time by *Apéritif*. By this method of reasoning, we find that
we are not only being governed from national to city administrations by
Communistic gentlemen, but that there is a hoard of howling office seekers
who, logically, must also be Red. This thought, plus the chronic, ponder-
ous warnings of the *Los Angeles Times* in regard to Upton Sinclair, Stalin
and the Roosevelt Brain Trust, has thrown us into an hysteria, and we have
been prodding the garden with a spade to find a soft spot to bury the silver.

Occasionally *Aperitif* crossed the line into scandal. For the year and a half
that *Apéritif* was published, Montecito society cringed on the eve of each new
issue hitting the news stands. The writer of an article that appeared in the *San
Francisco Chronicle* about the publication surmised that, while the aristocratic
set generally did not mind being satirized, it was different when the person
doing the satirizing was one of their own: "The lady in question, the beautiful, witty American Baroness Emily von Romberg, possesses a lot of energy, a
peppery personality and a mischievous mind that lately has thrown the members of the gilded set into a recurrent state of jitters. Shivers run along aristocratic spines, uneasiness persistently creeps into self-contained souls, and
well-massaged throats contract because of the monthly fear as to what Baroness Emily may do in her magazine *Apéritif* in gibing at the members of her
social crowd."[16]

Max, who had some ability with a camera, was appointed photography
editor. The art director for the early issues was Campbell Grant, a talented
designer and an animator for Walt Disney. Grant would eventually become
highly regarded for his work on the movie *Fantasia,* in particular the "Night
on Bald Mountain" segment for which he was both animator and story director. He was also the animator for *Pinocchio,* and *Snow White.* As a resident of
Santa Barbara just starting out in his career, Grant had considerable graphic
ability and his design for the publication was elegantly spare. Costing ten cents
on the newsstand, each issue had several major articles, short stories, poetry,
and regular sports, fashion, and book review columns.

Even when writing about new spring fashions, Emily could not avoid being
acerbic. For example, immediately after describing a crepe and satin opera
pump, she wrote about the end of Prohibition and its effect on fashion: "Years
ago the one and only Adrian announced that if repeal [of Prohibition] ever
went into effect a new romantic era in women's fashion would be the inevi-

table outcome. He probably based his prediction on the supposition that as soon as ladies' dainty feet could be pried loose from the brass rails of speakeasies the sooner they would cover them in flowing gowns. As usual he is right and hats and gowns this season should almost make men remember when Knighthood was in flower. This is probably too much to hope for but if the new fluttering bits of femininity can at least inspire them to keep cigars out of their mouths while in elevators they will have done their share."

The most infamous issue began when Emily got a mug shot of herself taken at the local police headquarters. Then, on a lark, she convinced several society acquaintances to have mug shots taken as well. According to a full-page newspaper article in the *San Francisco Chronicle* that appeared after the debacle, the pictures:

> looked awful! So Emily had a further idea, or maybe she'd had it all along. Wouldn't it be quaintly amusing to use a number of the photos in a police Rogues Gallery layout in her smart publication! She did so—and to add a touch of realism, she mixed up in the layout several actual mug pictures of real thugs and criminals! The idea was for the reader to guess who were society people and who were criminals. The idea increased readership, and most of the socialites so skewered took it good-naturedly, but not Eleanor Gould Stevens, daughter of multi-millionaire Jay Gould, whose blood pressure shot skyward into the lawsuit stratosphere when she saw her front view and profile identified by a faked convict number printed between photos of a leering pickpocket and a blonde, frowsy gunmoll. Since the magazine had already hit the streets, Emily took a rubber stamp and ink pad, went to all the news stands in the area and blotted out Mrs. Gould's face. But Emily was not contrite. "I still think it was a good idea. When one examines the pictures, it is surprising how little there is to distinguish the elect from the criminal." [17]

To emphasize just how uncontrite she really was, she gave the *San Francisco Chronicle* permission to reprint Eleanor Gould's mugshot to accompany the article on the scandal, thereby giving it far more attention than it got in *Apéritif*.

It was not only society people who came under attack. Emily also courted the opprobrium of artists and writers when she published a short story titled "Artists and Other Rats" by William Saroyan in which he criticized harshly the artificiality of the artistic crowd in a town vaguely reminiscent of Santa Barbara. Only twenty-six years old, Saroyan had a very high opinion of his own ability, to the point that he had sent the story to Emily with a note saying that she could only print it "word for word, just as it is, otherwise no-go." Emily's response, which she printed in a box accompanying the story, showed her typical wit: "O.K., Saroyan, here it is, word for word according to the hard-boiled terms laid down in your letter. For over a week, long-faced friends have warned us of the subscription cancellations that would surely follow the printing of your yarn. And maybe so, for the Lord knows the pure are always with us . . . In spite of that we think the story is great. If you are down our way look us up — the desk behind the stack of letters in the room marked Subscription Cancellation."

More surprising than her barbs at society people and artists was Emily's willingness to print controversial political articles. In May 1935, Carey McWilliams wrote an article titled "Bruno Hauptmann: In memoriam" attacking the "orgy of wildly gluttonous popular glee" over the trial of the man who on flimsy evidence had been found guilty of the murder of the Lindbergh baby. McWilliams was appalled by the 700 newspapermen and 129 cameramen who had descended on Flemington, New Jersey, for the trial and by the frenzy that had been whipped up by William Randolph Hearst, which had made a mockery of any chance for a reasoned decision. In a scathing attack on Hearst, McWilliams contended that "Mr. Hearst was a trifle confused about the trial. Not knowing whether it was to be a game or a show — and not wanting to take any chances, he sent his star sports writer, Mr. Damon Runyon, and his star Hollywood expert, Adela Rogers St. John." McWilliams was equally appalled by the German-baiting that had occurred throughout the trial, citing the prosecutor's bellowing statement to the jury that "no American could commit this." McWilliams added, "Think not that the Hauptmann trial is a trivial incident. For it demonstrates too clearly that ugliness and repressed violence lurk near the surface of the contemporary American mind. We are a violent — not a timid or weak — people. But we want our violence at a distance: we want to indulge our ferocious appetites by reading newspaper accounts of ferocities: we want, not to enact our sadisms, but to read about them. If the scene is placed at a distance, and if it can be witnessed in secrecy, the average middle class American will warm to the carnal indignities, the common bestialities, like a dog to a platter of bones."

Yet another provocative piece was a long review by Esther Blaisdell of Jakob Wassermann's book *Dr. Kerkhoven's Third Existence*. Wassermann, a novelist, had been a victim of Nazi persecution, and Blaisdell quoted his explanation of Jew-baiting by the Germans: "They want a scapegoat. Whenever things have

Emily and Max at a polo match. He holds the issue of Apéritif *that featured on its cover the cartoon of a rider (himself) being kicked into the air by a polo pony, signifying Emily's intent to kick him out of her life.*

gone badly with them, after every defeat, in every difficulty, in every trying situation, they shift the responsibility for their distress upon the Jews. So it has been for centuries."

In February 1936, Emily and Max separated for a third time for the same reason as before — polo — to which Max had once again returned, apparently with his abilities fully restored. A big article in the magazine section of the

Sunday Mirror splashed the news that behind a tale of insurmountable incompatibility was a tragedy of "horses, horses, horses." [18] To announce the separation to her readers, Emily put on the front cover of *Aperitif* a cartoon of a rider unceremoniously being thrown from a polo pony that had a satisfied look in its eyes. At the same time, the two announced that they intended to reverse the old adage of "living together and working apart." Instead they would work together and live apart and to underscore their new relationship, they printed a photo of the two of them reviewing copy for an upcoming issue of *Apéritif.* Unfortunately, the new arrangement did not work any better than the old, and Emily decided to cease publishing *Apéritif* totally.

One of the reasons for her decision to quit publication may have been her health. Years later, in 1969, when Emily was diagnosed with tuberculosis, it became clear that she had suffered a major attack as a young woman but that, because she, her sister, and her mother were Christian Scientists, she had never spoken about it to anyone but her sister. In a letter written in the summer of 1936, her sister Jane refers obliquely to Emily's serious illness. Jane had asked her own Christian Science practitioner (a type of teacher or spiritual facilitator) "to go to work for you at once," and adds, "that is why I was anxious to hear this morning if you became quiet and could go to sleep." After giving her pages of Christian Science advice, Jane wrote, "Keep saying over and over to yourself 'self, when I destroy the thought I'll destroy the thing,' you will find yourself, I am sure, gradually seeing this so called disease as nothing more or less than a product of wrong thinking. The doctors have painted a nice picture for you and you have been willing to accept it as real. Now change the thought. See it only as a product of mortal mind and not you."

Jane was so convinced that thinking the bad thought would bring the thought into reality that she never mentioned in her letter the nature of Emily's problem. The closest Jane ever came in any of her letters to naming tuberculosis were references to Emily's lack of energy and her lungs: "I do hope, dear, that you will not let Error shut out all the health and happiness that are in store for you by admitting that fear of lungs into your beautiful thinking." Even with all the "work" being done by Christian Science practitioners, Emily's health continued to decline. A year later, Jane wrote that she had "worked" Christian Science all night for Emily after having received a distressing letter in which Emily had told her of her health problems. Finally Jane called Emily "and heard your sweet calm voice and knew that you were much better than when you wrote the sad little frightened letter. Mortal mind with all of its usual arguments will try to cloud our vision and thinking but we must be good soldiers and take up our stand for the supremacy and infinite operation of good and not let in suggestions of fear and doubt."

While Emily was struggling with achieving a mind-over-body remission of tuberculosis, Max was up to his old dangerous ways. In August 1936, Max again came close to dying, an occurrence that was becoming commonplace. He and his cousins Roger and Ed Converse had planned a month-long hunting expedition on the Kenai Peninsula in Alaska. A remote place of icefields, glaciers, and fjords, Kenai jutted out from the mainland with Cook Inlet to the west and Prince William Sound to the east, while to the southwest rose Kodiak Island. It teemed with game, including bear and moose, but was difficult to reach. To get to Anchorage, located at the upper end of the peninsula, Max and his cousins had to go by rail. They rented what was called a "gas train car," which combined a diesel engine with a single compartment for gear and passengers. Because of the severe climate, the train had to travel long distances through snow sheds, structures rather like wooden tunnels that kept the tracks clear of snow in the winter. The train had lost time in the process, so, upon emerging from one of the snow sheds, the engineer decided to pick up speed. The car was traveling at forty miles an hour when it started out on the longest and highest trestle bridge in Alaska. Had the trestle been straight, that speed would not have been excessive; unfortunately it curved. As they began to go into the curve, the back wheels slipped off the track. The engine jumped the rails and careened along the ties until it bumped to a standstill on the very edge of a two-hundred foot drop. Unfazed, Max, Ed, and Roger dug their cameras out of their gear, walked out on the trestle, and took pictures of the engine teetering over the precipice. Soon another train came along, and its crew managed to put the engine back on the tracks. They resumed their journey with the baron curled up on one of the seats sleeping peacefully. Once in Anchorage, they hired the services of a bush pilot with a seaplane to fly them to Tustumena Lake, one of the numerous glacial lakes on the peninsula. They unloaded their gear, waved good-by to the pilot and set up camp, only to learn later that on its next flight out of Anchorage with another group of hunters the plane had crashed into a mountain, killing all on board. The rest of the trip went by without incident, and the three men returned safely to Montecito at the end of September.[19]

Only five months later, the next serious accident occurred. Max had just purchased a new plane, a single-engine, cabin-type Waco painted the von Romberg colors. His intent was to fly it to Alaska the following summer for another hunting expedition. Perhaps made uneasy by the crash of the plane that had taken him and his cousins into the peninsula, Max had decided that he would be at the controls of his own plane for the next trip. He was testing out the new model on short trips up and down the coastline. On January 25, 1937, while coming in for a landing on a small private field near the Santa Barbara Biltmore Hotel, he overshot the runway. Trying a second time for a landing, he "gave it the gun," as he told a reporter, but the motor misfired, sputtered, and died. "When I saw I couldn't make it and was going to crash, I cut all the switches and pancaked her in." The plane grazed a large boulder and then crashed onto the rock-covered beach just seventy-five yards from the hotel. Had Max been able to stay airborne a few more seconds, he could have set the plane down on a long stretch of sand. "I nearly made it," he said ruefully to a reporter. The impact folded the left wing down over the door, trapping Max inside. Immediately flames broke out. He exerted all his strength as the fire gained headway and managed to get the door open enough to squeeze through. "I just got out and was standing on a rock not ten feet away when the entire plane went 'whoof' in flames." Panic-stricken witnesses called in doctors and ambulances, but Max, though shaken and bruised, was unhurt. Only his hair was singed and he laughingly told the reporters and bystanders that he had been on his way to Los Angeles for a haircut anyway.[20]

An article appeared a few months following the accident with a five-column banner headline: "Love Trumps Jinx Card of Death: Wealth, High Adventure And Quarrels Threaten von Rombergs, But Somehow Baron Always Saves His Life — and Re-wins Wife!" The reporter wrote that some of Max's friends wondered if he wore an amulet or charm. "Because of the Baron's deep interest in aviation, his friends have decided that if he does wear some rare and ancient amulet, it is probably a miniature golden wheel, as a silent tribute to the sun god — the great red circle in the sky toward which he so often flies." Another reporter noted that every time Max had an accident, he and Emily reconciled. So it was to be this time as well. Perhaps to help cement the relationship, they decided to build a house. In a letter that Jane wrote to her mother in the summer of 1937, she raised the hope that the building of a house would change Max for the better. As with all her letters, she couched that idea in the Christian Scientist framework of thinking only the good thought so as to bring it into being. "Please, dearest Mummy, do not cross bridges, and try to know that what blesses one, blesses all. If it blesses Emmie to have a house, which I am sure it will, you will be blessed in some way too, perhaps by seeing a beautiful change in Max's thinking. Expect good — look for it, and in proportion to what you think will it be manifested in your own experience." Whether the building of a house brought about a change in Max's thinking is unknown. One thing is certain: it was no ordinary house that the two of them had in mind.

Throughout most of the United States, 1937 was marked by the unending Depression. People stood in breadlines in the cities, and men showed up by the hundreds outside any factory that advertised the availability of jobs. However, hard times were nowhere in evidence in Montecito where construction of the grand von Romberg mansion was about to begin. Construction alone would cost $116,000, not including the architectural fees, extensive landscaping, and interior design work. The total cost would exceed $150,000.

The architect that Max and Emily chose was a young woman named Lutah Maria Riggs who was already highly regarded in the Santa Barbara area. In his monograph, *Lutah Maria Riggs: A Woman in Architecture, 1921–1980,* David Gebhard says that the von Romberg estate was comparable to the great country houses built in Southern California in the more opulent teens and twenties and may well have been "the last California pre–World War II villa clothed in the Spanish Colonial Revival image." Riggs was an obvious choice to design the mansion because she had helped create many of those great estates when she worked as the chief designer for the renowned architect George Washington Smith. A graduate of the University of California School of Architecture, she endeavored to preserve Santa Barbara's environment while providing her clients "enough beauty to lift the soul." The house, which the von Rombergs would call Brunninghausen after Max's ancestral home, Brunn, in Wiesbaden, was to become one of Riggs's most famous designs.

Working closely with Riggs, Emily and Max were involved deeply in the design of the house, which went through at least twenty variations. Some were mere pencil sketches, but several were carefully drawn and rendered in large-scale perspective drawings. In her initial concepts for the house, Riggs toyed with the shape of a swastika, an iron cross, a snail, and what she labeled as a Ziegfield Follies design, which was a curving tower. One early design had the feel of a late fifteenth-century country villa in Italy. Others were classical Italian Renaissance, Venetian/Byzantine, and English Regency. Yet another she labeled Modern Classic. The scheme that finally was agreed upon was basically cruciform with a three-and-a-half-story keep, or tower, rising in the center from which the four arms were offset slightly. It retained an Italian-Spanish flavor with open loggia and walled courtyards, but it was cleaner in line, using the historical architectural ideas as if for reference. Riggs not only did masterful drawings, she also made an exact scale model, designed the pattern for the tile in the courtyards and the paneling in the study, and modeled the baron's coat of arms in clay. In his book about Riggs, David Gebhard wrote: "the roofs are flat and parapeted; and the walls read as expansive light surfaces broken by only a few penetrations. The cantilevered hood over the entrance has gone from a design which was quite specific in its reference to northern Italian Romanesque examples to a striking, simple abstraction. The interior of the house evoked the sensitivity of the then popular Regency mode. The one major exception was the exercise/retreat room within the upper reaches of the keep. Its story and a half space, reminiscent of Le Corbusier's version of the Parisian artist's studio, was pure Streamline Moderne."

The interior designer was Paul Frankl of Frankl Galleries in Beverly Hills, an exponent of Art Deco and Streamline Moderne. An article in the *Los Angeles Times* quoted Frankl as saying his work in the house was "genuine antique and genuine modern."[21] Wherever possible the von Romberg colors of maroon and gray were used. Even the pink, rose, and white cyclamen in the window boxes were chosen to harmonize. In Emily's bedroom pink and gray curtains hung straight to the floor, and a gray chiffon valence was caught back by rings covered in braided pink chiffon. The drawing room was dominated by a twelve-paneled allegorical mural extending almost to the ceiling and surrounding the fireplace, painted by Nicolai Remishoff in shades of vermillion, chartreuse, gold, pink, and gray. The only thing that seemed out of place in the house was the great stuffed head of a moose, a souvenir from a hunting expedition, that hung over the fireplace in Max's office. A reporter's description of the tower room is especially interesting: "Now to the Tower Room. After climbing a winding staircase one comes face to face with the most enchanting place! Rough textured walls in white and chartreuse plus a row of high windows in natural wood seem to allow the whole outdoors to empty barrels of sunshine into the room. Even a lovely white Cambodian rug adds to the lightness. One side of the room opens onto a terrace—a green hand-blocked linen wing chair of modern design is drawn up to the fireplace—and a very long sofa stretches along half a wall. In a convenient place—with a heavenly view off the terrace—is a modern desk in gray-green lacquer: The hobby room of the Baroness."[22]

For all its beauty, Brunninghausen was the subject of dark rumors as the aggression of the Third Reich increased in the late 1930s. Whether or not it was warranted, people with strong ties to Germany fell under suspicion during this period, especially if their names were preceded by titles such as Baron and Baroness. Emily protested these accusations but she could not quell the rumors completely because of certain features of the house itself: although the swastika and the iron cross had been rejected as architectural foundation schemes for the house, they were used in details, including the grillwork over vents. Riggs also designed secret rooms and hidden doors. Most surprising in this regard is a hidden circular staircase that starts in the basement and rises up to just below the roof line. It connects five small rooms and storage spaces: the wine cellar, a bar on the first floor (in which there is a peephole in the shape of the iron cross that gives a view of the front door), a closet, a tiny office that Max may have used as a dark room, and finally a half-height storage space under the roof. The rooms on the first and second floors are accessible by doors hidden in the ornate wooden paneling. Besides the iron cross peephole, another peephole, in the middle of the vaulted hall ceiling, allowed a person on the second floor to observe anyone who entered. There was also a trapdoor in a closet off the front hall. Riggs designed a shaft for an elevator that would go up into the tower, and built in space for it. She asked the Otis Elevator Company for an estimate on a price, but for some reason an elevator was never installed. There was a long passageway in the cellar, and there were five exits from the wine cellar.[23] There was also a sophisticated teletalk system installed throughout the house. Riggs's notes and letters indicate that this was designed and installed at the request of Max and Emily. The most innocuous of explanations is that they were intrigued with the idea of secrecy and the fact that European castles and mansions often had hidden rooms and peepholes. But against this is the rumor that they would hire only German firms to work on the house, a rumor that is partially borne out in the list of firms who were employed.[24]

One person who remembers distinctly the peculiarities of Brunninghausen is Burton Tremaine's daughter, Dorothy Tremaine Hildt (called Dee), who stayed there in 1944 prior to Emily's marriage to her father. She remembers as a teenager trying to find the secret rooms with the help of her father and her friend Mary. Emily had told them there were seven, but she did not tell them where they were all located.

We'd spend our time knocking on the walls and the studs trying to find the seven secret rooms. Two or three or four of them were known to us and there was one big one, sort of a tower room on the house which she used as an office which was not really a secret. Then there were I guess three rooms that went behind the master bedroom. There was a passage behind the closet that led downstairs, which put you over the bar area. Then you could go down into the basement and into the wine cellar and you could do the entire passage-way without being seen. In the library there were some enormous trophies that were mounted on the walls . . . My father used to love to get on the other side of the wall and pretend he was speaking through the moose and he would say to the children "well, the moose sees everything that you are doing." Of course they thought that was wonderful. There were apparently several other rooms that we never did find, as hard as we knocked on all the studs when she wasn't around. . . . I asked her when she sold the house if she told the new buyers where all the little places were and she said "certainly not."

Despite the fact that the house would not be completed until July 1938, Max and Emily began to move in some of their possessions during the late spring, planning to finish the task after Max returned from attending a wedding on Long Island.[25] Emily had considered going with him but at the last minute had decided to stay in Montecito overseeing the final details on Brunninghausen. On June 4, 1938, at 11:45 A.M., Max took off from Roosevelt Field, New York, and headed toward Red Bank, New Jersey, where he intended to play a weekend of polo at Monmouth Country Club. He was flying the Beechcraft biplane that he had purchased after his last crash just the year before. At 12:15 P.M. an official at the Red Bank Airport heard a plane circling overhead, but since the ceiling was only about four hundred feet he could not see it. For the next twenty minutes he and the other bystanders heard the plane circle and circle. Some bystanders reported that the engine seemed to be missing at times, but airport officials later said that was a common illusion when the clouds were low and thick. According to one eyewitness, suddenly the plane shot down through the clouds with its motor at full speed and plunged straight into the North Shrewsbury River. Upon impact, the baron's parachute opened and floated out of the cabin and up to the surface. When the volunteer firemen arrived just minutes after the crash, they attached a line to the canopy and pulled his body out of the wreckage, which lay in ten feet of water.[26]

It was the end of ten tumultuous years during which time—regardless of all the separations and reconciliations—Emily and Max had never stopped loving each other. Even during the last year their letters had indicated that they could live neither with or without each other: "I ordered a divine dessert set for $180.00 and have notes on other things to talk over with you, if you are speaking to me. All my love Emily." "If you are speaking to me, please wear the flower I'm sending with Elliot. All my love Butch" (Butch was yet another of Max's nicknames.)

In his last postcard to Emily, addressed to "Mein Puppchen," Max talked about the polo games he was intending to play and ended, "Last night a friend asked me if I would like a passenger west. That sounded nice until I found that the prospective passenger was female. I pulled the parachute gag about having only one and intending to use it if occasion arose. A nice graceful way of saying no. Adios darling."

The soul is emerging, refined by struggle and suffering. Cruder emotions like fear, joy and grief, which belonged to this time of trial, will no longer attract the artist. He will attempt to arouse more refined emotions, as yet unnamed. Just as he will live a complicated and subtle life, so his work will give to those observers capable of feeling them emotions subtle beyond words. — Wassily Kandinsky

CHAPTER THREE

THE DARK YEARS

In terms of art, Emily's life began to spiral upward after Max's death, but in terms of day to day circumstances, her life began to spin downward almost out of control. On August 10, 1939, a year and two months after Max had crashed into the Shrewsbury River, Emily impulsively remarried, entering a dark labyrinth from which she would not emerge until 1945, then somewhat chastened, less interested in seeking publicity, and more dedicated to art. According to Dee Tremaine Hildt, "Emily met him on the first day of Fiesta in Santa Barbara, which took place at the beginning of August every year. Everybody would go to the parades and there would be horses with silver saddles, cowgirls, and big parties that lasted for about three days. She saw him across a room, fell madly in love, and married him about a week later in Las Vegas. On her return, Emily went to tell her mother. Before being told the name of the groom, her mother said, "That's fine dear, but I only hope it isn't to Adolph Spreckels." Unfortunately it was to Adolph Spreckels. Heir to a sugar fortune, he was also three times divorced on the grounds of cruelty. Even worse, he was suspected of being a Nazi-sympathizer. Just as her marriage to Max had been fodder for reporters, so her marriage to and eventual divorce from Adolph would keep the press wires humming.

The fiesta in Santa Barbara is a celebration of Santa Barbara's Spanish heritage. Horses wear the heavy, ornate tack favored by rancheros; women don white flounced skirts and pin their hair up with tortoise shell combs; guitar music floats on the air; and señoritas ride on parade floats and throw flowers to the crowds. It is also a time to party heavily, and the fiesta in 1939 was no exception. In fact, the local newspaper dubbed it a "killer-diller" that left everyone yelling "uncle." The grandest party of all was thrown by Emily's good friend and fellow art collector Wright Luddington at his Italianate mansion Villa Verde. It was attended by Vincent Price, Walter Pidgeon, and other Hollywood stars who flocked up from Hollywood for the excitement. As a reporter told it: "When Santa Barbara's creme-de-la-creme filed past the Roman statues, they were so elaborate, they even made the marble figures blink their eyes for a second look. For instance the Baroness Emily von Romberg was so glamorous in a rumba outfit that Adolph Spreckels eloped to Reno with her not four days later."[1]

Decked out in a leopard coat and wearing a small cap on which was the polo pin from Cartier's that Max had given her, Emily was in too much of a hurry to worry about appropriate bridal attire. They flew into Reno early in the day and persuaded the county clerk to issue a license before regular office hours. When asked by the press whether he had married the two, Justice of the Peace Harry Dunseath said he had been sworn to secrecy but added "Of course, I can't deny that I performed the ceremony." There were only three witnesses: Barbara Boston, who had worked with Emily on *Apéritif* and was now a society editor for a New York newspaper, her husband, and a Reno attorney.[2]

Adolph was only twenty-seven years old. Emily was thirty-one, although she told the reporters that she was the same age as Adolph. It was his fourth marriage, the previous three having been short and acrimonious. His first wife, Lois Spreckels, divorced him in Reno in May 1935 after they had been married nearly three years, and gained custody of their child. At the age of twenty-three, he married his second wife, Gloria, on September 6, 1935. She was only 18 years old, and filed for separation within three months of their marriage, charging him with abuse, humiliation, and desertion while on their honeymoon, In retaliation he threatened to expose her diary, which he described as "hotter than Boccaccio's *Decameron*."[3] Unfazed, she went through with the divorce anyway. His third wife was his second cousin Geraldine Spreckels, also an heir to the sugar fortune. They were married in London in

July 1936, and separated the following May. She charged that he was "cruelly antagonistic, rude, insolent, surly and profane." The uncontested divorce was granted in November 1938.[4]

Adolph was young and handsome and, like Max, he relished living on the edge of danger. On June 14, 1936, three years before his marriage to Emily, he was injured seriously when he lost control of an outboard motorboat because its automatic throttle jammed. It raced up the beach at Green Lake in Seattle, hurtled through a crowd of spectators, injuring several people, and finally crashed on top of a sound truck. Adolph was catapulted into the air and impaled on a bar that jutted out from a telephone pole. His left arm was severely injured, his face required plastic surgery, and his jaw had to be reset. Just prior to the accident he had announced that he was "through with racing," but at the last moment he had borrowed a boat to enter the regatta. The surgery to his jaw made his face look as if it were locked in place. With his straight blond hair brushed back flat, he looked severely Teutonic. If there had been any glint of softness in his features before the accident, there was none after.[5]

Besides being a violent daredevil, Spreckels was an alcoholic and a drug abuser. He had been arrested in Havana, Cuba, in January 1933 for possession of marijuana, an incident serious enough to be reported in the *New York Times*.[6]

On September 1, 1939, less than a month after the marriage of Emily and Adolph, Germany invaded Poland, and England and France declared war. To be openly pro-German was no longer socially acceptable. To be openly pro-Nazi was scandalous.

Adolph could be very pleasant as long as he was sober, but when he drank, which he did frequently, he became belligerent and even violent. He and Emily seemed to lead the high life, both at his home in San Francisco, and in Brunninghausen. However, what appeared in the society columns and what was happening in reality were entirely different, as divorce papers later made clear. For example, in January 1940, they attended the Diamond Ball in New York City, a masquerade party for the benefit of the Beaux Arts Institute and the American Ambulance Corp. Even though the Rockefellers and the Morgans and other people of immense wealth were in attendance, it was Emily who got the most press coverage, because she was bedecked in $500,000 worth of diamonds: there were diamonds on her turban, diamonds on her fingers, and diamonds on her wrists. For further dramatic emphasis, she had pinned

Adolph and Emily Spreckels
at the races.

four black orchids to her halter top. A newspaper photo (a pin-up-type shot) showed her perched on a bench smiling beguilingly, with her hands tilted on her crossed knees to show off her glittering rings to best advantage.[7] But according to her divorce petition, one of the most mortifying moments of her life had occurred just the week before when she and Adolph went to dinner at Luchow's, the largest and best-known German restaurant in the city. Adolph had pulled out a Nazi flag and placed it in a prominent position on the table. Someone shouted "Hitler is a heel. Heel Hitler!" and a hissing spread through the restaurant. When the management requested that Adolph remove the flag, he refused to do so, at which point he and Emily were asked to leave the restaurant. The divorce suit said that the incident caused Emily "to be grievously humiliated and to be shunned and avoided as un-American by many of her former friends and acquaintances, and has caused said plaintiff to be publicly insulted and embarrassed." [8]

At a hotel the following month Adolph began to drink, and when Emily tried to get him to stop, he attacked her, blackened both her eyes, wrenched her arm, injured her wrist, broke her nose, and lacerated her tongue and mouth. Her injuries were extensive enough to require medical attention. He beat her again on their first anniversary, August 10, 1940. Dee Tremaine Hildt recalled that, "Emily told me that at one time she was terrified because she had hidden in one of the secret rooms in Brunninghausen to get away from Adolph because he was coming after her with lighted cigarette butts. She had gotten into one of the secret places but was terrified that she wouldn't be able to get out or that the door had closed permanently. Anyway she did finally get out, but it was a little claustrophobic in there. So she had a few little safety places because she did like mysteries." Emily also told Dee that she had to hire what she called "a keeper" for Adolph. "The keeper lived in the guest house and when Adolph got too terrible, Emily would call him. He would come up, give him a hypodermic and put him out."

On August 25, 1940, just two weeks after their first anniversary, Emily left Adolph and shortly thereafter filed for divorce. The headline in the *New York Times* said it all: "Says A.B. Spreckels is Associate of Nazis: Fourth Wife Accuses Sugar Heir of Entertaining German Agents." [9] In another article titled "All His Sugar Millions Couldn't Sweeten That Swastika," the reporter took the slant that Emily's charges were humorous:

> Bang! The war spreads some more. Right here, in the United States, Adolf Hitler has succeeded in blasting the happy home of Adolph Spreckels, spectacular sugar millionaire. In fact Mrs. Emily Spreckels virtually names him in her divorce suit, as a sort of political co-respondent—a Fifth Column, right in the bosom of the family. These fifth column activities are alleged to have begun right after the honeymoon, followed by a Blitzkrieg, with plenty of terrorism, including a broken nose, black eyes, cut lips, bruises and a call for the ambulance corp. Even the Nazi flag was hoisted on American soil in a German-American restaurant where, promptly, it had to be hauled down amid hisses. No airplanes or bombs seem to have been involved, though if Mrs. Spreckels's description of her husband's drinking is accurate, there was one formidable "tank" thundering around. Poor little Norway must pay $3,000,000 a day to Germany for daring to resist the

invader but Emily, far from paying anything, is demanding $2,500 a month indemnity from her Adolph. This is assuming that he will win every battle but the last. The fight is going on in the Superior Court of Santa Barbara, California. All depends, of course, on the sugar heir's reply which, like Hitler's invasion of England, was postponed.[10]

Despite the reporter's mocking tone, Emily's charges were extremely serious: besides the physical abuse, she charged that from the time of their marriage Adolph, "had consorted with and entertained people under the employ of the Nazi government of Germany" and that he had compelled her to entertain such persons in their home. Had the United States already entered the war, Emily's claim that Adolph had turned Brunninghausen into a quasi—West Coast base for Nazis would have led to charges of treason. Emily's lawyer said he wanted to keep "the sordid details from becoming a matter of public record" but that Emily was prepared to bring additional charges of extreme cruelty if it became necessary.[11]

Adolph fired back that Emily herself had pro-Nazi leanings. His claim was buttressed by a photograph, reproduced with the article about the divorce, showing Emily holding Swastika, her dachshund. Adolph also pointed to her title, the name of her house, the swastikas built into it, and the German flag flying out front. She tried hard to defend Max's reputation (and thereby her own) by telling reporters that although he had been a German of ancient lineage, he was, as she bluntly put it, "no Nazi." Her divorce suit began with the words "That your said plaintiff, Emily Hall Spreckels, is an American girl, born of old American stock." But her protestations of innocence were ineffective. She was the former Baroness von Romberg whose father-in-law was a World War I German war hero—that alone was sufficient to put her under suspicion of being a Nazi sympathizer and to undercut her charges against Spreckels. Furthermore, in the United States at that time political differences, no matter how severe, were not considered a valid reason for granting a divorce. As a result, Emily reluctantly withdrew her suit "without prejudice," and the divorce did not go through.[12]

The closest parallel to Emily's predicament was that of Baroness Hilla Rebay, director of the Solomon R. Guggenheim Museum of Non-Objective Art, who had come to the United States in 1927. Germanic in bearing, autocratic in style, and insistent on the use of her title, Rebay was denounced as a spy during the war but cleared herself after an investigation. She later discovered that the false rumors that she was a Nazi had been spread by Rudolf Bauer, a painter whom she had championed in the United States, because he was jealous of her position.[13]

It is only conjecture as to what was Emily's stance on Nazism. However, *Apéritif* should not be overlooked as a source of clues. There was a political savvy about the publication that ran counter to its status as a society magazine. Its editorial tone was iconoclastic toward all political systems and politicians. Worthy of note is the article about Jakob Wassermann and his eloquent opposition to anti-Semitism; so also is the article on the Lindbergh trial in which Carey McWilliams excoriated people who allowed themselves to be caught up in mass hysteria.

Perhaps in an effort to counteract the Nazi rumors, Emily served on the American Field Service Committee during the war, raising money for the European front. Her sister Jane (then married to J. Bennett Noble, a retired Navy commander) threw parties at Glen Oaks for convalescent soldiers from Hoff General Hospital. However, it was not until Emily shed the names von Romberg and Spreckels and took on the name Tremaine that she finally was clear of suspicion. By that time, the war had ended, and anti-German sentiment had begun to abate.

For a while following the aborted divorce, Emily and Adolph seem to have resolved their problems. A picture of them attending a play together appeared in the Santa Barbara newspaper early in 1941 under the headline "A Reconciliation."[14] But it did not last long, and the two soon separated for good. A divorce did not actually go through by default decree until early in 1945, at which point the divorce papers stated that they had been living apart for more than three years.[15] A friend recalled that it took that long because Emily could not locate Adolph in order to have the papers served. Emily did not get a monetary settlement, but neither did she need it, considering that her estate included not only her own sizeable inheritance but Max's fortune.

Emily's severe marital problems were not the only ones she faced during this period. Her mother, Purdon Smith Hall, who had instilled the love of art in Emily, died on December 26, 1941. Years earlier in a letter to her sister Sue Etnier, Purdon had written that she was afraid Emily would "marry some brute who would not appreciate her fine nature." Purdon's concern had been prophetic. Although Adolph was no longer in Emily's life, he had hurt the entire family.[16]

Even after her terrible experiences with Adolph, Emily did not choose to settle down to a quiet life. On the contrary, she was known as a bit of a feminine rake who had many glamorous Hollywood friends. Her parties were legendary; she even had an opium pipe with her name inscribed on the side. There were rumors of love affairs, including a spectacular one with Johnny Weismuller, the Olympic swimmer who became famous playing the part of Tarzan in the movies. Most of the outrageous stories about her are cited at second- and third-hand, and have about them the fuzziness of myth rather than the crisp lines of truth. However, they all contain a standard feature— Emily occasionally liked to shock people. Katie Goodrich, a niece of the Tremaines', heard the following story about Emily from her mother who lived in Montecito. "She made a rather dramatic appearance one evening at a large formal function that was taking place at the casino in the club ball room and all Who's Who were of course there. Emily made her entrance into the ballroom in a mink coat, very finely bejeweled and coifed and came into the middle of the room and at the right moment, with the most precise timing, just grand gesture, threw off her mink coat and was stark naked underneath." [17]

Emily met Burton Gad Tremaine in 1944 through his brother Warren, who had a home in Santa Barbara as well as one in Scottsdale, Arizona. Six years older than Emily, Burton was tall, handsome, and gregarious. In a letter to Emily, dated February 8, 1944, Warren's wife, Kit, wrote: "Burton is interested in painting and I think Warren hoped you might be able to arrange for him to see some of the good collections."

Burton's father (who had the same name but was often called either B.G. or Lucky B.G.) was on the board of directors of General Electric. He also had extensive financial interests in several companies. He had developed a large industrial park, the first such facility in the country, in Cleveland for General Electric, and owned a lighting fixture manufacturing firm called the Miller Company, which was based in Meriden, Connecticut. [18] In 1934, displeased with the executive team at Miller, which had run up an excess inventory of over a million dollars, B.G. decided to make his son, then only thirty-two years old, president of the floundering firm. Young Burton had already shown business acumen five years earlier, when, just months before the stock market crash, he had sold at a handsome profit the Superior Screw and Bolt Company, located in Cleveland. As a result of this transaction, Burton was in a good position to move from Cleveland, where he had been born and raised, to Madison, Connecticut. Burton had the money for whatever he desired, but he had a serious business side to his personality, and under his guidance the Miller Company had weathered the Depression.

At the time Emily and Burton met, both of them were recovering from previous marriages and affairs, and Burton also was recuperating from pneumonia. On the surface, it hardly seemed the ideal match: the East Coast businessman and the West Coast femme fatale. However, on another level, it was an excellent match. There had always been a practical side to Emily and a party side to Burton. She knew art; he liked it and wanted to learn; they both loved to travel. Unfortunately he also loved women and a good time (two things for which he never lost his taste), but, unlike Adolph Spreckels, Burton was warm, not abusive; he appreciated Emily and enjoyed her company. Burton had learned to drive his father's electric automobile at age twelve, navigating it through the streets of Cleveland to take his brothers to school. He had received his pilot's license in his early twenties and loved operating motor boats. However, he was too sensible to take the extreme chances on the water and in the sky that Max and Adolph had. As for horses, he loved to ride, having been taught while a student at the Evans Ranch School near Mesa, Arizona, but he never played polo.

While Emily was waiting for her divorce to become final, Burton and his daughter, Dee, often visited her at Brunninghausen. A teenager at the time, Dee was fascinated with Emily, who was unlike anyone else she had known. Everything about her was glamorous, including her Hollywood crowd. Once, when Dee had a friend with her, Walter Pidgeon came to a party at Brunninghausen. "He kissed my friend's hand and she didn't wash it for a week," Dee recalled. Dee was also impressed by Emily's wardrobe and her attention-getting flair for dressing. One day she and a friend went to the Biltmore Beach Club for lunch. They were "sitting on the beach which was a little patch of sand on one side of the pool and Emily came in through the front doors of the club and she was wearing short red shorts and a red and yellow bando sweater, one side red and one side yellow. To finish the outfit she had on a pair of high-heeled shoes, one of which was red and one of which was yellow. It was quite a sight as she walked into the beach club amidst all the more elderly matrons."

At the time that Emily was introduced to Burton Tremaine, her friend Louise Lynch Getty (known as Teddy) was staying periodically at Brunninghausen. Emily occasionally would visit with Teddy at her home in Santa Monica. Teddy was the fourth or fifth wife (it was hard to keep track) of the oil magnate J. Paul Getty, from whom she was then separated. Although both Paul and Teddy were friends of Emily's, she was annoyed at Paul's constant womanizing. Emily wrote to Burton on March 22, 1944:

> Burton dear—It's so heavenly here this morning. There is a wonderful soft breeze and the sun has the water looking like Tiffany's window (see how my mind works)—you have no business being in Cleveland.

Jeanne, Victor and Teddy have gone to town so here is a peace passing understanding which may last for exactly two more hours at which time Paul arrives on the Chief [a train] and all I have to do is to tell him he is a perfidious, black-hearted, wife-beating, contemptible sex maniac, that his wife has left him, he is not to come to the beach, and no one is going to see anyone without a lot of advice from a lot of counsel.

Because I'm two-faced, I'm trying to get an apartment in town so he won't have to freeze in dix-huitême ciecle splendor at the Wilshire House, although my instructions at the moment are to see he sleeps in the gutter where he will doubtless be among friends and where he goddamn well belongs. After I take the apartment and add to my gray hairs hearing Paul's side of it, they will, of course, end up in bed here, and I will be thrown out as the false friend who tried to get Paul to take an apartment and not come home to his poor little wife who never for a moment ever doubted her wonderful wonderful Paul except when that schematizing Spreckels woman filled her full of mistrust. . . . You should have seen the rat-leaving-ship sequence this morning when it developed the last one here tells Paul, and this rat, of course, with two broken cylinder heads, wins the beautiful ivory eight ball. Anyway, Teddy's made a pretty good super-colossal out of a B script and I think is loving it.

Darling, you will never know how I've loved your calls. Your voice is always so sweet and assuring, just hearing you gives me such a sense of security. You are so strong and wise and dependable, it's a comfort to know we are in the same world. I've expressed myself awkwardly. I don't mean by that I want to cling to you and choke you like the ivy on Mother's trees, but because you exist and I know where, it's that feeling that there's principal in the bank. So you see you don't have to worry because I've been brought up not to draw on principal.

Paul has arrived! I must close. If you get near Hattie Carnegie, be a pet and order me a blue satin double breasted restraining jacket. Dearest Love Emmie.[19]

Burton never purchased that "blue satin double breasted restraining jacket." Instead he bought Emily orchids and asked her to marry him. On May 5, 1945, V. E. Day, Emily married Burton Tremaine at Warren and Kit's house in Scottsdale, Arizona. Their marriage would last forty-two years, until Emily's death in 1987.

I must, therefore, create a new sort of beauty, the beauty that appears to me in terms of volume, of line, of mass, of weight, and through that beauty interpret my subjective impression. . . . I want to expose the Absolute.
— Georges Braque

CHAPTER FOUR

THE GENESIS OF THE COLLECTION

Beginning in October 1944, Emily shifted her focus from Montecito to New York City, where she began to concentrate on art collecting. During the six-month period before her marriage to Burton, Emily acquired masterpieces by several well-known Europeans including Piet Mondrian, Joan Miró, Paul Klee, and Wassily Kandinsky. Then, as if to prove decisively that her days as a novice collector were over, she acquired the works of a number of highly talented but lesser known American artists, including Stuart Davis, Milton Avery, Harry Bertoia, and Ralston Crawford.

What appeared on the surface to be a radical change in Emily was actually the culmination of a gradual process begun in her childhood and continuing through her two marriages, during which time art had provided Emily with a modicum of solace for all her tribulations. The significance of the year 1944 is that it marks the point in Emily's life when art collecting changed from a pastime to a passion.

An inventory of Brunninghausen made a month after Max's death in 1938, already showed the genesis of a unique modern art collection, international in its scope and sublime in its yearnings. There were two paintings, *Sleeping Girl* and *Still Life with Bird,* by Frederic Taubes, a Polish painter who had emigrated to the United States in 1930 after studying at the Bauhaus, the famous German school that sought to encourage experimentation in art and architecture. In the living room hung the masterful cubist still life *The Black Rose* by Georges Braque. There were two Surrealist works, *On the Beach* and *Rampant Horses,* by Giorgio de Chirico. *Picking Horses* by Yasuo Kuniyoshi, which Emily sometimes claimed was a portrait of her, shared wall space with her formal portrait (in which she held the dachshund Swastika) done by Cecil Clark Davis, a woman painter who wintered in Santa Barbara. There was also *Family at the Seashore* (later re-titled *On Gilbert Head*) by Emily's cousin, the painter Stephen Etnier. Finally, there was the twelve-paneled allegorical mural by Nicolai Remishoff that surrounded the living room fireplace, extending from floor to ceiling. All of these paintings were representational. Emily had not yet purchased the first work that was, as Piet Mondrian put it, at "the edge of the abyss," one which made a total break with the material world—black roses, seashores, horses, and people—in an effort to visualize the immaterial world.

Whenever she analyzed the factors that led her towards art in the 1930s, Emily included her interest in philosophy, frequently quoting Aristotle: "The aim of art is to represent not the outward appearance of things, but their inward significance; for this and not the external mannerism and detail is their reality." According to her, this definition helped "to simplify an acceptance and some understanding of the meaning of abstraction." For Emily, gaining this understanding was an evolutionary process of looking, reading and contemplating that would take a lifetime. Were it to be plotted, the line would begin at *The Black Rose* and Braque's struggle to break through the limitations of perspective, and it would end in the 1970s with the art movement aptly named Earth Works. By then, Emily had become fascinated by art that was struggling to break through the limitations of subject matter, technique, and the material of art itself: canvas, paint, brushes, even the hand of the artist. But at the beginning, she was still attracted to art in which roses looked like roses and horses looked like horses, and paintings were decorously bounded by frames.

Behind all great art collectors there is usually an *eminence grise* (whether a dealer, another collector, or an artist) who provides expert advice and guidance, thereby influencing the nature of the collection. When Emily first started collecting in the 1930s, her *eminence grise* was her close friend Chick Austin, the director of the Wadsworth Atheneum, whose help she readily acknowledged and deeply appreciated. "I think Chick actually had more influence on me and the kind of direction our collection was taking than anyone. Chick's

Brunninghausen was designed by Lutah Maria Riggs in an Italian-Spanish style with open loggia and walled courtyards.

enthusiasm was infectious. He opened my eyes more than anyone," said Emily.[1]

To know Chick Austin was to have access to an entire world of collectors, artists, sculptors, architects, dancers, composers, poets, set designers, and choreographers. There was hardly a form of artistic expression in the United States at that time in which he was not interested. Some people took him to be a dilettante who had strayed far beyond his original area of expertise, which was Italian painting of the seventeenth and eighteenth centuries, but no one disagreed that he was the nearest thing to an artistic impresario this side of the

Atlantic. His flair for the dramatic was most obvious in 1934 when he staged the world premiere of the opera *Four Saints in Three Acts* (which actually had fifteen saints and four acts) with music by Virgil Thomson and illogical words by Gertrude Stein. It was directed by John Housman, and acted and sung by an all-black cast, chosen on the supposition that they could vocalize with spirit the nonsense words better than could white singers. This production coincided with the opening of Avery Memorial Hall, the new addition to the Wadsworth Atheneum designed in the International Style. To draw further attention to the new building, especially its spare white interior court, Chick gathered together a large selection of paintings, prints, and drawings by Picasso as a retrospective. Such a conjunction of art, architecture, drama, and music was a rare aesthetic event, and the fact that it took place during the Great Depression made it rarer still.

Henry-Russell Hitchcock, an historian of art and architecture who would eventually work closely with Emily on the first exhibition of the Tremaine collection, said about Chick, "There was a peculiar excitement spreading from him in connection with almost everything he touched. His was not the systematic approach of the critic or scholar, but the antennae of his sensibility were very long and incredibly responsive. To vary the image, he seemed to know by osmosis all that was going on in the world of the arts and to have the happy talent of realization—sometimes almost impromptu realization—of ideas which others could cope with only more ploddingly and at a further remove from actuality." [2]

Chick piqued Emily's interest in abstract painting by explaining to her his reasons for mounting the first Picasso exhibition in America. He introduced her to the strange, unsettling art of Eugene Berman and Pavel Tchelitchew and even attempted to talk her into hosting a Surrealist ball in Santa Barbara in the style of Salvador Dali, as he had in Hartford. Emily found that idea repugnant. "Chick had a great dramatic thing that was moving him which I didn't have nearly as strong. I could appreciate and I loved his sense of poetry, and I loved to be with him when he was doing a performance," she said. "However, I was always much more architectonic in my tastes, more direct. I was never really taken by the Surrealists."

Chick also introduced her to other modern art collectors, including Wright Luddington, who lived in Montecito. These introductions were crucial in shaping the type of collector Emily would become. "At that time [Wright] had what I thought to be very exciting pictures," Emily explained. "As I look back on them now, they are terribly well-behaved and not that exciting. But

Georges Braque. The Black Rose *(1927). Oil on canvas, 20" × 37".* The Black Rose *was the first major painting that Emily acquired. Braque considered the still life to be the triumph of one of his most creative years in painting. In private collection.*

they are good pictures. He has some marvelous early Picasso's. Every time I went to his house I was enriched and my eyes were opened more."

Emily made what she considered her first major art purchase when Wright Luddington invited her to see works that Dalzell Hatfield, a dealer in Los Angeles, had brought to his home. "After a while, I decided I was really going to be brave and buy a picture [which] I loved and could not get out of my thought." Her choice was Braque's *The Black Rose* (1927). Braque himself considered *The Black Rose* to be the triumph of one of his most creative years in painting. Along with Picasso, Braque helped to define Cubism beginning in 1908, the year Emily was born, but, unlike Picasso, he never deviated significantly from Cubist principles, always finding renewal in a nonscientific perspective that enabled first the painter and then the viewer to see beyond the eye's limitations, yet that acknowledged the two-dimensional surface of the canvas. It is intriguing to contemplate *The Black Rose* both as the leitmotif of what would become the entire Tremaine collection and as a reflection of Emily herself. It has both a surface presence and a withdrawn quality. It is a still life of common but ineffable objects. There is an element of mystery in the painting, imparted by lines that resemble automatic writing. In a quiet, somber composition, the yellow of the lemons sparks the darker hues, and the standard idea of the beautiful — the rose — has been subtly transformed by the rose's color: black.

Having made the purchase, Emily began to worry about what her mother would think. Although Purdon Hall loved art, her taste had not progressed much further than the Impressionists. Furthermore, the painting had cost $3,250, a significant amount in the middle of the Great Depression. Emily recalled, "I kept it hidden from my mother for several weeks, removing it from the wall when I expected her to come to our house. But the inevitable unexpected visit came and she was jarred. When she learned what I had paid for the picture, her only comment was, 'Thank heaven your father left your money in trust.' When I went to New York the next time, she said 'would you loan me that crazy picture you bought? I want to look at it some more.' So I sent it over to her house. When I got back, she said 'I don't want to let that picture go. It is really marvelous.' So she didn't."

This acquisition made Emily aware of the joy of collecting. "I had owned it only a very short time when I received requests to loan it to one or two museums, and several friends who heard I had acquired the work telephoned me and asked to see it. To me there was never any joy in anything I could not share; and with this awakening—that the world was asking that it be shared—I think I became a collector." [3]

The Black Rose never left Emily's collection except when it was out on loan, or at her mother's. Braque himself selected it as his single representation for the important still life exhibition at the Orangerie, "La Nature Morte: de l'Antiquité à nos Jours," in 1952. This event crystallized for Emily the pride of possession. She recalled, "A very exciting moment in my life came about 20 years later [after the purchase] when driving from the airport into Paris on a dreary winter day, I became suddenly aware that on every few lamp posts hung a poster bearing a magnificent reproduction of *The Black Rose* announcing a still life exhibition being held at the Orangerie. Of course, I knew the picture was at the Orangerie. I had been told it had been selected by Braque himself for the exhibition. But I had not been told it would be on the announcement. No stage mother has been more excited seeing her child's name in lights than I was on that otherwise bleak morning in Paris. The pride of possession, or as Aline Saarinen phrases it in the title of her book, *The Proud Possessors,* is a facet of collecting not to be overlooked." [4]

Aline Saarinen's insights, not only into the pride of possession but also into the moral component of art collection, help to explain why Emily, steeped in Christian Science, would be attracted to collecting in the first place.

Art is conveniently endowed with exactly the right characteristics to make its pursuit not only pleasurable, but also wise and virtuous. . . . In addition, wisely chosen, art has again and again proved in the long run to be a sound, often an extraordinarily profitable, investment. Waste is a sin; but the purchase of art can be rationalized as a prudent, rather than a reckless, act. Art has other less mundane and less practical merits. It stands for beauty, which, like truth, is on the high plateau of the good. It can be considered educational. And its personal accumulation can be justified in terms of its future public benefit.... Thus, happily, the craving to be intimate with and surrounded by lovely objects can — like few other desires of the senses — be gratified without loss of virtue.[5]

About the same time that she purchased *The Black Rose*, Emily bought two paintings by de Chirico, one of the few Surrealists she collected. *On the Beach* and *Rampant Horses*, are not in the same vein as the dark, troubling works of de Chirico's earlier years, during and immediately after World War I, in which there is a heavy presentiment of cultural doom. *On the Beach* and *Rampant Horses*, still mysterious, are lighter and less brooding. Even so, Emily did not keep them in her collection, but donated them eventually to the Corcoran Gallery.

Until the Braque and de Chirico purchases Emily had been interested in art nouveau and art deco. She owned as well "some fine academic seascapes," explaining, "I had been enchanted with these as a child and grew out of them very quickly and I'm afraid I haven't grown back into them." From the start of her collecting, she was interested not only in the art of Europeans or Americans, Cubists or Fauvists; in fact, she came to feel strongly that anyone who so limited a collection was shortsighted, confined in what she called "a subservient state" to a particular place or period.[6]

Besides Wright Luddington, her other West Coast mentor was Grace Morley, director of the Museum of San Francisco (now San Francisco Museum of Modern Art), who introduced her to the works of Georges Rouault, Amedeo Modigliani, and Juan Gris, among others. "She arranged some very good exhibitions. I always tried to see them although San Francisco was 300 miles away. In the thirties that was the only place on the coast I knew of that was interested in showing something new." Even though she liked living in Southern California, Emily found the area to be culturally sterile. She considered San Francisco more advanced than Los Angeles, due in large measure to the influence of Morley, who was a tireless champion of contemporary art worldwide, but Emily felt that neither place could compare with New York City.

As Emily's knowledge of modern art deepened and her perception of quality became more acute, she looked more and more toward New York, becoming acquainted with its galleries and museums, especially those that focused on twentieth century art. Whenever she had the chance, she asked artists, collectors, and gallery owners for their advice. Having purchased a painting from Frederic Taubes, for example, she wrote to him for advice about several other artists, including his assessment of Salvador Dali. He replied, "I am working at present under great pressure and strain—experiments and more experiments, and who knows where they may lead. . . . Dali painted I think horses, although as part of a surrealistic composition. Although they all call him a "pompier" in France, if he is one, then certainly a King among the pompiers. . . . My very best to you and Max, your always devoted Taubes."[7]

In many ways the years 1936 and 1937 mark a watershed for Emily's evolving artistic perception. In 1936, Cecil Clark Davis painted the portrait of Emily titled *The Baroness and Swastika*. It was typical of the paintings that a wealthy individual in Europe or the United States commissioned to idealize and memorialize herself. Emily peers out at the viewer haughtily, almost disdainfully, her left hand on her hip, her right arm holding the dachshund and its looped leash. She wears gauntlets, as if she has just come inside from taking the dog for a walk. A heavy gold cross stands out dramatically against her black dress, which has a high white collar that flares out just below her chin. On her head is a small black cap in a Robin Hood style, from which sweeps down a long red feather that matches the shade of the lipstick on her perfectly pouted mouth. In the upper right-hand corner, also in red, appears the von Romberg crest.[8]

Whereas the portrait painted by Davis reached backward to nineteenth-century realism, the supposed portrait painted by Yasuo Kuniyoshi a year later reached forward to twentieth-century abstraction. Born in Japan in 1893, Kuniyoshi had come to America in 1906. A trip to France in the late 1920s had enlarged the scope of his work and prompted him to return to working with models on his return to the United States. His *Picking Horses* (also titled *Picking the Ponies*) shows a young woman who looks like Emily studying the racing lists in a newspaper. There are strong parallels to the Davis portrait: she is wearing a hat and a high-collared dark dress, with a white scarf setting off her face; she is angled to the left, although the perspective is slightly from above, and her hands are gloved.

Emily loved to be seen as enigmatic and mysterious. The uncertainty about whether *Picking Horses* was, in fact, her portrait was due entirely to her own efforts at obfuscation. Dee Tremaine Hildt recalls, "I admired the Kuniyoshi painting and I used to think it was of Emily, but she would shrug her shoulders and with an air of mystery say 'oh, do you think it looks like me?' She never said yes or no, so you were left wondering." Emily told another friend that she had gone to Kuniyoshi's studio and picked out the painting which she said was called "A Homely Girl Wearing a Hat." In 1984, when Emily was working with Gregory Hedberg, a curator at the Wadsworth Atheneum, on the catalog for the exhibition *The Tremaine Collection,* she directed him to print the portrait by Kuniyoshi instead of her photograph. That should have laid any doubts to rest except for another incontrovertible fact: there is a receipt for *Picking Horses* dated March 1937 from the Downtown Gallery in New York City.[9] Although the subject shows a striking resemblance to Emily, *Picking Horses* is not a portrait.

About the same time that Emily was in New York buying *Picking Horses,* she was also shopping for antiques, furnishings, and modern art for Brunninghausen, which then was under construction in Montecito. She wrote to Max about several paintings, including one by the French artist André Derain, a founder of Fauvism along with Henri Matisse and Maurice de Vlaminck. "Sunday I went to the Metropolitan and spent several hours in the contemporary painting gallery. I saw no Derain's that compared with the one I am considering. . . . Steve Etnier says he will try to drop by the gallery with me tomorrow and pass on the Derain. He says it is dirt cheap, if any good at all should be $1,500. I saw the most beautiful Matisse I have ever laid my eyes upon but it was $7,000, and Picasso's are out of sight, $10,000 and $13,000. I wish you could talk Wright Luddington out of his *Sleeping Woman* which is a Picasso blue period and a wonderful example."[10]

Besides seeking advice from Chick Austin, Emily frequently turned to her cousin Steve Etnier. In 1922 Steve had entered Yale University with the intent of preparing for a career building water turbines at S. Morgan Smith Company, the family business. However, he found the prospect of following in his grandfather's industrial footsteps so unappealing that he ran away to South America. When he returned, he transferred to fine arts before dropping out of Yale altogether. He chose to study instead at the Pennsylvania Academy, although even there, by his own admission, he was too bored to work very hard. Not until he heard a lecture by Rockwell Kent, in which he said that all the painting theory the students had painstakingly acquired was based on Impressionism and was "baloney," did Etnier truly begin to paint. From 1933 to 1935, Etnier and his wife lived on a schooner, sailing up and down the Atlantic coast from Nova Scotia to Charleston. Eventually they bought an island off the coast of Maine on which they built a house, which Chick Austin had demanded be "Doric" and perfectly white. Boats, lighthouses, and life along

Emily stands outside the door to her study located in the "tower room" of Brunninghausen.

the shore became Etnier's subject matter, and he had several successful exhibitions of his art work.[11]

Etnier wrote to Emily in April, 1937 congratulating her on the purchase of *Picking Horses* and encouraging her to learn all she could about art: "I'm sure of course that you'll like the Kuniyoshi. I do hope that you will really become interested in the stuff—that is painting—there is more fun in it than one would normally suppose. I still have in mind your request for some books [about art], and I promise you that I will get around to it before long. . . . *Modern Art* by Thomas Craven and *Ananias or the False Artist* are both worth looking at, but they are frightfully opinionated, and I don't agree with a lot of their opinions."[12]

As Emily's comprehension of and commitment to art grew, wealthy art patrons in Southern California invited her to see their paintings and encouraged her to build her own collection. The collection of Walter and Louise Arensberg, both of whom had inherited great wealth, was particularly fine. Covering every wall and stuffed into every corner of their mansion in Hollywood were works by Wassily Kandinsky, Paul Klee, Joan Miró, Pablo Picasso,

Max Ernst, and Robert Delauney, to name just a few. African and pre-Columbian objects jostled with Shaker furniture and Oriental rugs in a rich visual stew.

Emily was also invited to see Ruth Maitland's eclectic collection displayed in her mansion in the Bel Air section of Los Angeles. From her father, Maitland had inherited French, nineteenth century paintings, to which she had added works by Henri Matisse, Georges Braque, Paul Cézanne, and Paul Klee, among others. She made a point of making her collection accessible not only to her friends but to art enthusiasts, an approach that Emily would adopt when her own collection became large enough to warrant attention.

Nearer at hand for Emily was the remarkable collection put together by Mildred and Robert Woods Bliss. Bliss was a well-known diplomat who owned Dumbarton Oaks in Washington, D.C., but who also had a summer home, named Casa Dorinda, in Montecito. Emily found Mrs. Bliss to be especially encouraging. "Their house was directly across the road from mine, and for many years she allowed me to share the services of an extraordinary physical therapist she had found when they lived in the Argentine, and who then traveled wherever they went. As soon as Mrs. Bliss discovered that my interest in painting surpassed my interest in gymnastics, she at once began sharing this facet of her life. Musicians, artists, and art scholars were frequent visitors at Casa Dorinda, and Mrs. Bliss invited me to luncheons and gatherings where I learned what was of interest at such temples of wisdom as Harvard or the Tate, or perhaps I would just be invited to participate in a decision about a purchase."

With an insider's access to such collections, Emily was able to learn how avant-garde collectors made their artistic choices. They listened carefully to dealers and accepted guidance but they did not become pawns. In her childhood, Emily may have become aware through her friend Huguette Clark that collecting for the sake of collecting could become obsessive. William Andrews Clark's vast, yet in many respects mediocre, collection had cost him dearly. Hung in a mansion of grandiose design, the collection was a testament to ego, not to quality. But the Arensbergs, the Blisses, and the Maitlands were not like Clark. They knew how to avoid the danger of being possessed by their possessions, and how to make up their own minds. From them Emily learned that the secret to putting together a great collection was a true love of art. The pride of ownership, financial savvy, and social status all played a part, but they were secondary. Once, while on a tour of a collector's home with a good friend, Emily became annoyed when she discovered that there were no paintings on the second floor; they were all displayed on the first floor where guests could see them. "They're not collecting for the love of art. They're collecting to show off!" she muttered, not attempting to conceal her disdain. To her, collectors lacked integrity if their sole intention was public display rather than private appreciation.[13]

As her collection grew, Emily did begin to share it with other people. With the typical zealotry of the newly converted, she often attempted to persuade her friends to collect. She made such an effort with her good friend Walter Pidgeon, the actor, but to no avail.

> Collectors are proselytizers. They cannot stand not to have their friends get into the act. Some years ago the oldest friends Burton and I have, the Walter Pidgeons, bought the Maitland House in Bel Air. I was sure those incredibly beautiful pictures had been a strong attraction and I was sure, whether he knew it or not, that when Mrs. Maitland moved away with her pictures, Walter at long last would apologize to me for all the awful things he had said about our pictures, and would beg and plead with me to help him restore the vacant walls to their original splendor. It did not quite work. After much persuasion on my part, I got him to give an afternoon to look at pictures in New York. I confided the problem to Pierre Matisse [an art dealer and son of Henri Matisse] who assembled as many pictures as he could that would approximate the Maitland collection. Beautiful Mirós, Matisses, Kandinskys, and Braques were paraded before the completely taciturn Pidgeon. Pierre was worn out when we got up to leave, but graciously, to break the tension, said "Mr. Pidgeon, it has been a pleasure to meet you, I have always enjoyed your pictures." Walter stirred a modicum of his famous charm and replied, "I'm sorry, Mr. Matisse, I cannot say the same for yours."[14]

During the late 1930s and early 1940s, Emily began to add significantly to her collection at exactly the point that modern art was taking a strange turn, precipitated by world events. Established European artists were flocking to the United States, either to get away from the crushing lack of artistic freedom in Germany or from the looming prospect of war that hung over all of Europe. Along with them came people such as Peggy Guggenheim, the flamboyant collector of modern art (and modern artists) who established a kind of European outpost in New York City with her new gallery called Art of this Century, located at 30 West Fifty-seventh Street. Designed by the architect Frederick Kiesler, the gallery was in itself a modernist statement that attracted press attention, thereby drawing attention to the art. It had surrealistic curved walls made of gum wood, and the paintings were illuminated by blinking spotlights.

In addition to showcasing the work of European artists such as Jean Arp, Alberto Giacometti, Jean Hélion, and Theo van Doesburg, Peggy Guggenheim exhibited the work of upcoming young American artists including Jackson Pollock, Robert Motherwell, Hans Hofmann, Clyfford Still, Mark Rothko, David Hare, Adolph Gottlieb, Hedda Sterne, and Ad Reinhardt. She helped to forge a creative connection between well-established European artists and young American artists who were struggling to find a new means of expression in opposition to what they saw as the stale realism of the 1930s. Shows at the Museum of Modern Art and at the Solomon R. Guggenheim Museum of Nonobjective Painting, which had opened in 1939 in rented gallery space on 54th Street, also helped to build a bond between the two groups of artists. Under the leadership of Baroness Hilla Rebay, the Guggenheim showed works principally by the Dutch de Stijl Group and the Bauhaus artists including Mondrian, van Doesburg, Klee, and Kandinsky. Like Peggy Guggenheim, Rebay became the mentor of a group of young American artists. By 1942, the Guggenheim collection included works by Balcomb Greene, Alexander Calder, John Ferran, and Irene Rice Pereira. Pollock, who was hired by Rebay as a carpenter and janitor for the museum, spoke of the influence the European artists in exile had on his work: "I accept the fact that the important painting of the last hundred years was done in France. American painters have generally missed the point of modern painting from beginning to end. . . . Thus the fact that good European moderns are now here is very important, for they bring with them an understanding of the problems of modern painting. I am particularly impressed with their concept of the source of art being the Unconscious. This idea interests me more than these specific painters do, for the two artists I admire most, Picasso and Miró, are still abroad." [15]

Another benefit of the close contact between the Americans and the Europeans was that it helped to demystify and humanize the latter. When Mondrian shared a bottle of beer at the bar called Spec's Place with Charmion von Wiegand, or when Ernst poured a drink for Jackson Pollock in Peggy Guggenheim's apartment, not only were they personally accessible but so also was their work — and that which seemed accessible could be exceeded. Therefore, it was not only the exchange of ideas that gave the Americans a boost, it was the realization that they were capable of achieving their own vision and no longer had to genuflect in uncreative awe before the Europeans.

Although Emily did not visit New York as often as she wanted to during this period, she did become friends with Peggy Guggenheim. In her own inimitable way, Peggy indicated that friendship by eventually naming one of her much loved Lhasa apso puppies after Emily (although, she said that the name was also meant to memorialize Dickinson, Coleman, and Brontë). The other person with whom Emily became friends during the war years was the artist and dealer Betty Parsons. "I remember it was at Wright Luddington's that I met Betty Parsons during the war. Later she started her gallery in New York and my husband and I were there often. We liked her as a person and also liked the artists she represented. She had a very advanced vision, far more advanced than ours. We loved to be with her."[16] Parsons was a member of that unusual group of dealers who were also artists in their own right. As a result, she was very sensitive to the personalities of the artists that she represented. Not only did Emily purchase art through Parsons, but she eventually owned art by her, including *Four With Stripes* (1967).

The artists whose work Emily collected during this seminal period were mostly European and represented the theoretical fathers of modern art, a role they earned not simply by their work but by their writings and teachings about art. For example, in 1940, Emily bought from Le Corbusier his painting *Watercolor* (1928), which was a small, collage-like study of bottles superimposed on rectilinear forms. She also collected the work of Mexican artists, including Carlos Merida and Rufino Tamayo. However, it did not hold her attention, and she eventually gave those paintings to museums, as she did with most of her Surrealist paintings.

An exception to the pattern of acquiring European work was Emily's purchase of *Midnight* by Perle Fine, a young American Abstract Expressionist (although that term was not yet in standard use) who was barely making ends meet living on a small stipend from the Guggenheim Foundation. About the painting, Fine wrote that she "employed limited color and means in an effort to create the drama of the play of these forces in space, and then suddenly, the tensions of these forms as they seem to be arrested in their play at a single moment — midnight."[17]

The exhibition that changed forever the way Emily looked at art took place in 1944. Sidney Janis, a New York-based art dealer and patron, put together an exhibition called "Abstract and Surrealist Art," which came to the Santa Barbara Art Museum in July of that year. As part of that exhibit, there was a group called "American Works by Artists in Exile." The artists represented included Marc Chagall, Salvador Dali, Marcel Duchamp, Max Ernst, Fernand

Léger, Jacques Lipchitz, Roberto Matta, and Yves Tanguy, all of whom had fled Europe and were working in New York. Included as well was one unfinished experimental work painted in 1942 by Piet Mondrian—his groundbreaking *New York City*.[18] Five months before the exhibition came to Santa Barbara, Mondrian had died of pneumonia, leaving on his easel his unfinished masterpiece *Victory Boogie-Woogie*. In *New York City*, a precursor to *Victory Boogie-Woogie*, Mondrian asked of himself aesthetic questions that he began to answer in the later painting. Emily remembered, "I almost lived in the museum while that show was there. On the second floor in a room that wasn't easily available was this Mondrian. I think I ran up those stairs fifty times to see whether what I saw was still there. My cousin Stephen Etnier was there and I said 'Stephen, look at this. This is marvelous.' He said. 'Oh, that's just a trick. It's just a hypnotic trick. It's ridiculous.' Then the next time I came east, I went to Hartford and over Chick's desk was a beautiful Mondrian and I said, 'Well, Chick that doesn't seem like you.' And he said, 'that picture is having a very radical effect on my life. I'm going to stop being a director. Where does western art go from here?'"[19]

In his *New York* series of paintings, Mondrian experimented with replacing the sharp black lines that had become almost a signature in his work with colored lines and planes in multiple grids. In the painting exhibited in the Santa Barbara Art Museum, he had not abandoned the use of black lines altogether, but had modulated their effect by using white lines as well. He had also begun using paper tape on his canvases as a way to experiment with the precise placement of the lines before he actually painted them. He believed strongly that the point of transection was crucial to the integrity of the painting as a whole. Unlike many of his earlier paintings, which were called simply "compositions" (e.g., *Composition with Red, White and Blue* and *Composition with Black Lines)* to avoid connecting them to a concrete world, the ones from this period had titles that referred to places and music.

Regardless of the turmoil of World War II and of his own exile, Mondrian had found New York to be a very exciting place in which to create. When asked by a journalist if he thought that the skyscrapers were a little too tall, Mondrian replied "No, not too tall, they are just right as they are."[20] He was also enchanted by the constant bustle in the streets, as well as by popular American music, especially boogie-woogie, with its incessant bass beat in the left hand. In his quest to express the universal both in his art and in his dense philosophical and spiritual writings about art, Mondrian found in New York a kind of life force that was uninhibited and uninhibiting. It appeared to him that Americans were always in the process of destruction and creation, which he saw as a strength, unlike Europeans who were focused on preserving the past, which he saw as a weakness. Mondrian carried that belief into his work, stating that "the destructive element is too much neglected in art." This was one of the reasons he was trying to deconstruct the black lines during the final years of his life, moving instead toward color planes. "Only now I become conscious that my work in black, white and little color planes has been merely 'drawing' in oil color. In drawing, the lines are the principal means of expression. . . . In painting, however, the lines are absorbed by the color planes; but the limitations of the planes show themselves as lines and conserve their great value." [21]

By the fall of 1944, when Emily moved to New York to wait for her divorce to go through so that she could marry Burton Tremaine, all the elements were in place for her to begin putting together a stellar art collection. She was no longer in need of a mentor such as Chick Austin, although she would continue to ask him occasionally for his opinion. As one friend appreciatively observed, Emily had acquired a good eye as well as a good ear.[22] From here on, she listened to everyone, read everything, and most important, visited artists' studios, no matter whether they were out of the way, or in run-down neighborhoods. She carefully studied what she saw. Then she made up her own mind, occasionally in complete opposition to what she had read and heard. "Sometimes I think the artists know less, especially of their own work," explained Emily. She also said, "I think very often the thing they want you to buy is probably the least interesting thing they ever did, not always of course. I try not to listen too much to the dealer or the artist. I try to find my own insights."

Emily did not vacillate: she went after what she wanted with a sense of authority. On November 20, 1944, she purchased for $10,000 from the Valentine Gallery (also called the Valentine Dudensing Gallery) *Woman with a Fan* by Picasso, *Le Chat Blanc* by Joan Miró, and *Figure Composition* (later renamed *Fencers*) by Milton Avery. *Woman with a Fan* is a monochromatic cubist painting, begun in 1911, over which Picasso later superimposed areas of flat blue and vigorous straight black lines. *Le Chat Blanc* is a Surrealist painting with a sense of humor: the long curving whiskers indicate that the white blurred circle against a soft, brown background is actually a cat.[23] Avery was just starting his career at that time and the inclusion of his painting with those of Picasso and Miró indicates Emily's nascent interest in younger American artists. In January 1945 she purchased *Stability Animated* by the Russian painter Wassily

Kandinsky from the Nierendorf Gallery. Just as Mondrian wrote about the nature of art, thereby extending his lines far beyond the edges of the canvas into the minds of future artists, and as Le Corbusier influenced an entire generation of architects with his teaching and his radical designs, so also did Kandinsky. His book *On the Spiritual in Art* is considered a small masterpiece, and it had enormous influence on other artists. Given Emily's evolving interest in the expression of the universal in the specificity of art, Kandinsky's work was an obvious choice. He wanted his art to "lead to an all-embracing synthesis, which will ultimately extend far beyond the boundaries of art into the realm of union of the human and divine."

In February 1945 Emily purchased from the Nierendorf Gallery *Departure of the Ghost* by Paul Klee, as well as three mono-prints by Harry Bertoia and yet another painting by Kandinsky titled *Zig-Zag*. Of these, *Departure of the Ghost* was to become a cornerstone of the entire collection. Forced to leave the Bauhaus in 1931, Klee commemorated his regret, as well as the increasing fear and uncertainty of the times, by means of the ghost plaintively waving good-bye.

In his insightful book *An Art of Our Own: The Spiritual in Twentieth Century Art,* the art historian Roger Lipsey identifies a class of painters whom he calls artists-metaphysicians, people who saw their work as deeply spiritual:

> The century has been dominated by science and material progress, distorted by world wars and totalitarian regimes, and unsure of its metaphysics — so much so that most professional philosophers, let alone most literate people, have discarded the very word "metaphysics." Yet many of the artists understood their art to be an avenue of search, not just for "form" or originality but for deep meaning and penetrating vision. Kandinsky sought an art endowed with what he called an "inner sound," and the work of his middle years culminated in poetic images of a universe sacred or almost sacred, alive with gorgeous color and stately motion. Brancusi sought to embody an elusive "essence" in works of stunning simplicity and formal sophistication. Mondrian intuited "the universal that towers above us" and wished to bring it into our world without denaturing it; he too sought to release the essential from the world of accidental appearances. Morris Louis never committed to words what he sought, but the evidence is there in a glowing icon that combines many things into one — sacred mountain, rainbow covenant, veil — and yet remains a thing apart, a new vision.[24]

Eventually, Emily owned works of art by all of the artists that Lipsey mentions, except Brancusi — artist-metaphysicians who attempted via abstraction to reach beyond themselves and beyond the discernable world for something higher, better, and purer.

Behind all her activity was Emily's belief in Christian Science, that she read and studied daily. For her, Mary Baker Eddy's book *Science and Health* functioned as a kind of compass rose, its needle pointed toward pure spirit. According to Eddy, "The physical senses can obtain no proof of God. They can neither see Spirit through the eye nor hear it through the ear, nor can they feel, taste or smell Spirit. . . . The only real senses of man are spiritual, emanating from divine Mind."[25] That quote from Eddy could have come just as easily from the writings of Kandinsky or Mondrian. The first rhapsodized over his struggle "for a world in which pure ideas can be thought and proclaimed without becoming impure." The second proclaimed, "Man has an inherent urge to regain the original unity of his duality," and attempted to replicate that unity on his canvases by means of line and plane.[26] Different credos, but one artistic trajectory. For Emily, it was all summed up in one painting — *Victory Boogie-Woogie* by Piet Mondrian.

The life of truly modern man is directed neither toward the material for its own sake nor toward the predominantly emotional; rather it takes the form of the autonomous life of the human spirit becoming conscious . . . Art . . . as the product of a new duality in man, is increasingly expressed as the product of cultivated outwardness and of a deeper, more conscious inwardness. — Piet Mondrian

CHAPTER FIVE

THE VICTORY BOOGIE-WOOGIE

From the moment that Emily saw Piet Mondrian's *Victory Boogie-Woogie* in the fall of 1944, she wanted it. Mondrian had died of pneumonia earlier that year, leaving the great diamond-shaped canvas unfinished on his easel. Paradoxically, its incompleteness offered intriguing visual possibilities to a perceptive viewer such as Emily, who had studied Mondrian's art and philosophy. She recalled, "I was in the Dudensing Gallery one day and Valentine said I should see one of the most exciting things I'd ever seen, and he brought out *Victory Boogie-Woogie*. I will never forget the impact. I don't think anything has ever hit me as hard as that and I said, 'Oh, how much is it?' And he said 'It's not for sale. I've got my own ideas about this.' I called Chick right away and I said 'Chick, you come down here. I've seen a picture where every door that Mondrian closed he has opened again. There's a whole century of inspiration and art and ideas and vision in this thing. I just see a little bit, but it's there.' When he came down, he saw it, said 'yes, isn't it true! He's just opened every door.' " [1]

Mondrian had started working on *Victory Boogie-Woogie* in 1942, after dreaming of its composition one night and doing a quick sketch when he awoke. He showed it to Charmion von Wiegand, a young artist and writer who had made his acquaintance the year before when interviewing him for an article. Because she was already an abstract painter, and her father had been a theosophist, as was Mondrian, she felt an immediate affinity with him. Not long after being shown the small sketch, von Wiegand wrote in her diary on June 13, 1942:

> Yesterday I received a letter from Mondrian. He asked me to come last night or any night this week-end. . . . . I got there at 5:45 and planned to go to a movie, if there was no answer. I rang three times and again three times and the door clicked. Mondrian came out wearing his new blue smock and seemed a little sleepy—he had been napping. Almost immediately he asked me to look at the pictures. The big diamond stood against the south wall, but it had not yet been painted white. We began to discuss it. "I want to balance things too much," he said, pointing to an old square canvas and the one with the yellow square. He was struggling to solve both of these with small rectangles on the extreme edge like radiating blocks. But then he began moving tapes on the new diamond one, which is really very wonderful. It was close and sticky inside and confusing at first. After an hour I got into it, and had him move the picture into the alcove where we had more distance. Back and forth he trudged in his slippers, sticking little tapes over the lines—changing them so they went over or under. . . . Each small dab of tape changing a color at the intersection changes all the relationships. . . . Mondrian wants it to be free, asymmetrical, and equilibrated with no classic balance. "How I make you work," he would say. Today I could tell him what I thought and make suggestions freely. He tried them all. "No, I don't like that—it's less victorious," he said when the long red vertical balancing the yellow central axis was changed.
>
> I told him how someone had said that he would as soon call in a plumber or the ice man and ask them what to do with his composition, because it made no difference anyway; all he wanted was a human sounding board to test his own convictions, and anyway he knew what he wanted. "Yes, I am always sure," he said, laughing when I told him. But he was also very impatient that he could not get rid of the classic structure and create a more dynamic one.[2]

Two weeks before his death on February 1, 1944, Mondrian told von Wiegand that the *Victory* was essentially finished, but after she left his studio he perceived another way to arrange the small colored rectangles that would set them in syncopated rhythm with the larger gray and white planes. Mondrian had not used the color gray since he had been a young man in Holland trying to paint the essence of trees and the ocean. Yet in the *Victory Boogie-Woogie* he found it conveyed a sense of calm, as if the sharp black and pure white, so common in his work, were diffusing into light. Especially at the top point of the canvas, the gray seemed ethereal and unbounded, imparting a sense of unending space on a two-dimensional surface. In comparison, he felt that the rest of the canvas was too static; it needed a more dynamic quality that would transcend classical balance.[3] Furthermore, the yellow squares troubled him; they overpowered the blue. So, with irregular pieces of colored tape, he began once again to overlay what he had already painted, intending to remove the tape and paint the underlying canvas as soon as he was satisfied that it had "more boogie-woogie."[4] He had not been feeling well, but he did not want to take the time to see a doctor. The *Victory Boogie-Woogie* was driving him. It was almost done, yet "there was still too much of the old in it."[5] It needed more work.

Von Wiegand did not see Mondrian again until she found him in bed gravely ill, waiting for the doctor to arrive. She recalled that:

> I went into his studio to look at *Boogie-Woogie* and I was startled by the change in the ten days—the picture which had seemed to me complete was covered with small tape and looked as though he'd been working on it in fever and with great intensity. It had a more dynamic quality and the little squares seemed to be more and in various colors. The earlier picture seemed to be more classical, more serene and less complicated, but this effect of a more dynamic intensity and restlessness may be due also to the fact that the papers were put on, because there were practically no papers on the canvas when I had seen it previously; it was all painted. . . . Fundamentally I don't think there was any great change other than this intense staccato movement that came from it.[6]

In those final days Mondrian struggled with the most fundamental ideas of all art—line and form. "It is so difficult to express, to paint what you feel. It is a great struggle," he told a reporter for the newspaper *Knickerbocker Weekly* in the last interview he ever gave, just a few weeks prior to his death. "I know that it would really be torture if I shouldn't get it on canvas. I feel never free—there is always this compulsion driving me on. When a picture is finished, I am satisfied for a short while and then the pressure comes again. It is always going on."[7] However, referring to the *Victory Boogie-Woogie*, he said "I feel better about this one." In fact, he felt that the *Victory* was so close to completion that publication of the interview was held up so that a photograph of the finished painting could be included.

When Emily saw the *Victory Boogie-Woogie* at Valentine Dudensing's gallery eight months later, she felt that Mondrian had almost achieved the dynamics for which he had yearned. She made up her mind to acquire the painting, even though the pieces of tape might fall off. But Dudensing was not interested in selling, despite Emily's insistence:

I got it in my mind I wanted that picture more than anything in the world and I'd keep talking to Dudensing and he said "nobody appreciates Mondrian today. I couldn't get a thousand dollars for this picture today, but someday I'll be able to sell it for enough money to get out of this business. I don't like being a dealer. I'm going to buy a chateau in France and I know where the chateau is and as soon as that picture brings that to me, that's what I'm going to do." I came home and told Burton the story and Burton said "Well, how much is the chateau?" And I said "oh, I didn't ask. I suppose it's the Petit Trianon or something." He said "ask him. You seem to want this more than anything." So I went down again and said "how much is your chateau and he told me and I thought [to myself] 'that's a lot for a Mondrian, but it's not much for a chateau.' I told Burton and he said "All right, if you really like it that much. Write out the check and tell him he has to cash the check within two or three hours or the deal's off, because I know that man. He'll call up every other collector in New York and auction that picture."

I went down and it was a cold, rainy day and [Dudensing] had a scarf on; he was miserable. I said "If you're really serious about your chateau in France, here's the check, but it has to be cashed (the time was about two o'clock) by five o'clock this evening." He called his wife and said "Bébs, I have this check here. Do you want it?" And she said "Oh, take it Val."

When I got home Burton said "They're not going out of business any more than you're going to stop collecting. Val's got it in his blood." But in a month they were out of here and they got their chateau. I visited them a few years later. They didn't even have an object trouvé in the place, nothing, no art at all. They had cows and vineyards, and that's where they stayed until they died.[8]

Regardless of Emily's statement that Dudensing claimed he couldn't get more than a $1,000 for it, the price tag was considerably higher — $8,000 to be exact. This was far more than the $1,250 that an anonymous purchaser had paid for the *Broadway Boogie-Woogie* in 1943 (afterwards donating it to the Museum of Modern Art), which was the most Mondrian had ever received for one of his works.[9] Harry Holtzman (Mondrian's friend and fellow artist and executor of his estate) was dismayed that Dudensing sold the painting to the Tremaines for so high a figure. According to Holtzman, Mondrian's paintings "usually went for $200; $400 was a lot." Dudensing had not taken a commission on the sale of the *Broadway Boogie-Woogie* in 1943 and so Mondrian had promised to give him his next picture. Holtzman thought that Dudensing wanted to keep the *Victory* for himself. "I didn't know he wanted it for money." Clearly, Dudensing knew the *Victory's* worth. He told Emily that the day would come when "Mondrian will be greater than Cezanne."[10] Forty-three years later in 1988, the *Victory Boogie-Woogie* sold for $11 million.

No other painting was more important to the Tremaine collection, nor did any other sum up Emily's philosophy towards life and art as succinctly. It was ironic, therefore, that Emily felt a need to defend the painting from the moment that she purchased it. Although she and Burton later split the purchase cost, it still was one of the biggest financial risks Emily ever took. Not only was the price far higher than had ever been paid for a painting by Mondrian, but there was deep disagreement among artists and critics as to its worth. Had Mondrian flung open a window to the transcendental, or had he just changed the color of its shutters? Compounding the problem was Emily's status as a Southern Californian relatively unknown in New York. She did not yet have a reputation as a savvy collector.

A more immediate concern for Emily was the painting's precarious physical shape: "Almost from the day it arrived, this collage began to tremble and I realized that even losing one element might throw the whole thing off that Mondrian was working on, he was so exact." In March 1945, Emily loaned the painting to the Museum of Modern Art for a memorial exhibition of Mondrian's work. After the show closed in May, Emily asked Monroe Wheeler at the museum whom she should hire to preserve the painting. He consulted the curator of the show before sending her a recommendation, which Emily described in a letter:

> Mr. Sweeney, who directed the exhibition, feels that the best possible person to do the work is Mr. Fritz Glarner, who has photographs of the painting taken before the pins were removed and would therefore be able to restore it to its original condition. He was Mondrian's closest friend and is a painter himself. We asked Mr. Glarner to look at the picture and to give us an estimate on the work involved. He feels that it would take at least two weeks and would cost about $125, depending on the time required. He says furthermore that there is no way in which the painting can be permanently

preserved, that is, there is no surface covering which can be put over the painting to keep the pieces of paper from drying out and buckling at the edges. The scotch tape would undoubtedly have to be changed every five years or so. The oil painting color underneath eventually comes through the scotch tape put over it and changes the colors. There is bound to be some buckling and rolling of the edges since canvas and paper do not dry in the same way. Some of the pieces were placed incorrectly when the thumb tacks were taken out, these Mr. Glarner will be able to straighten out according to the photography." [11]

Instead of approaching Glarner, the Tremaines asked Holtzman to help stabilize the tapes. They loaned the painting in 1946 to the Gemeente Museum in Amsterdam. Concerned that the pieces of colored tape would again come loose and fall off, the director wrote to Emily asking for permission to make an exact copy. Emily turned to Alfred Barr, director of the Museum of Modern Art, for advice, and he agreed that it would be wise to make a copy. He recommended Fritz Glarner, Harry Holtzman, or Burgoyne Diller for the job, because their technique would be similar to that of Mondrian. His preference was Holtzman. He wrote to Emily that Holtzman "was closest to Mondrian during the period in which the picture was painted, has—as I wrote you— the very paints that Mondrian would have used, and would do it largely as a labor of love. He proposes a fee of between $500 and $1,000, which is very much less than Glarner's estimate of $3,000." [12]

Holtzman was the obvious choice for the job for several reasons, the principal one being that Mondrian considered him more like a son than a friend. Holtzman had gone to Paris in 1934 specifically to meet Mondrian, whose work he greatly admired. In 1939, Holtzman was responsible for bringing Mondrian to the United States, footing the bills himself, finding him an apartment, and helping him make the transition to a new life. Following Mondrian's death, Holtzman reverently kept Mondrian's studio open for a month so that artists could come and see the space (which was designed as if it were one of his paintings) and study the *Victory Boogie-Woogie*.

When the *Victory* was finally shipped back following the exhibition in Europe, Emily wrote to Holtzman, "As you may know, the *Victory Boogie-Woogie* just returned from an extended loan to Holland and Switzerland. It has been on loan in this country almost continuously. Museums in our experience are not as careful as they might be, and, too, the shipping is rather hard on paintings. The *Victory Boogie-Woogie* is a rather delicate painting due to the scotch tape. I have reached the point where I hesitate to allow it to travel much more, as I feel the painting is of great historical value and I would hate to have anything happen to it. It has been suggested to us that we have an exact copy made, eliminating the scotch tape and using in its place the exact colors." [13]

Another reason for Emily's desire to have a copy made at this time was that she had begun to put together an exhibition of the Tremaine collection, to be titled in honor of Mondrian *Painting Toward Architecture*. In an interview published just after his death, Mondrian said that "the future is more and more for the new architecture and for the young painters who are trying to unify painting and architecture." Because the idea of "painting toward architecture" was Mondrian's, Emily was emphatic that the *Victory Boogie-Woogie* tour the country with the exhibition, but she knew that it could never withstand the strain of traveling to twenty-four museums over a period of two to three years. If the *Victory* were to go on tour, it would have to be a facsimile and not the real thing, hence the need for an exact copy.

Holtzman apparently started on the project, at least in so far as buying the linen and paint, but for some reason (possibly a disagreement over price or length of time allowed for completion), he did not follow through. The Tremaines decided instead to hire Perle Fine whose painting *Midnight* Emily already owned. They asked Fine to complete two paintings, the first a precise copy and the second an interpretation, based on a thorough analysis of the painting, in which the unfinished work would be completed.[14] The same age as Emily, Fine had been one of the group of artists, including Jackson Pollock, with whom she became friends, who received a stipend from the Guggenheim Foundation during the war. Fine incorporated geometric and organic shapes into her paintings. Her first solo show was at the Willard Gallery in 1945, with subsequent shows at the Nierendorf Gallery. She shared with Emily a worshipful yet cerebral appreciation of Mondrian, whose neoplastic principles she had studied carefully.

The transition from Holtzman to Fine did not proceed smoothly, in part because Holtzman was very possessive of everything having to do with Mondrian. A disgruntled Fine wrote to Emily, "In the matter of the copy, I made it quite clear to him (though I don't see now why I need have troubled myself) that it would be as conscientious an interpretation of a great work, that I, in all humility and love for that artist's work could make. Furthermore, since it is to be an interpretation upon which my integrity as an artist who has studied and practiced the laws of plastic spatial art as propounded by Mondrian stands, I stand ready to defend it, should it be necessary, to the fullest extent." [15]

In beginning the project, Fine was meticulous about materials. "Mondrian used pre-war unattainable cadmiums, permanent blues, etc., which very fortunately I have stocked up well on." She told Emily that Holtzman had gone on and on about the enormity of the task, "the canvas being so large, bending over, the great skill needed to match the colors perfectly, the fumes of the turpentine, etc. Of course, I know it's going to be a big job and one that cannot be hurried." [16]

To compound the enormity of the undertaking for Fine, Emily wanted her to do a complete analysis of the painting accompanied by meticulous annotated charts.[17] She had her secretary send Fine a dictaphone so that she could record carefully "all the changes you feel Mondrian would have made in completing the picture. We would like it made also in scale diagram drawn off in small sections so that in your completed discussion of your work on the version you will be able to refer specifically to particular passages with which you are dealing." Emily hoped that Fine's diagrams and her written analysis could be combined with reproductions of the *Victory* in a brochure that would be made available to artists, thereby increasing its impact on the direction of modern art. (See illustration, pg. 88.)

Both women had a sense of mission in keeping alive Mondrian's accomplishments as embodied in the *Victory*. This shared sense of mission is clear in a letter that Fine wrote to Emily regarding another suggestion by the director of the museum in Amsterdam that a "map" of the painting be made based on geometric measures. Fine was insistent that such a map would be a "disservice rather than a service to such a great man and to what is undoubtedly his greatest painting." Explaining to Emily Mondrian's extreme sensitivity to color, rhythms, and counter-rhythms, she closed by writing, "The indebtedness I feel to this artist impels me to write this. I believe we should all be on our guard to protect the principles to which he so successfully devoted his life. Let us make sure at least that we present him always at his best." [18]

According to Emily, Fine "worked in her studio, in a pure white room, with north light, and discovered that the apparent whites in the painting are not white at all, but the opposing colors to those dominant in a certain area, carried to their highest attenuation on the scale of tints toward white." Emily agreed with Fine that the variety of whites gave the painting a "marvelous breathing quality" that was intentional on Mondrian's part. "Miss Fine numbered the brushes Mondrian used—found they were very different for every size of plane. Those are all stroked in different directions; it's really a very painterly painting." [19] But even on the issue of the white tints, Emily and Fine were fighting an uphill battle in convincing other artists, critics, and connoisseurs. Carl Holty, a friend of Mondrian's and a painter who knew Mondrian's work very well, felt that Mondrian would have over-painted all the white areas with a heavy coat of pure white at the end. Emily and Perle Fine were convinced that although he would have done so in his earlier paintings, in the *Victory* he was breaking new ground. They believed that to gauge this final painting by what Mondrian had done before was to fail to see the uniqueness of the *Victory Boogie-Woogie*.

Fine struggled with several other aspects of the painting, not just the tint of the whites. She pointed out to Emily that "while the method used by Mondrian and all those who practice pure plastic painting concerns itself with "down, up, left, right" movement, (these were used to create depth as opposed to the idea of perspective), one must take care not to overlook two other movements, that is, straight *into* depth, such as is suggested by the white rectangle, and straight *out* of depth, as is suggested by the red and yellow complex." In undertaking the final conceptual painting Fine wrote, "I should like to add at this point that the painting may reveal movements quite other than those to the spectator because it certainly *has* so many; the important issue is that it awaken in him at least *some* of its plastic qualities. When one considers that by the mere act of placing a simple rectangle anywhere on a sheet of paper, one has created simultaneously not *one* but *six* movements to deal with in the process of painting, even without the disturbance of a second rectangle to change the tensions, it must become immediately apparent how a painting such as this one is so rich and pure in its myriad plastic elements and how it may then mean so many more things to the spectator who has become sensitive to such qualities."[20]

Fine agreed with Emily's assessment that the *Victory* was a greater painting than the *Broadway Boogie-Woogie*. According to Fine's analysis, the motif in the *Broadway* was limited to the box and the little "box within the box," while the *Victory* had at least four motifs "making for a much fuller symphonic conception and this without any loss in achieving an equivalent of the opposing forces, which are, on the contrary, so magnificently integrated that . . . it often is difficult to tell to which one or the other belongs."

However, for all her meticulous work, Perle Fine's completed interpretation, which toured with the *Painting Toward Architecture* exhibition as Emily had intended, did not capture the essence of Mondrian. Emily told one interviewer that although Fine worked very hard "the copy just doesn't have the life of the original; the charts don't seem really to explain it."[21] Indicating as an example the plane at the top that appears to extend upward beyond the canvas, Emily found in it "a metaphysical suggestion" that she believed was common in Mondrian's work and that was impossible to replicate. In spite of the fact that she prized Fine's interpretation, she was scrupulous about differentiating it from the original: "What he had, the spirit, the vision, isn't there. That was an interesting experience for me to see that it wasn't there because no one could have tried harder and I wouldn't give Perle Fine's document up for a million dollars."

An illuminating family story is told by Emily's step-grandson Burton G. Tremaine, III (called Tony to avoid confusion with his father and grandfather). Fine's precise copy of the *Victory* hung in Emily's office at the Miller Company, and her interpretation of the finished painting hung in the boardroom. Many years later, Tony Tremaine had the chance to study Fine's interpretation carefully and slowly and then to compare it with the original:

> In 1982, I was on the negotiating team for The Miller Company for a labor contract, and things weren't going well. We were spending enormous time in our board room and as the custom is, for whatever reason, when you sit down at a table, you tend to own that chair for the duration of the event; no matter how many times you come and go, you always come back to that chair. So for some reason I picked a chair that looked across the board room at Perle Fine's interpretation of what the *Victory Boogie-Woogie* would have looked like if Mondrian had lived long enough to complete it. Because there was no window to look out of, I sat there and studied that picture for four months. Finally the strike was over and I went to see my grandparents whom I hadn't seen since the strike started. Walking into their New York apartment, I knew right where the *Victory Boogie-Woogie* hung; so I wheeled around the corner, and I was almost thrown off my feet by its power. I was jolted by having studied the interpretation and then seeing the original. It was so much more powerful. Mondrian was a pure genius. An artist sitting there trying to copy this picture perfectly hadn't been able to come close to its power. So I learned a lot in that experience of what modern art is all about.

Accurate reproduction continued to be a problem even after Fine's major effort, not only with the *Victory* but with *Composition in Red, Yellow and Blue* (later renamed *Composition, 1935–42*) which the Tremaines acquired in 1945. As Emily explained it:

It's amazing how poorly reproductions show the qualities of these paint-ings. In the *Composition in Red, Yellow and Blue,* the lines go off the canvas, giving a dimensional quality not picked up in reproduction. The surface has a [patina] of strokes.

The *Victory* eludes reproduction. In addition to the subtle paint quality, it has the tapes, of irregular cut or tear, over colors showing through — overlapping one another. Some are shiny, some matte; most are primary colors, some beige, which adds a different kind of warmth from the yel-low. I believe that he was trying to take some of the yellow color out. He told Charmion von Wiegand that it had too much yellow. That's entirely possible because I think the *Broadway Boogie-Woogie* has too much yellow in it.[22]

Restoration was just as great a problem as reproduction, both technically and philosophically. Emily was troubled that the originality and uniqueness of Mondrian's art would be destroyed by restorers. "We sent the *Victory* to Europe only once. Not anymore. No matter how well they take care of it, a picture suffers," said Emily. "Often with a Mondrian, a restorer, in order to clean it, just covers it with paint, which also covers the brush strokes he used, which I feel are all important to his conception. Now that I am aware of this, I will not let our Mondrians get in a condition to require that kind of resto-ration. His paintings tend to craze on the surface, however, because he used so much paint."[23]

The first major restoration was undertaken in April 1949 when the Tre-maines discovered that more pieces of tape were coming loose. After consult-ing with several chemists, conservators, and manufacturers (including Min-nesota Mining Company) as to the type of glue to use, the Tremaines sent the painting to Sheldon and Caroline Keck, well-known restorers. In April, Caroline wrote to Emily that they would wait until "after Easter" to begin the arduous work. "It is one of those jobs which can only be worked at when nothing else is going on in the place. The funny thing is we have two paintings with flyaway headaches — yours and a Modern Art Futurist school which has loose sequins to be reattached. Both are jobs where a sudden motion or a draft of air can set you back a couple of hours. There are moments when I think restorers shouldn't have children; our boys have excellent studio manners but they are still boys and burst in with their routine woes at some pretty grim moments!"[24] Before the Kecks re-glued the tapes, they informed her that there was a finished painting underneath and asked whether they should proceed.

The Tremaines acquired Premier Disque *from Sonia Delauney, the widow of Robert Delauney, in 1953. "I feel that Robert started it and Mondrian took it as far as it would go with the* Victory," *she explained to the Tremaines. She also presented them with this photograph of her husband in his workshop with the* Disque *leaning against the wall.*

Although her feeling was that the collage should be preserved instead of the finished painting, Emily again sought Alfred Barr's opinion. She recalled the conversation: " 'I know what my answer is, I won't touch one piece of collage, but as a scholar, do you think it should be put back into its original completed form?' He said 'No, if you preserve that collage, that is the greatest.' " [25] The Kecks then went ahead and re-glued the tapes.

So central was the *Victory Boogie-Woogie* to the entire Tremaine collection that several paintings were acquired specifically because of their relationship to it, the most important being *Premier Disque* by the French painter Robert Delaunay. In 1953 Sonia Delaunay, his widow, approached the Tremaines to see if they were interested in purchasing *Premier Disque* because she wanted it exhibited with the *Victory Boogie-Woogie*. In that way, the apotheosis of Orphism would hang alongside the apotheosis of Neoplasticism — two of the great art movements of the twentieth century exemplified by two of its greatest works. Delaunay had painted *Premier Disque* in 1913–14, thirty years before Mondrian conceived of the *Victory,* and had felt that in it he had broken "through to the actual, nuclear problem of painting. I found the essential technique of color."[26] Emily loved to tell the following story about why she and Burton were offered the painting:

> We got the *Disque* because of the Mondrian. In 1953 in Paris, we visited with Michel Seuphor, who wrote the Mondrian catalogue raisonné. He wanted to talk to us about the *Victory*. While we were there, he said that Madame Delaunay had asked him to bring us by her studio because she too had questions on the painting. So we went and had a marvelous time, and, at the end of the afternoon, she went off into another room and brought out her husband's *Premier Disque*. Burton and I were so impressed with it. I told her I felt it was the beginning of Modernism, that so many things start in that painting, even to eliminating the frame, everything. Then Madame Delaunay looked at us and said "Would you like to own it?" But of course! "Well, I would like it to be with the Mondrian," she said. "I feel that Robert started it and Mondrian took it as far as it would go with the *Victory*, even to leaving the piece unfinished, the final enigma. . . . Always keep the two together." And Burton and I promised that we'd try—and we have.[27]

The Tremaines were delighted to be able to acquire the *Premier Disque*, and although they moved their paintings around a great deal in their New York apartment (partially because paintings were often out on loan to museums), as often as possible they kept their promise to Madame Delaunay: the target-shaped *Premier Disque* hung on the left side of the fireplace (which was itself an austere black square) and the diamond-shaped *Victory Boogie-Woogie* on the right, while in between on the mantel stood African art—a Senufo female form and an antelope head from the Upper Volta. Carefully placed on the coffee table in the foreground were two small red spheres that functioned as vanishing points, uniting the entire end of the room into the equivalent of a single canvas.

The interview with Mondrian published in the *Knickerbocker Weekly* just after his death prompted Emily to seek out the work of Stuart Davis; Mondrian had said that Davis was the most abstract of the young Americans. In the spring of 1945, Emily and Burton visited Davis in his New York studio and bought *For Internal Use Only* (still wet and unfinished), which incorporated several ideas from Mondrian, specifically the black grid, vertical orientation, and color-within-color blocks. Davis had first met Mondrian in 1941 at the home of their mutual friend Charmion von Wiegand. When asked by Emily if the painting had been inspired by Mondrian, Davis said that he had painted it in homage to the older artist and that he missed their experiences listening to jazz together. He pointed out to Burton and Emily the abstracted marquee of the New York jazz club called Spec's Place, and the piano keys, bow tie, and face of Spec himself, who was one of Mondrian's favorite boogie-woogie pianists.[28]

Other paintings purchased around the same time that to Emily bore a relationship to the work of Mondrian were *Flying* (1929/1935) by Josef Albers, *Composition* (1934) by Jean Hélion, *Perpendiculars and Diagonals* (1945) by Ilya Bolotowsky, *Space-Time Construction No. III* (1923) by Theo van Doesburg, and *No. 22* by Ad Reinhardt. In 1948 the Tremaines also purchased Mondrian's *Pier and Ocean* (1914) from Charmion von Wiegand. It was one of a series of paintings in which Mondrian began to replace curved lines with straight, moving from a naturalistic viewpoint to an abstract one. A colored gouache and ink on paper, *Pier and Ocean* shares with the *Victory Boogie-Woogie* an experimental, unfinished quality because some of the black lines are obviously overpainted in white.

When Richard Tuttle, an artist and sculptor, first visited the Tremaines' apartment in the late 1960s, Emily and Burton had recently purchased a huge painting by Larry Poons on which curving lines of red and blue dots shimmered across a brilliant red ground. Tuttle thought it "a 1960's rock n' roll painting" and was surprised at Emily's enthusiasm about it: "It was like watching a 70-year-old tap her foot to the beat of the Rolling Stones music. I guess I had a quizzical look on my face and she read my look. She said to me, 'Come here, I'll show you how I got that painting.' And she took me over and stood me in front of Mondrian's *Victory Boogie-Woogie* and said to me, 'That's how I got that painting.' What she was saying was that what Mondrian was giving us in his painting was rooted in the same source that this young painter [Poons] is seeing too. She had a real intelligence of seeing."[29]

Emily was so certain of the *Victory's* profound worth and so convinced that "it belongs to the world" that she and Burton loaned it through the 1950s and 1960s to the Museum of Modern Art in order for it to be accessible to young artists. Seeing its influence especially on the works of Mark Rothko and Ad Reinhardt, Emily contended years later that Mondrian actually had been the prime mover behind Abstract Expressionism, the dominant art movement of the late 1940s and 1950s: "Ad Reinhardt told me that he, Pollock, and the others saw that painting in the Museum of Modern Art all those years. He said 'As Abstract Expressionists, we got our courage toward the unfinished, toward the Japanese unintentional theory of drip from this.' Bridget Riley, when she came here from England for the Museum of Modern Art exhibition *The*

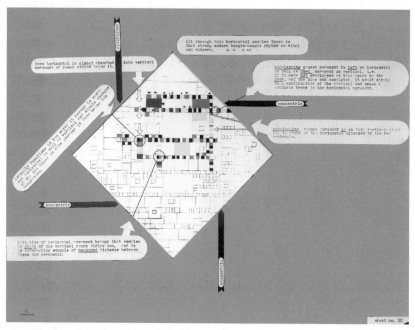

As she painted an exact copy of Victory Boogie-Woogie, *Perle Fine kept meticulous notes and drew up a series of analytical charts. The intent was to increase Mondrian's influence on artists, but the charts were never published.*

Responsive Eye, came to see the painting. She said she had seen it in Belgium and it was the greatest influence on her work." [30]

By the early 1970s, Emily was becoming disenchanted with museums and was uncertain as to what should be done with her formidable collection in the event of her and Burton's deaths. This disenchantment centered in part on the *Victory Boogie-Woogie.* From the day she had acquired it, Alfred Barr, who had been a principal advisor to her as well as a close friend, believed that it was inferior to the completed *Broadway Boogie-Woogie,* which the Museum of Modern Art owned. As a result, the museum alternated showing the two, putting the *Victory* in storage when not on view. Barr's actions irritated Emily, especially when she found out that some artists had come to New York specifically to see the *Victory* and were not given access to it. This was the beginning of a low-key feud between Barr and Emily that eventually soured her toward the Museum of Modern Art, even though she remained very active on its International Council throughout the 1960s and 1970s. "They were favoring their own pictures and I wasn't committing the *Victory* to them. I was always very fond of Alfred. I knew he was as extreme as he could be, but I loved being with him. But Alfred was always jealous of his own collection, and as much as he knew how great the *Victory* was, until he had his name on it, he was going to show the *Broadway* and downgrade this picture. That's one of the things that annoyed me, that he couldn't be objective, because if I felt that the *Broadway* was a better picture I'd be the first one to say 'well, the *Broadway* is the best.' But there's no question, the *Victory* is it. This was a culmination of everything that Mondrian ever thought. Unfortunately, if he'd lived another week or two, we'd have had it right; but even so, the struggle there [on the unfinished canvas] is important."

Emily was quick to make the point that Mondrian himself was not pleased with the *Broadway Boogie-Woogie* and that the only reason he did not change it, as he did the *Victory*, was that after it was exhibited, it was sold and donated to the Museum of Modern Art, so it was no longer his to revise. But he had told fellow artist Carl Holty that its effect was weakened by a preponderance of yellow. Holty believed that the colors had looked clearer and more distinct in Mondrian's small studio than on the museum's walls, where the yellows seemed to bleed off against the whites.[31]

After their disagreement with the Museum of Modern Art about putting the *Victory Boogie-Woogie* in storage, the Tremaines took the painting back. Emily hung it on the wall of their living room in Manhattan for the rest of her life, but not without some guilt. "It's still fantastic. I think it does not belong here. It belongs in the public domain. Every time I walk in the door, I'm covered with guilt, but I just haven't been able to part with it. I will. I'll make myself."

Over the span of her life, Emily would find great joy in many paintings and sculptures that were far removed from Mondrian's neoplasticism. However, it was always the *Victory Boogie-Woogie* that for her was the quintessential work of art: "I feel that the *Victory* was an intense breakthrough that was the culmination of Mondrian's whole life. The experience of it is wonderful; there is drama caught in it. It's like Beethoven's Ninth Symphony—the full orchestration—the chorus forcing octaves almost beyond human ears. Mondrian felt that nothing is ever finished—always proceeding from the material to the spiritual, just as high as you are able to go with it. There is no beginning and no end."[32]

Paradoxically it would be Burton, not Emily, who would acquire for the Tremaine collection in 1948 an aesthetic response to the *Victory Boogie-Woogie*—Barnett Newman's defiant *Euclidean Abyss*. In this painting, a fluid yellow line, the "zip," flows across a black atmospheric ground (the abyss) opposing a yellow reverse L that defines the right edge. Even though his artistic yearnings were every bit as transcendental as Mondrian's, Newman felt that geometry was dead and that it was time to move through the window that Mondrian had managed to crack open.

It is obvious that in their search for purity of form, [painters and sculptors] have deprived their art of certain traditional values; yet it is their passionate and concentrated investigation of form which has made painting and sculpture valuable to architects as never before in the history of art.
—Alfred H. Barr, Jr.

CHAPTER SIX

PAINTING TOWARD ARCHITECTURE

When World War II finally ended, European artists, collectors, museum curators, and gallery owners began to assess the damage and to bring works of art out of hiding. Some artists had died; many collectors had been killed in the death camps; paintings had been destroyed or stolen. Disoriented, and appalled at what had been irretrievably lost, artists struggled to start over.

Many of the artists who had fled to the United States before the war, including Max Ernst and Fernand Léger, returned to Europe, but several of the architects had found secure positions and chose to make the United States their permanent home. Among these were Walter Gropius, Marcel Breuer, and Martin Wagner, who all were ensconced at Harvard, and Mies van der Rohe, who was at the Armour Institute of Technology in Chicago.

It was a perfect time for the Tremaines to collect art. Besides her visual acuity, Emily had the ability to analyze what she heard and read; Burton had the gut instinct; they both had the means; and the art world had shifted from neutral into high gear, with New York City as its base of operations instead of Paris, although the importance of that shift would only be revealed in hindsight.

It was also a perfect time to promote architecture. The nation's postwar economic vitality was coupled with the catalytic presence of European architects. There also were several American

The Painting Toward Architecture *exhibition opened in December 1947 in the Avery Court of the Wadsworth Atheneum.*

architectural giants still working at the top of their form. The most famous was Frank Lloyd Wright, whose creativity was not diminished by the fact that he was about to turn eighty. The iconoclastic Buckminster Fuller, only in his fifties, sought for efficient ways to make the best use of natural resources to promote the well-being of all humans, which had led him to study forms that occur in nature, specifically the hexagon. From this arose his idea of the geodesic dome. Such favorable conditions for architecture had not prevailed since the Roaring Twenties. But, unfortunately, an entire generation of architects who had received their training in the two decades following World War I had seen their prospects wither during the Great Depression and World War II. Now that the way was finally clear, they lacked inspiration and resolve. The International Style that had predominated in the 1920s and 30s seemed dated, art deco was passé, and what would take their places was uncertain. Yet there was excitement in the air, fomented by the economic conditions which promised that what could be dreamed actually could be built.

It was during this period that Emily came to see herself and Burton not as passive collectors adorning their walls solely for their own pleasure, but as catalytic patrons who could strengthen the bond between architecture and art in the United States. To help achieve this, she decided to mount a nationwide touring exhibition of the Tremaine collection under the name of Burton's firm, the Miller Company. Calling the exhibition *Painting Toward Architecture* in homage to Mondrian, in whose voluminous writings the idea of the transformative power of art appeared frequently, Emily took on the role of advocate—not of a particular artist, but of an artistic ideal.

By the end of 1947, when the exhibition first opened in the Wadsworth Atheneum, the Tremaines had added to their collection several seminal works besides the *Victory Boogie-Woogie.* These included Fernand Léger's oil-study *Le Petit Dejeuner,* in which three massive women, who look as if they have been extruded by a machine, personably share tea amidst the comforts of chairs, a book, and a cat; Alexander Calder's lyrical mobile *Bougainvillea,* which moved sinuously in the wind like the tendrils of the plant for which it was named; and the huge canvas by Matta titled *Splitting the Ergo,* which seemed to defy geometry. Emily also included in the exhibition *Pattern of Conflict* by Mark Tobey, whose art was influenced heavily by his belief in Baha'i and Zen. Tobey believed that "the dimension that counts for the creative person is the Space he creates within himself. This inner space is closer to the infinite."[1]

Art critics were uniformly dazzled by the exhibition. Writing in the *Art Digest,* Alonzo Lansford voiced the majority opinion: "Last month there started on tour, a new kind of art exhibition—an exhibition the importance of which to artists, to architects and industrialists, and eventually to the general public, can hardly be over-estimated. . . . It is a pioneering effort which promises a unique and highly practical tie-up of the fine arts and industry, without compromise on the part of the artist."[2]

Painting Toward Architecture included thirty-seven paintings and eight pieces of sculpture, which were exhibited alongside architectural drawings

and photographs of buildings to show the correlation between art and archi-
tecture. Among the buildings represented were Frank Lloyd Wright's Hickox
House in Kankakee, Illinois; Le Corbusier's Savoye House in Poissy, France;
J. J. P. Oud's Cafe de Unie in Rotterdam, Holland; and the Bauhaus in Dressau,
Germany, designed by Gropius. Although European artists predominated in
the exhibition, there were fourteen American artists and sculptors represented: Alexander Calder, Perle Fine, Lyonel Feininger, Mark Tobey, James
Guy, Mary Callery, Harry Bertoia, Charles Sheeler, Ilya Bolotowsky (who had
emigrated from Russia at age sixteen), Stuart Davis, John Marin, Georgia
O'Keeffe, José de Rivera, and Irene Rice Pereira. The earliest work (other than
a woodcut by Japanese artist Kunisado) was *Woman with a Fan* by Picasso
begun in 1911 and finished in 1918, followed by Juan Gris's *Still-Life with Pears,*
dated 1913. Calder's *Bougainvillea,* Mary Callery's *Water Ballet,* and Charles
Sheeler's *On a Theme of Farm Buildings* were new works, completed in 1947.

Artists, architects, and students unable to see the exhibition in person
prized the catalog, with its brilliant text. "To me it had a kind of Book of Genesis look, the first wonderful steps of a new version of Creation," remembered
the art historian Robert Rosenblum, a version that "could at last destroy and
replace a crumbling, moribund world inherited from the 19th century." He
recalled:

> In 1948, my first year as a graduate student in the history of art, I stumbled
> upon a book that had just been published. It was called *Painting Toward
> Architecture,* and it could boast on its title-page the participation of two lus-
> trous names known even to a beginner like myself — Alfred H. Barr, Jr. and
> Henry-Russell Hitchcock. What lay inside had, for me, almost the char-
> acter of a thrilling manifesto, a sweeping overview that, with the help of
> discussions of specific works of art, summed up the most adventurous and
> progressive feeling and thinking of the first half of our century. Its timing —
> three years after the devastating conclusion of the Second World War — was
> both poignant and optimistic, for it still conveyed the pre-War belief that
> the heroic innovations of modern art somehow reflected the possibility of
> creating the cleanest and purest of slates, and one uniquely appropriate to
> our century. Moreover, it persuasively suggested that the three tradition-
> ally major arts — painting, sculpture, architecture — had joined forces in a
> common endeavor to materialize, even if for the moment more on draw-
> ing boards and in museums than in the real world, a dream of a Utopian
> society founded on an alphabet of new forms.[3]

Sponsored by the Miller Company, the Painting Toward Architecture *exhibition was designed to encourage architects to appreciate the interrelationship between modern art and architecture.*

The initial impetus for mounting a nationwide exhibition under the name of the Miller Company was decidedly practical—encouraging architects to specify Miller fluorescent lighting in their designs. Yet underlying that impetus was the Bauhaus philosophy that called for a synthesis of manufacturing and art to benefit society as a whole, and not just the wealthy cultural elite. The largest subset of artists in the exhibition had been associated with either the Bauhaus or the Constructivist Movements. It included Mondrian, Klee, Kandinsky, Feininger, Moholy-Nagy, Albers, Schwitters, and van Doesburg.[4]

The project began when, not long after their marriage, Emily became art director of Burton's lighting firm. Convinced that architects were interested in art, one of Emily's first ideas was to make silkscreen prints of some of the paintings in the collection for the sales people to use as gifts to clients and prospects. She was influential in hiring Josef Albers, then at the Black Mountain School in North Carolina, to begin work on redesigning the corporate logo, and Serge Chermayeff to redesign all the stationery, including bills of lading and packing slips. Drawing on her publishing experience with *Apéritif*, she simplified type, made it consistent, and subordinated it to abstract design, moving away from realistic representation. Having purchased Josef Albers's painting *Flying* in 1945 under the Miller Company name, Emily suggested that it be used on the cover of an advertising brochure for the fluorescent lighting division, because its linear design was analogous to the new ways that lighting was being used. Later she recommended that a sculpture by José de Rivera, with its swirling forms suggestive of heat waves, be used on the cover of an advertising brochure for the division that made oil burners. According to an article that appeared at the time the exhibition opened:

> When one of [the advertisements] won a National Advertising Agency Network award, Miller ad men felt reassured and now they wholeheartedly support the flexible checkerboard, asymmetric scheme designed for this year's campaign by Serge Chermayeff, Director of Chicago's Institute of Design. . . . Miller engineers began to take notice of a kind of art they had never looked at or cared about before, because they saw it could speak their language. In planning arrangements of fluorescent lighting fixtures they began to derive inspiration from the patterns of the pictures in the collection. Many of them requested paintings for their own offices. One of them bought himself a Stuart Davis; others have begun purchasing lithographs and prints.[5]

Under Burton's guidance, the company had moved more aggressively into the production of fluorescent lighting fixtures specifically for business and industry. In the 1940s fluorescent lighting was still a relatively new form of illumination. The Miller Company had installed it in aircraft plants as well as many other plants during the war, but now that peacetime had returned, they wanted to encourage architects to include it in their plans for commercial buildings. Because continuous fluorescent lighting was a component of a hung ceiling, instead of an appendage, it needed to be included in the architect's initial drawings as a structural element. Achieving their goal required that architects be educated about fluorescent lighting and its design potential. The ancillary step was to encourage them to specify lighting by the Miller Company. Calling the concept "Ceilings Unlimited," the Miller Company had begun designing various patterns of fluorescent lighting, but they did not know how to get the attention of architects. When Burton asked Emily for her advice, she replied, "Whenever I'm around museums, I certainly meet a lot of architects and whenever I talk to them, they are very interested in art. . . . I think if you would put an exhibition together that would be oriented toward architecture, it would attract the architect who would get to know your company name." Emily always claimed that in terms of making decisions about art, Burton was "very courageous, much more courageous than I am." In this situation, he told her, "Go ahead. We would ordinarily put twelve ads in *Fortune*. I'll give you what the twelve ads would cost the company to do it your way." Emily immediately called Chick Austin to get his opinion. "Oh, I think it's a great idea. Come over and we'll have Russell Hitchcock to lunch," he said.

By this time, Chick had left the Wadsworth Atheneum to take the position of director of the John and Mabel Ringling Museum of Art in Sarasota, Florida, but he had kept his stage-set-style house on upscale Scarborough Street in Hartford. It was there that Emily probably first met Henry-Russell Hitchcock, a great bear of a man with a ferocious intellect and an encyclopedic knowledge of architecture. Fifteen years earlier he and Philip Johnson had collaborated on the influential book *The International Style: Architecture Since 1922*. While traveling with him on a research trip through Europe, Johnson had written to his mother that Hitchcock was "tenderhearted, enthusiastic and brilliant intellectually. . . . his mind works like mine in disconcerting jumps, but he really knows a lot and can synthesize his knowledge. . . . He knows everything there is to know about traveling. . . . does not fit in America, and does not feel at home there. He is much too strange, with his great Socrates face under a great messy red beard. But he is terribly sensitive. A great many people dislike him, but real people are always eminently dislikeable, and he has many warm friends."[6]

Burton had not been a collector prior to marrying Emily. However, he had moved rapidly and wholeheartedly into her camp, and now threw his full support behind her idea for the exhibition, including hiring Hitchcock to help bring it into architectural focus. When the exhibition opened in December 1947, art critic Aline Louchheim interviewed both Emily and Burton and reported the following story about Burton's first personal purchase, which in his ever-practical way was related to his company: "I was at the Non-Objective Museum and I saw one picture and suddenly I thought of our combustion engineer — and I said to myself — that picture shows just how his mind works. That particular canvas wasn't for sale, but we went to the artist's studio — and I bought my first Perle Fine."[7]

Having won over her husband, Emily met with the company's board of directors, advertising executives and engineers who were at first quite skeptical about the idea of an exhibition. She explained about Le Corbusier in France and Mies van der Rohe in Germany, and pointed to the *Victory Boogie-Woogie* hanging in her office, attempting to illustrate the enormous influence of twentieth century art on typography, layout, and architecture in Europe. "In our fluorescent lighting equipment business today we are concerned with problems of architecture, structure, and design," she explained. "This indicates a direction we must follow, and one to which we must introduce those architects in America who will use our equipment." Emily assured the company's executives that for a lower cost the exhibition would attract more attention than the planned advertising campaign.[8]

With the board's reluctant concurrence, Emily and Hitchcock selected the paintings to be included and began to work on the text for the catalog. Because Hitchcock was teaching at Wesleyan University in neighboring Middletown, it was convenient for Emily and him to meet regularly. "We'd discuss how we could make a point without forcing [a painting] into architecture." They decided that no art would be commissioned specifically to support the thesis. Paintings purchased included Le Corbusier's *Still-Life,* Moholy-Nagy's *Farb-gitter No. I,* Ben Nicholson's *Still Life,* and Theo van Doesburg's *Space-Time Construction No. III.* According to Emily, the fact that none of the works was commissioned was one of the exhibition's greatest strengths. It was composed of art created for purely aesthetic reasons, instead of commercial or academic reasons. "I don't know of any company except the Miller Company that never commissioned a work," said Emily. "We bought what we thought was truly said, what the artists truly wanted to say."

Emily then hired a team to put the entire exhibition together, including the young historian Vincent J. Scully, who was at Yale University, and Mary Chalmers Rathbun, who had been working at the Addison Gallery. The renowned graphic artist Bradbury Thompson, also at Yale, designed the catalog, incorporating shapes from the works of Jean Arp and John Tunnard into the jacket and frontispiece. An image of a painting by Ben Nicholson was embossed in gold on the black cloth cover. In the foreword to the catalog, Alfred Barr stressed the problems of economic insecurity and lack of freedom of expression that often hampered architects, and applauded the Miller Company for its enlightened efforts, ending with the benediction — "may its enthusiasm prove contagious." Early drafts were read by Barr and James Thrall Soby, a friend of Chick Austin and an influential modern art patron who had written about Picasso, Dali, de Chirico, and Tchelitchew. Although the exhibition had been her idea, Emily's name appeared only on the acknowledgments page, where she was listed as Art Director of the Miller Company, a position for which she did not accept a salary. Only the printing of the catalog fell short of her quality standards: the print registration was off on Léger's *Le Petit Dejeuner* and Mondrian's *Composition,* causing green lines to shadow the black lines (a flaw that would have rankled Mondrian, were he alive, because he felt that green was an impure color).

To make the connection between art and architecture even more apparent, Hitchcock prevailed on Emily to buy a woodcut done in 1805 by Kunisado. It was titled *Japanese Actors,* and was an example of the type of art that had influenced Frank Lloyd Wright. Hitchcock was an expert on Wright's work. In the catalog the print appeared opposite the text, and the concentric squares in the kimono of one of the actors seemed to pop out from the page. Hitchcock's text was dense throughout. However, his writing style was never turgid, and this particular juxtaposition of art and subject gave him a chance for insightful eloquence:

> It remained for Wright to apprehend in the Japanese print—and not as has sometimes been supposed in Japanese buildings—wholly new abstract possibilities for architecture. He saw that the simple geometric elements, so carefully disposed in the Oriental woodcuts, created a compositional interest independent of the subject matter of the prints. By this time this was indeed recognized by many European and American artists and critics. But Wright also realized that this sort of abstract or pattern interest was capable of analogous exploitation in architecture.[9]

Of the forty-five works in the exhibition, Hitchcock and Emily chose to exclude the following seven in the catalog, only listing them at the end: Harry Bertoia's mono-print *Composition,* Josef Albers's *Flying,* Perle Fine's *Climax* (her *Midnight* was included), Leo Amino's *Spring,* a sculpture made out of polystyrene, and Picasso's *Drawing, 1916, New Hebrides Mask,* and *La Femme au Chapeau. La Femme au Chapeau* was a major addition to the Tremaine collection, purchased in 1947, for $5500, but it did not fit Hitchcock's thesis easily.[10] Paintings such as Charles Sheeler's *On a Theme of Farm Buildings,* and Georgia O'Keeffe's *New York Night* had buildings as their subject and were clearly architectonic, but *La Femme au Chapeau,* finished by Picasso the day the Germans marched into Paris in 1939, was difficult to categorize, at least from the standpoint of the connection between art and architecture.

The exhibition opened in December 1947 in the Avery Court of the Wadsworth Atheneum, an especially appropriate space because it had been designed, at Chick Austin's insistence, in the austere International Style. Then the exhibition traveled to museums in twenty-four other American cities, going first to the Walker Art Center in Minneapolis, followed by the Akron Art Institute, and the Baltimore Museum of Art. In every city that it visited, there was a gala reception to which local architects were personally invited. In Hartford and Baltimore, Hitchcock was on hand to deliver an opening night lecture. Given his renown among architects, attendance was excellent.

Extending the reach of the exhibition was publicity and at least three major articles: two by Aline Louchheim for the *New York Times* and *Art News* and one by Serge Chermayeff in *Art and Architecture*. There were also articles in *Art Digest, Newsweek, Harper's Bazaar, Saturday Review,* the *New Yorker,* and the *Herald Tribune*. Whenever the exhibition opened in a new city, there was local press coverage. For example, articles appeared in the *Christian Science Monitor,* the *Los Angeles Times,* the *Minneapolis Star,* and the *Milwaukee Journal.* To further increase the interest of architects, the entire exhibition went on display at the Greenbrier Hotel in White Sulphur Springs, West Virginia, for the annual meeting of the American Institute of Architects. Emily also made certain that colleges were on the itinerary, including Yale University, the University of Michigan, Rhode Island School of Design, the University of Tennessee, and Smith College.

The exhibition brought The Miller Company to the attention not only of architects but of the country at large. Shortly after the exhibition closed, the publicity the company had received was appraised at $200,000 for a single year. Because the length of the tour was two and a half years, the full value was approximately $500,000. It also created interest—and some introspection—about the role of corporations as patrons, the new "Medici," as one reporter put it. Before that time some large corporations, including Pepsi and the Container Company, had amassed collections, but few had underwritten exhibitions of any kind. Furthermore, the art that corporations owned was firmly conservative. One reviewer expressed tongue-in-cheek dismay that in the Miller collection there was "not one landscape! Not one nude! Not one cuddly baby! Not one house! Not even a marine! Obviously, unlike the average company collection, it was not assembled to meet the approval of the masses, not unless we assume the Miller advertising executives to be hopelessly incompetent." The reviewer concluded that they knew what they were doing and hoped others would follow their inspired lead.[11]

Serge Chermayeff was impressed that the exhibition pointed to fundamental affinities, rather than superficial similarities, between contemporary painting and architecture. "A more vivid humanist vocabulary for architecture emerges in which the rich, free form as an element stands as a complement to the rectilinear severity of line and plane. Qualities of texture, color and translucency of both natural and synthetic material are clearly recognized and are exploited as integral elements of composition by architect, sculptor and painter alike." He believed that the exhibition would help acquaint the public with this new vocabulary of architecture, which would in the long run make it easier for the architect to convince clients of the value of the new. Chermayeff was hopeful that it would even lead to "lasting friendship between the public and the contemporary artists." [12]

By the time the exhibition closed in June 1950, the Miller Company had made a name for itself, but, unfortunately, the nature of architecture and fluorescent lighting had begun to change. By the mid-1950s, the company decided not to market to architects by means of art. It also had come to realize that to use art that it had not commissioned specifically for marketing or advertising was to operate in a gray area ethically. There were no laws on copyright of art at the time, but the custom was for a company that owned art and wished to use it in this way to pay the artist an additional sum, over and above the purchase price, commensurate with the commercial value of the advertising or marketing campaign of which it was to be a part. At the very least, a company owner was expected to inform artists of their intentions and to obtain approval.

Acting in good faith, the Miller Company had acquired Josef Albers's painting *Flying* early in 1945 for $300 from the dealer B.J. Neumann who had purchased the painting for himself personally several years before. In April 1945, Shirley Naysmith, vice president of engineering at the Miller Company, wrote to Albers to inform him of the purchase, tell him that the company had produced a silkscreen, and ask if he would be interested in designing a trademark. [13] Albers was interested in the proposal, and the relationship began amicably. Then, early in November, Naysmith wrote to Albers about plans to use the painting on the cover of a brochure and asked him to sign a release. Albers felt that he should be compensated for the commercial use of the painting. To gain support for his position, he immediately telegraphed fellow artists and designers Paul Rand and Herbert Bayer asking for their opinions. Rand responded, "I quite concur with your views and I believe that you should ask for $5000 for use of your drawing." Rand recommended that to protect Albers's integrity, a clause be added requiring the Miller Company to consult Albers "as to the fashion in which your drawings are to be employed. In any event this will preclude any indiscriminate use. I don't think that royalties work out very well. It would involve endless complications and legal ramifications." Bayer also responded promptly by telegram: "Unwise [to] allow Miller to print anything without first submitting to you for approval or rejection. For permission to use your painting for advertising purposes, ask $500 to $1000 depending on size of company advertising. We have checked business rating and found them A1. No chance for royalty basis. Negotiations more businesslike if handled by your agent."

With this support for his position, Albers refused to sign a release unless he was compensated and was given the right to approve the design of the brochure. He wrote to Naysmith, "Through purchasing a painting the buyer acquires the physical ownership of the painting. In the case of recognized artistic value, it appears as a matter of course that the artistic merits of the painting remain with its originator. Thus the owner has the moral, if not a legal obligation, towards the artist as to the use of the painting, just as the artist is equally entitled to pursue the proper use of his work."

Albers chose Rand's estimate of $5,000 as fair payment, not Bayer's suggestion of $500 to $1,000. Naysmith politely responded, quoting case law, that unless Albers had stipulated in the original sale any "special or unusual rights," the owner had the right of reproduction because "the unconditional sale carried with it the transfers of the common law copyright and right to reproduce." However, Naysmith offered Albers $150, "which represents one-half of what we paid for the painting, as this we understand is in line with what some dealers are trying to make the commercial practice now and which has nothing to do with the law or the conditions under which your painting was originally sold." In the closing paragraph of his letter, Naysmith once again asked if Albers would be interested in designing a logo or in selling the company another painting to be used as a corporate logo. "While on the subject, we return to the thought which we left with you in one of our previous letters, and that is, we would be interested in purchasing a further painting from you which in your opinion would be somewhat characteristic of our product which is modern illumination on engineering lines." Anticipating a continuing amicable commercial relationship with the Miller Company, Albers eventually settled for $300, signed the release, and began work on the corporate logo. However, the relationship again turned sour in 1947, and the company turned to Serge Chermayeff to take over the task of redesigning the logo and the stationery.

Albers's design was a series of concentric circles, basically a target, over which the name Miller was superimposed. Two elongated lower-case letter l's in the name were meant to indicate factory smokestacks. When Chermayeff took over the job, he eliminated the circles, which the Miller Company executives had found distracting, but kept the elongated l's. Albers apparently felt that his idea had been usurped without adequate compensation, and this time the relationship between artist and company was completely severed. This helps explain why *Flying,* which toured with the exhibition, was not included in the catalog, except in the list of paintings at the end. Perhaps the Miller Company feared yet another request for compensation from Albers if they linked his work to their product in print.

Being a corporate patron of the arts was turning out in some respects to be a difficult proposition. Several critics applauded the Tremaines' efforts to translate abstract art into the objects of daily life. But, what some people saw as enlightened self-interest, others saw as putting the arts at the service of the marketplace. In support, Aline Louchheim wrote in *Art News,* "The Tremaines have made abstract and non-objective art intelligible in terms of application. They have seen its coherent design, the relations of its colors, and its experiments with new materials not as ends in themselves, but as starting points for ultimate translation into the most widely seen and understood (and the most living) twentieth-century art forms — architecture and advertising layout. In that application they hope it will be approached and understood by many people who have heretofore dismissed it as anything from sheer mathematics to incomprehensible doodling." [14]

In another article, published in the *New York Times,* Louchheim said that the use of Albers's painting and Rivera's sculpture on the brochure covers demonstrated that Emily had "recognized quite frankly that in an age of scientific approach and in an art style predicated on intellectual theories much painting is primarily laboratory research in design. Thus some of it has been adapted without feelings of sacrilege."

One of those people who would have disagreed strongly with that statement was Barnett Newman whose painting *Euclidean Abyss* the Tremaines had purchased in 1948 while the collection was on tour. Apparently they considered adding it to the exhibition, but Newman was opposed to the painting being associated in any way with a commercial venture.

By the early 1950s, the Miller Company had decided to back off from the entire endeavor. From then on it took a standard approach to advertising. The main reason was purely economic: it no longer made marketing sense to focus heavily on architects. There is one interesting footnote to all this. Many

At the California Palace of the Legion of Honor in July 1948, Calder's Bougainvillea *was placed on a low table at the center of the room.*

years later, when the Philip Morris Corporation underwrote a retrospective of Jasper Johns's work, the Tremaines were asked to lend *White Flag* and *Three Flags;* indeed, the retrospective would have been incomplete without them. At first Emily flatly refused, because she was totally opposed to the use of tobacco and felt that Philip Morris actually was advertising its products via its sponsorship of the retrospective. She eventually relented, when appealed to by Johns himself. Because of the *Painting Toward Architecture* exhibition, no one knew better than Emily the effectiveness of linking a corporate name with art.

In the final analysis, it is questionable whether the exhibition achieved anything besides advertising success for the Miller Company. Paradoxically, Emily's efforts at increasing the influence of art on architecture and graphic design, specifically in advancing Mondrian's principles, tended to result in at best an attenuation and at worst a debasement of those principles. Without overemphasizing the importance of the exhibition, perhaps it succeeded too well. Writing forty years after the exhibition, at a time when Mondrian's influence had become part of the cultural background, Paul Brach, a New York artist and critic, concluded an article about Mondrian with a telling observation about "the failure of modernism to bring us better lives": "Mondrian felt that the application of his principles would free humanity from 'subjectivity' and would create happier lives. When the uninitiated see in a later classical Mondrian a design for linoleum or for a crisp graphic layout, this is not a travesty of Mondrian's intentions, but more like an askew version of his aspirations. Nowadays, it requires an act of faith to separate Mondrian's aspirational message from the artifacts of designers' studios."[15]

The *Painting Toward Architecture* exhibition would not have been particularly noteworthy had it been the Tremaines' only major effort to become patrons of the arts and architecture during this period. However, they went one step further and decided to commission architects to design buildings that would embody the confluence of art and architecture. In one year, 1947–1948, they hired five: Lutah Maria Riggs, the architect for Brunninghausen, to design a ranch house for the Bar T Bar Ranch; Buckminster Fuller to design three identical houses, the first to be built on a New York rooftop, the second on the ranch, and the third in Montecito; Oscar Niemeyer, a young Brazilian architect, to design a beach house in Montecito; Frank Lloyd Wright to design a visitor center and observatory for Meteor Crater near Flagstaff, Arizona; and Philip Johnson for a plethora of projects, from the design of fluorescent lighting systems for the Miller Company to barn renovations. With the exception of Riggs, all these architects were either famous already or would be shortly. Yet, regardless of the extraordinary concentration of talent, the Tremaines rejected every design except Johnson's. Their relationship with him would span twenty-three years and would include the exterior designs of the factory for the Miller Company's phosphor bronze rolling mill (1965) and its lighting fixture plant (1970).

The Tremaines had been very pleased with Wright's and Niemeyer's designs and had rejected them on the basis of cost, not quality. Emily, therefore, made certain that they were published, so that they could influence other architects. The conceptual drawings for Wright's Meteor Crater observatory and Niemeyer's beach house were published in the *Painting Toward Architecture* catalog. Niemeyer's plans and presentation model also were included in a 1949 Museum of Modern Art exhibition curated by Philip Johnson, entitled "From Le Corbusier to Niemeyer, 1929–49," as well as in the publications *Interiors* (April 1949) and *Arts and Architecture* (March 1949).

The Tremaines' first architectural endeavor involved the 300,000 acre Bar T Bar Ranch near Flagstaff, Arizona, which Burton, his brother Warren, half-sister Bertine, half-brother Carl, and the heirs of his deceased brother Alan owned in partnership with the Chilsons, a local ranch family. In his constant efforts to expand his sizable holdings, Burton's father, Lucky BG, had purchased the 100,000 acre Pitchfork Ranch, which surrounded Meteor Crater (also known as the Barringer Crater) in 1939. Bar T Bar Ranch later signed a 199-year lease to the crater itself. It was owned by the descendants of Daniel Barringer, an engineer who had attempted to mine iron from the remnants of the meteorite that had struck the earth approximately 50,000 years before.

In Burton's mind, the crater, almost a mile wide and 550 feet deep, was worthless in terms of iron ore but a potential goldmine as a tourist attraction. This plan would require new roads to make the remote site accessible and the construction of a visitor center and observatory. But before they undertook that project, Burton and Emily wanted to build a ranch house on the Bar T Bar for themselves. Emily's choice for an architect was Lutah Maria Riggs, who had been endlessly patient with Emily and Max (very demanding clients) in the building of Brunninghausen. Highly regarded in Southern California, Riggs did not have a national reputation, nor did she seek one, but that did not matter to Emily, who had great admiration for Riggs's ability to turn a three-dimensional structure into an abstract sculpture within which one could live comfortably.

Respectful of the region's architectural style, Riggs chose the shape of a ring as her motif for the ranch house. The living area occupied about half of the circumference, three tack rooms and a hitching rail completed the other half, and a round swimming pool was in the center. From the front, the ranch would appear to be a one-story structure sided in rough-hewn vertical logs from which a rustic shed roof slanted in a gradual angle. Unusual only in its curvilinear shape, the ranch was to look as if it had been built years before, and to seem as natural a part of the landscape as sagebrush and sand. However, from the rear the ranch would reveal smooth white modernist walls interspersed with large expanses of glass curving around the pool. Instead of being jarring, the juxtaposition of rustic and modern was designed as a subtle interplay. For example, the rugged outside walls were to be broken by sleek jalousie windows, and the smooth interior space was to be enclosed by split rail fencing.[16]

It is only conjecture why Riggs's design was never built. Certainly Emily's taste had already turned more toward an abstract austerity free of detail, which is why the Tremaines' eventual choice of Philip Johnson as their architect was so appropriate. For whatever reason, Riggs's plans were shelved, and Emily turned next to Buckminster Fuller, whose philosophy toward life interested her as much as, or more than, his designs. She had first become aware of his work in the early 1930s when she and Max were in Cambridge. Fuller's unique Dymaxion house had been included in the "4D" Exhibition hosted by the Harvard Society for Contemporary Art in 1929. The title stood for the fourth dimension, and the highly unusual structure that was the centerpiece of the exhibition did everything it could to break out of the first three. Drawing on the engineering principles used in suspension bridges, Fuller had suspended the hexagonal house from a center mast, and then had combined the concept of compressed air with materials unusual to architecture including casein, rubber tubing, and balloon silk. It was in all respects an utterly new domestic architectural creation.[17]

Since that exhibition, Fuller had continued his efforts to develop new ways to use materials that would benefit everyone, not just the wealthy. At the end of World War II, anticipating that there was going to be a serious housing shortage and aware that thousands of aircraft workers would be laid off with the cessation of the production of warplanes, Fuller made a deal with Beech Aircraft in Wichita, Kansas, to build a prototype of his redesigned Dymaxion house in preparation for mass production. Soliciting the support of labor leaders for the idea, he argued that it might solve the housing shortage and provide permanent employment "because there is no basic difference between the fabricating of aluminum parts for the Dymaxion house and for the fuselages of B29's." [18]

Hoping to purchase one of the Dymaxion houses, Emily wrote to Fuller while he was in Wichita in March, 1947. "We have been anxious to hear how the Dymaxion is progressing, and of course have been looking forward to seeing you again, too. So do please keep in touch with us. And maybe we can get together before too long. If you happen to be east in the late spring, it is lovely here in the country. Believe me." She wrote to him again in June reiterating her invitation. But the Dymaxion house was not to be. Even though a prototype was built and was enthusiastically received by the people who toured through it, Fuller could not get the major funding he needed to go into full mass production. Beech Aircraft had decided to turn their attention back to the building of private aircraft, and the idea of an entire house, weighing only 6,000 pounds, that could be built for the price of an expensive car did not fit in their business plans. Also, the nation was not terribly interested in Fuller's visionary ideas. In 1947 Fuller was way ahead of his time and out of step with the workings of capitalism, in which job growth came from building bigger, ever more expensive houses using raw materials that seemed limitless in supply. As a result, funding for the Dymaxion house dried up, and the Tremaines' plan of purchasing one came to an end.

Undeterred, the Tremaines approached Oscar Niemeyer. Influenced by Le Corbusier, Niemeyer was noted for using reinforced concrete in a fluid, sculptural way. He first came to the attention of Americans in 1939 with his design for the Brazilian Pavilion at the New York World's Fair. In 1942 the Museum of Modern Art put on an exhibition called *Brazil Builds*, highlighting his work. Rapidly gaining in international fame, Niemeyer would within a year of the Tremaines' project be appointed to the team of architects selected to design the United Nations complex overlooking the East River in New York City, an assignment that would give him a chance to work closely with Le Corbusier.

Emily owned property on the Pacific Ocean in Montecito that had been owned earlier in the century by Robert Louis Stevenson's stepdaughter, Isobel Fields. Situated on a small bluff, it was lush with transplanted vegetation from the South Seas, including ginger, rubber plants and jasmine. The Tremaines decided it was the ideal location for a beach house designed by Niemeyer. When asked by a reporter why they did not hire an architect closer at hand, Emily told him they had enormous admiration for Niemeyer's work and wanted to have an example of it right at home.[19] Since Niemeyer was unable to visit the site or to meet with the Tremaines in person, the Tremaines decided to hire Lutah Maria Riggs to provide the working drawings, draw up the specifications, and supervise the construction of the house.[20] She was to be Niemeyer's on-site alter ego.

For the spectacular site chosen, Niemeyer conceived of something far more grand than a typical beach house. Low and horizontal, with plenty of glass "to take maximum advantage of the marvelous view offered by the Pacific Ocean," as Niemeyer wrote on the plans, it was designed specifically for major Southern California-style entertaining. Even Burton, who loved parties, good times, boating, and everything else that went along with those activities, found the plans too ambitious. An article in *Interiors* (April 1949) stated the problem succinctly:

It is considered fundamental in this field that a designer should never proceed with any project without first becoming thoroughly acquainted with both client and site—at first hand. Oscar Niemeyer, one of Brazil's outstanding young architects, failed to comply with the letter of this rule in producing the design illustrated in this article. Niemeyer met his clients only by mail; saw their California acres only in photographs. Nevertheless New York's Museum of Modern Art has seen fit to exhibit the model and plan of this house. The design is not only an exceptional performance in itself, but a milestone in modern architecture. Two concepts—one esthetic and one functional—that have long been taking shape, are here clearly realized. Before going any further, we must explain that the house will probably not be built in its present form because it is larger and more lavish than the clients want, but this error in scale does not invalidate the principles expressed in the design. It is an exhilarating example of what can happen when a first rate architect finds intelligent clients with a beautiful site, even though they are 6,000 miles away.[21]

Certain peculiar (for the times) touches marked the design as distinctly Niemeyer's: he called for three "Quonset huts" to be joined together to make a garage; however, the mention of Quonset huts as specified on the drawings is misleading, because what Niemeyer really envisioned was a three-arch structure that would visually provide a vertical ripple against the rectilinear main house. This play of wavy motion against straight also was captured dramatically in the shape of the first floor, which curved out like a long tail from underneath the rectangular second floor. Since Niemeyer conceived of the grounds and gardens as part of the house, he suggested to the Tremaines that they hire his colleague in Rio de Janeiro, Roberto Burle Marx, to design them. Burle Marx was a renowned landscape architect who saw the design of gardens as an art form. His sense of color was as exquisite as Matisse's, his sense of form as developed as Arp's. With a deep appreciation for both the play of light on water and the serene sound of falling water, Niemeyer adopted the practice of designing pools and fountains with interconnecting streams that harmonized with the gardens.

As a writer for *Arts and Architecture* put it (in text that reiterated the *Painting Toward Architecture* thesis), the result of their partnership was a house that "represents today's final synthesis of two important Twentieth Century stylistic trends: the strict mechanical formalism of Le Corbusier and the Cubist, constructivist movement, and the organic shapes and free form fantasy of the tradition of Miro and Arp. . . . The process of cross-fertilization by which creative influences are transmitted in the arts remains a mystery despite all that is written about them. Yet the study of the models and drawings may help to suggest how contemporary architecture has arrived at its characteristic visual forms." Still, instead of asking Niemeyer to reduce his design in size, the Tremaines decided not to build the house. His plans were shelved along with those of Riggs.

While all this was going on, the Tremaines began to make plans to build the visitor center and observatory at Meteor Crater. At Henry-Russell Hitchcock's suggestion, they approached Frank Lloyd Wright, who, Emily contended was "the only architect who could make man-made things really fit with that kind of nature," by which she meant dramatic landscapes.[22] In response to a letter asking if he would be interested in undertaking the project, Wright sent a telegram: "Dear Mr. Tremaine. I would be happy to discuss the building in relation to the Great Meteor Crater near Winslow [that] Russell Hitchcock mentions. Seems interesting."[23]

Drawn to the austerity of the Arizona desert, which he described as a "titanic, ancient battlefield" that revealed the slow, violent forces of nature, Wright had built his second headquarters, Taliesin West, in Scottsdale, Arizona, in 1938. To him, the erosion of the parched landscape under the light of a fierce sun gave a sense of life-and-death struggle. Such environmental agony was utterly alien to the peaceable surroundings of his first headquarters, Taliesin East, located in aptly named Spring Green, Wisconsin. If violent drama stirred Wright's creativity, then the cataclysm caused by a meteorite spinning out of the heavens at approximately 40,000 miles per hour and crashing into the earth with enough force to fracture the bedrock a half mile beneath the surface should have inspired the apex of dramatic design. And indeed the feeling conveyed by Wright's drawings is of a stone projectile thrust deeply into the rim, almost as if it had been hurled from the skies. Jutting out of the edge of the crater at an incredible angle, the observation tower gave even the most stalwart of individuals vertigo simply from looking at the architectural sketches.

The tower was to be built out of local stone to heighten the effect of its emergence out of the landscape. What intrigued Hitchcock about the design was Wright's view of architectural materials as elements that "must take their place in the landscape and be subject to the natural action of time and weather.

He knew that architectural materials, having their own organic life in the world of nature, ought not to be treated merely as abstract fields of color. That organic life must be understood and respected by the architect if his work is to grow in grace as it matures."[24]

However much Hitchcock thought the project might "grow in grace," Burton was uneasy with the design. His uneasiness increased when on a visit to Taliesin West in April 1948, he realized that Frank Lloyd Wright's mailbox looked similar to his design for the Meteor Crater Project. Burton suspected that Wright had developed the design years before and had merely been waiting for the appropriate site to come along to take it out of the drawer. Burton also was concerned about the scope and potential expense of the project, a concern he expressed to Wright on receiving the preliminary designs in late May of 1948. As he later wrote to Wright, "I think both Mrs. Tremaine and I assured you we were overwhelmed and delighted with your ideas from an aesthetic point of view, at the time you showed them to us at the Hotel Plaza in New York. I expressed at that time some doubt as to our ability to carry into effect a building of this size."

In August 1948 the Tremaines' concern rose to alarm when Wright submitted a bill for "3% of $50,000, $1,500." The Tremaines had set aside $50,000 for the entire project including roads, wells, power plant, fees, and so forth, with a maximum of $35,000, up from an initial $20,000, earmarked for the building itself. Wright had based his design and fees on $50,000 for the building alone. There was also major disagreement about how much it would cost to build the structure. Wright's plans called for an 11,000–square-foot building with 4,000 square feet of terrace and walks. When Burton sent the preliminary drawings out to engineers for cost estimates, they calculated construction figures of $10 per square foot for the building and $5 per square foot for the terraces and walks, for a total of $130,000. Burton wrote to Wright, "I am afraid that the $10 figure is much too low. My judgement is that this structure would run to at least $200,000." This was obviously far more than the $35,000 they had planned for, and Burton was probably correct in his higher estimate, given that there was no bedrock on which to build; the impact of the meteor had pulverized it. Wright had a reputation for being disdainful of engineers, builders, and other architects, and rarely considered the cost and difficulty (even feasibility) of construction and ongoing maintenance of his designs. The construction and maintenance problems with his Fallingwater project near Pittsburgh, Pennsylvania, were well known. Cantilevered over a waterfall, this house was considered both an aesthetic wonder and an engineering nightmare. Because Wright was as autocratic as he was brilliant, the disagreement with the Tremaines over the cost of construction and the scope of the project was a run-of-the mill occurrence for him.

In an effort to resolve the dispute and get on with the project, Burton wrote to Wright on March 11, 1949, suggesting that he reduce the size of the building to 2,700 square feet. Burton's tone was very conciliatory. "While we were at Taliesin," he wrote, "we saw your small Kybab slab. It is a wonderful form. We hope you will take another look at the drawings in view of the above [size] requirements, and see if you can't work it out for us. . . . Nothing would please Mrs. Tremaine and me more than to see you in April with the problem solved. We are in earnest in wanting the project to be completed this year."

In his reply, Wright started out in a conciliatory tone but ended up in an angry one, subtly deriding both Burton and Philip Johnson, who, he surmised, was advising the Tremaines, for knowing nothing about building. Along with the letter he resubmitted his initial bill, which he thought he was amending steeply downwards from three percent of $150,000 to three percent of $50,000. He later admitted that he had made an error and that the two bills were the same.

Dear Mr. Tremaine,

Our stories don't match. I understood you to say you had about twenty thousand dollars, could get fifty, did not know what you wanted or how much to put into the project eventually—wanted me to submit sketches suggesting possibilities that would leave you go as far as you could at one time but in the general direction of a fine thing, not fantastic in outlay. I said I could do just that and I did. The fee was not mentioned in that connection. Well, I have done my best for you in the circumstance. Of course, the opus could be made much smaller and still retain significance and dignity. It could also be built in three sections each one seeming complete, leaving you to go as far as you wanted to or your money went.

Your estimate of $10.00 per foot sounds like Phil Johnson who knows about as much about this kind of construction as you do—or even any contractor.

If you read the term sheet given you (copy enclosed) you will see that we regard the usual contractor's (or architect's) estimate as worthless. Our buildings (there are hundreds of them) stand next to their neighbors at about one third less cost—accommodation for accommodation considered—$10.00 a foot means nothing.

What merit they possess as works of art none pay for. That comes to them as a labor of love. That is true.

Now, perhaps in the circumstances, I should have sent you a bill for 3% on only $50,000 and charge the rest to educational influence for better or worse. So that is where we are. The fee is $1,500 to date. I feel that then I have done all I should do or could be expected to do until the fee on that basis is generously and gracefully paid. The amended bill is herewith.

Sincerely yours Frank Lloyd Wright.

At an impasse, Burton sent Wright a check for $750, half the amount of the bill, and Wright accepted it, replying on April 12. "My dear Tremaine, you offer an admirable solution. I am $750.00 ahead of where I was afraid I was. I have no more tremors . . . Correction. I said your contractors probably knew nothing about my plans. The reason for the statement being that for 56 years I've been busy eliminating what they knew about building from my plans. To Mrs. Tremaine—greetings. To Russell—apology. I wish you all better luck next time. Sincerely Frank Lloyd Wright." This was followed by yet another telegram in which he alluded negatively to Niemeyer's work, saying the Tremaines should try "Brazilian Rococo."

With the project at a standstill, the Tremaines and their business partners the Chilsons decided to turn to the person whom Wright had derided: Philip Johnson, a young architect whom Emily had met through Henry-Russell Hitchcock. Johnson had been an authority on modern architecture ever since the early 1930s. He was chairman of the department of architecture and design at the Museum of Modern Art and was a member in good standing of Chick Austin's circle of influential friends. In the late 1940s, he was just beginning to design buildings of his own and, in fact, did not yet have his New York architectural license. Independently wealthy and not physically required or emotionally driven to support himself by means of his architectural skills, in 1940 he returned to Harvard, from which he had graduated, to undertake his graduate architectural studies under Walter Gropius. However, his aesthetic allegiance at the time was to the architecture of Mies van der Rohe, about which Hitchcock had written in *Painting Toward Architecture,* "the arrangement of the extremely simple elements of his facades often seem to approach very closely the rigid discipline of Mondrian." Emily's devotion to Mondrian made the choice of Johnson natural. The paradox was that Johnson was elitist to the core; he despised functionalism, appreciated monumentality, and cared little about design that would benefit the masses, whereas Mondrian had longed to reach beyond elitism to a universal principle in which art was a moral and spiritual force throughout society. In May of 1951 Johnson was asked by Peter Blake, his former assistant, what factors Johnson believed to be the chief obstacles to the continuation of the architectural renascence currently under way in the United States. Johnson's response could have been lifted from the text for *Painting Toward Architecture:* "There are no obstacles to an architectural renascence except the various theories of functionalism which keep people's eyes turned away from the art of architecture." [25]

Beginning in 1948, Johnson undertook several projects simultaneously for the Tremaines including designing the Miller Company's executive offices, a recreation room for the home of Burton, Jr., and the redesign of the Tremaines' home in Madison, Connecticut. He also designed fluorescent lighting systems for the Miller Company's product line. In fact, the Tremaines kept him so busy during this period that in a letter in 1951 to Nelson Rockefeller, the president of the Museum of Modern Art, Burton wrote, "Mr. Johnson has been advising us for some three years on product design. We, at this point, have come to consider him as part of our organization." As a result of Johnson's help and the help of Alfred Barr in writing the foreword to the *Painting Toward Architecture* catalog, Burton added that the Miller Company "would like to make the Museum a gift of the lighting equipment involved in their new building and, accordingly, please consider this letter as a credit in the amount of our invoice: namely, $4,927.10."

Johnson's first major project for the Tremaines was the design of the visitor center and observatory at Meteor Crater. Ever since Wright had cast aspersions on Johnson's and Hitchcock's 1932 exhibition and book *The International Style: Architecture Since 1922,* Johnson had experienced a love/hate relationship with him. Johnson was a welcome visitor at Taliesin West, yet the two men often did not see eye to eye. They both were capable of subtle and not-so-subtle invective, as evidenced by Wright's telegram to Burton saying Johnson had no idea about cost, and Johnson's later declaration that Wright was "the greatest architect of the 19th century." [26] Not surprisingly, Johnson's ideas for the crater were diametrically opposed to Wright's. "I'll never forget meeting him on his trip to Arizona to see the site," recalled Burton's son, Burton Jr., who by then had joined his father on the governing board of the Bar T Bar ranch. "We got together in Chicago and boarded the Super Chief. Philip was wearing a reversible coat, tweed on the inside, raincoat on the outside. The train was about to pull out of the station when we asked where his luggage was. After all, we were going to be there a week. 'Oh, I don't need any luggage,' he said. He reached into his pocket and pulled out his razor and shaving things and some soap. 'My clothes are drip-dry. I wash them out and hang them up.' That's how the man traveled, and still does, I suppose."

The next morning they all went out to the crater and Johnson walked around the site, peering down into the bowl, lost in thought. While Wright's idea had been to angle the main building out over the void, the idea on which Johnson was working was meant to give viewers a sense of stability coupled with a dramatic thrill when they looked into the crater for the first time. According to Burton Jr., "Soon he had the whole concept figured out; he was tremendously talented. 'This is a desert, so you need an oasis,' Johnson explained. 'You need to build something you can get inside of and be protected from this wind and this vast open space. Visitors shouldn't see the crater until they come right up to the rim, so we need walls to make that happen.' "

To achieve that, Johnson fell back on his favorite building materials of steel, stone, and glass. There would be glassed-in spaces along the walls of the museum permitting visitors to look out, and a platform extending over the edge for outside viewing. Telescopes mounted along the rim would give close-up views of the crater's interior. The first building in the planned complex was constructed in 1951, but it was totally destroyed in a windstorm in 1955. Later in the same year, the Tremaines replaced the building and constructed the rest of the complex.[27]

Johnson remembers that he got along more easily with Burton Sr., than with Emily, but that it was she who "lit up the collection" and who principally made the art and architecture decisions: "I liked him very much although he was secondary in the basic artistic choice business. He was a very helpful guy indeed, [but] it was really her leadership. . . . He used to come without her sometimes. He'd bring girls and things, he got around. We became pals, but I never became a pal of Emily. Tough lady but I liked her eye. I enjoyed talking with her about art."[28]

At the same time as he was designing the visitor center for Meteor Crater, Johnson began redesigning the farmhouse that the Tremaines owned in Madison, Connecticut. Located on Long Island Sound, Madison is a typical New England town, with colonial homes and white-steepled churches. Although there was plenty of wealth in the area in the 1940s, it remained basically rural, with acres of farm fields and rolling woodlands.

Built in the mid-1700s, the Tremaines' small, wood-framed house was neither grand nor very comfortable. On the first floor there was only a living room, a small dining room, a guest room, a tiny kitchen, and an enclosed porch. Positive attributes included the seventy-six wooded acres on which it was located, and the pond and waterfall directly across the road. At the beginning of the century, a previous owner had turned the eighteenth-century barn on the property into a kind of recreational space. He had built large fieldstone fireplaces at either end, as well as a balcony in Tyrolean-style woodwork, which gave the old place a vaguely European air that bordered on kitsch. Even with the renovations, the barn was drafty, dark, and cold, and it was unsuited to displaying art.

The house was no more suited for art than the barn. There were low ceilings on the first floor and angled ceilings on the second, created by the gambrel roof and dormers. Windows, doors, wood paneling, built-in china cabinets, a steep stairway, and narrow hallways added colonial charm but presented a major challenge to displaying canvases such as Matta's eight-foot wide *Splitting the Ergo.* Meanwhile the works of the Abstract Expressionists, which the Tremaines were beginning to collect, were getting larger and larger. Some of Jackson Pollock's murals, as they were aptly called, were so big they practically defied a collector to keep them. It was rumored that Barnett Newman was working on a painting eight feet by eighteen feet. Franz Kline's dynamic black-and-white paintings were not only large, they were visceral in impact. These were not domain-friendly paintings that happily blended with Limoges china and Ming vases. Even collectors such as Nelson Rockefeller, for whom space was not a problem, had to confront the difficulty of displaying such enormous works of art, for they were like visual magnets, pulling attention away from other equally fine but less dramatic works.

For all its architectural drawbacks, there were some advantages to the house in Madison: The location was both pleasant and convenient. It was only an hour and a half from New York City and half an hour from Meriden. Burton, who liked to go boating, could keep his cabin cruiser nearby on the Sound. He also liked the idea of its actually being a farm, even though the barn was reserved for parties, and the only animals that had been on the place since he bought it in the early 1930s were some pigs and a couple of sheep. The farm was to his liking, and he had no interest in selling it after his marriage, even though it was hardly of the caliber of Brunninghausen. But, from Emily's perspective, the house needed a major overhaul; she didn't buy paintings that could be nailed on any old walls, painted any old color. She did not buy sculpture that could be plunked down on the terrace, out of balance with the angle of the lawn and overwhelmed by unpruned trees. A painting or a sculpture needed to be surrounded by harmonious elements, so that the viewer could savor it at leisure, whether while sipping a cup of coffee with dawn light flooding in an eastern window or while listening to Chopin in the evening. In museums, paintings were lined up on white walls—sometimes grouped by period, sometimes by subject, often by artist, but rarely by visual and spiritual compatibility. But in a private home, a collector motivated by the desire to achieve a totality of beauty could attempt to harmonize all the elements of the environment.

The question for Emily was how to achieve this aesthetic harmony in a place built by practical New England farmers. There was one aspect to the place that held out hope: the barn was large and spacious. If it could be renovated, Emily would have the answer as to what to do with the burgeoning collection. For this task, the Tremaines once again turned to Johnson, who was working at the time on his own house in New Canaan, Connecticut, from which he would borrow several design ideas for the Madison renovation. Of the utmost simplicity, Johnson's house was a single room totally enclosed by glass and framed by eight steel piers. It was designed to bring the outside in and turn the inside out. The lawn around the windows, the placement of the trees and the shade they cast, the uninterrupted view of the Rippowam Valley—all were intended to be as much a part of the structure, which came to be known as the Glass House, as its walls, roof, and floor. To make the outdoors more perfect in relation to the house, Johnson removed many trees, opening up the space, and improving the view. He sheared low branches from the remaining trees to give them a greater impression of verticality and cut away the understory to achieve an airy openness on the land.

Renovations to the Tremaine home in Madison took place in stages over a five-year period, beginning in 1951 with the barn. According to Johnson, the whole thing "evolved": "All I remember is we'd sit around of an evening and we'd say, 'Wouldn't it be nice if we had a swimming pool here or a place to put pictures over there, or this living room is really awfully small, isn't it?' So the pleasantest days an architect can spend are with friends, are with people who are sympathetic to your ideas. As far as I can remember, Burton [and I] never had an architectural disagreement. We never had one of those 'Well, that's very nice Mr. Johnson, but I asked you to do *that!*'"[29]

Borrowing heavily from his ideas for the Glass House, Johnson replaced one of the barn's sides with a thirty-five-foot long and two-story high expanse of glass and installed a smaller two-story window in the opposite wall. He retained the rustic chestnut boards used in the ceiling, as well as the tremendous fieldstone fireplaces. However, he covered one chimney completely with dry-wall to provide additional space to hang large paintings. Johnson had tall bookcases built beside one fireplace, while he tucked a very small efficiency kitchen beside the other, reshaping the masonry to make it fit. Just outside the enormous window, he designed a bluestone terrace. Typical of Johnson, the barn was not totally practical. The glass was not thermal-pane, there was no insulation, and dampness was a constant concern, especially in the winter. But since functionalism was of no concern to Johnson, these problems did not bother him. Architecture had to be art even if that meant it did not incorporate any design concepts that would have made life a little easier for people who had to work on the premises. A small example: for all the extensive changes to the barn and house in Madison, Johnson never redesigned the main kitchen, nor did Emily ask him to; in fact, he made the dark unworkable space even worse by constructing a high wall only a few feet outside its single small window. The reason was simple—the Tremaines had servants and rarely used the kitchen themselves.

After the renovations on the barn were completed, Johnson began on the house, removing the porch and adding a large room surrounded by glass on three sides. Johnson specified that it have a bluestone floor that would be visually continuous with the outside terrace, playing with the idea of interior and exterior as he had with his own Glass House. Four years later, Johnson designed a sculpture garden bounded by an imposing eight-foot-high bluestone wall that extended out from the house in the shape of a block-lettered J. The long side closed the house off from the road. One short side (broken by a large opening) divided the house and patio from the barn, guest house, and servants' quarters. The other short side (the upturn on the J) defined the start of a lawn that sloped up to the woods. The wall's rough texture and dark color made a perfect backdrop for sculpture. Deciding that the wall cried out for a smooth and curving form, Emily approached Jean Arp to cast a bronze version of *Human Lunar Spectral* specifically for the site. Completed in 1957, the biomorphic sculpture stood in front of the wall as if it had sprung naturally out of the ground. Soon *Family Going for a Walk* by the British sculptor Kenneth Armitage claimed the space leading to the barn. A gentle piece, thirty inches in height and width but only a single inch in depth, it conveyed a feeling of timeless congeniality. Armitage had once said, "A life-time is so very short anyway, and the time-scale of art enormous. I sometimes look at a small engraving on a reindeer antler figment in the British Museum with an age estimated at 11,000 B.C.—which might have been made by a very good artist last week. . . . This easy communication across race, language, and vast spans of time is comforting in an age when indifference to art seems general."

Just such "easy communication" seemed to be occurring in the Tremaines' sculpture garden. Over the years many other pieces would join that original group, and the sculpture garden would spill out of the terrace and spread up the hill, with Antoni Milkowski's twelve-foot *Salem #7, 1966,* built of Cor-Ten steel, commanding the crest, while, at the edge of the clearing, as if it were a mythical beast lumbering out of the forest, stood Alexander Liberman's equally huge *Gyre, 1966.* Gio Pomodoro's bronze *Expansion, 1960–1961* was inserted into the middle of an evergreen hedge to hide its supports, so that it appeared to float. However, in 1957 all those sculptures were in the future. Johnson's design had given the Tremaines the opportunity for harmonious expansion. He had also encouraged Emily and Burton to clear more land behind the house and to trim the lower branches off the trees and clean out the understory as he had done in New Canaan.

At the same time as the wall was constructed, Johnson designed a fifty-by-fifteen foot reflecting pool, meant to be filled to overflowing. It was lit from underneath by four spotlights, and four fountains shot water in a low horizontal arc across the surface. Set precisely on the edge was Mary Callery's sculpture aptly named *Water Ballet.* The pool also was an automatic attraction for Burton Tremaine's four grandchildren: the twins Tony and John (born in 1947), Janet (1950), and Sarah (1954), the children of Burton, Jr., and his wife, Sally. John later remembered one occasion when the pool proved to be too much of an attraction.

They had these beautiful glass balls that were from Japanese fishing nets, which floated in the perfect rectangular reflecting pool. Being bored, Tony and I, aged ten, picked them up and threw them as close as we could to another ball in the pool, so that the splash moved the floating ball to the other side. We then retrieved it so that we could throw it back at the others in the middle of the pool. Emily and Burton were engaged in conversation with somebody and at one point they came out and suggested that we not do that because something could break. But we assured them that we had a precision throw down cold. Well, only a couple of throws later one of us missed our timing a little bit and two balls collided. All of a sudden there was nothing but a big huge pile of glass on the bottom of the pool. Boy, did we get in trouble for that because it required a team of workers to get the glass out.

Johnson also designed an entryway with large glass windows looking out on a brook that meandered across the lawn. Always concerned about how a person would move through a structure, Johnson had intended for everyone to enter what had now evolved into a compound through an imposing wooden gate in the bluestone wall, but Emily preferred as a starting point the new side entry, where one would be struck first by the art. It was one of the few things about which they openly disagreed. Johnson felt that Emily occasionally could be contrary. "But I liked that. I'm rather contrary myself," he admitted. "She liked architecture, she was interested, so as far as working [together] goes, she was fine. She had a will of iron. She wanted me to do over the barn. When we put that little porch on the front entrance she was very picky but very clear and everything worked out. . . . She was grand in every way. Although we were not really friends, architecturally it was all the way from her private needs to monumental things. Incredible."

Besides the house in Madison, Emily and Burton maintained an apartment in New York City where they lived for six months each year. In a psychological way, Madison was Burton's home and Manhattan was Emily's. They divided their time between the two places, the summer being devoted to Madison and the winter to New York. In 1955 Emily and Burton moved into an apartment on Park Avenue. Faced with the recurring problem of inadequate wall space, given the size of their canvases, they once again asked Johnson for his advice. Although he was not responsible for the redesign, he did suggest to the Tremaines that they eliminate all detail, including moldings, mantels, and several doors. He also recommended that they curtain the existing long bank of windows and hang pictures against the curtain. That suggestion, which they followed, gave them room over the years for such paintings as Mark Rothko's softly glowing *Number 8*, and for Willem de Kooning's equally large *Villa Borghese*, the two separated by Frank Stella's even larger *Luis Miguel Domínguin*. In their white bedroom Jasper Johns's *White Flag* hung over the beds, and Wassily Kandinsky's *Stability Animated* was hung on the far wall, along with art by Ad Reinhardt, Jean Dubuffet, Robert Rauschenberg, and John Marin and near sculpture by Jacques Lipchitz and Norbert Kricke. Visitors to the apartment were impressed not only by the art but by the Tremaines' deep pleasure in living in the midst of it. According to Emily, "It's an enormous joy to come into this apartment and be so tired I can barely drag my feet. The beauty and vitality that greet me is just pure joy. I love it, and I guess that's enough to ask of anything, isn't it?"

Visitors were struck by Burton's childlike enthusiasm about their

ecil Clark Davis. *The Baronness*, Emily Von Romberg. Oil on canvas, 45″ × 39″.

In the Tremaines' living room in New York City, Piet Mondrian's *Victory Boogie-Woogie* was balanced by Robert Delauney's *Premier Disque*. Between them were displayed an antelope head from the Upper Volta, Brice Marden's *Marble #14*, and a Senufo female form.

A painted ladder by Bruce Robbins served as a vertical foil for Mondrian's *Pier and Ocean* and Jim Dine's *The Hammer Acts* in the master bedroom in the New York apartment. Emily and Burton disagreed as to which side of the ladder should be on view. She preferred the side painted a metallic pastel shade, while he preferred the side with the rungs painted black.

A mix of primitive and modern filled the New York dining room. L. to r.: Jackson Pollock's *Frieze*, completed shortly before his death, and Picasso's *Woman with a Fan*. The glass-topped table was supported by two Austrian Baroque putti.

Also in the New York dining room were Léger's *Le Petit Déjeuner*, a huge tam-tam from the South Pacific, and Calder's *Bougainvillea*, which moved in the breeze as people walked by.

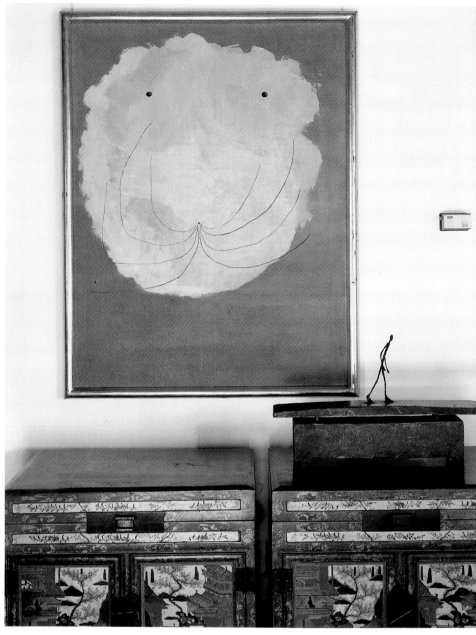

Paintings, sculpture, and furniture were juxtaposed to create thought-provoking combinations. Nothing was accidental. *Le Chat Blanc* by Miró hung over *Man Walking Quickly Under the Rain* by Giacometti, which was set on a red lacquer Mandarin chest.

mall works of art were interspersed with books or set on shelves. Works by Duchamp, Le Corbusier, and Miró shared space with *Stone on Wood* (second shelf) by John Tremaine, Emily's tep-grandson.

Emily constantly added to her wall of miniatures. Top, l. to r.: *New Hebrides Mask* by Picasso, *Blue Composition* by Reinhardt. Middle: *Printemps* by Riopelle, *Yellow Woman* by de Kooning, *Spanish Elegy Number 17* by Motherwell, *Silver and Black* by Pollock, *Moon Garden Series* by Nevelson. Bottom: unidentified paintings by Duchamp and Man Ray.

Marden's *Elements I* and Yasuo Kuniyoshi's *Picking Horses* flanked the door into the Madison dining room, which was painted entirely red, creating a dramatic backdrop for Warhol's *S & H Green Stamps*.

Renovations to the eighteenth-century farmhouse took place over a five-year period beginning in 1951. Johnson's specifications for the large glass-enclosed room included a bluestone floor that would be continuous with the outside terrace. He also designed the reflecting pool.

Redesigned by Philip Johnson in 1951, the barn in Madison was perfect for the display of large works of art. Foreground: Raoul Hague's *Swamp Pepperwood*. On wall: Lichtenstein's *I Can See the Whole Room*, Rauschenberg's *Windward*, and Jim Dine's *Crescent Wrench*. Beside fireplace: Hilary Heron's *Girl with Pigtails*.

As he had done with his own Glass House, Johnson opened up the side of the Tremaines' barn t[ ]
provide maximum light. At night, Matta's *Splitting the Ergo* and Franz Kline's *Lehigh* could be
seen through the expanse of glass.

To Emily, Mark Rothko's luminous *No. 8*, acquired in 1953 from Betty Parsons Gallery, was "one of the most glorious things we own."

An early visit to Claes Oldenburg's Ray Gun Store in Manhattan opened Emily's eyes to the power of Pop art. The Tremaines purchased several works by Oldenburg, including *Strong Arm.*

the entry room in Madison, the Tremaines placed Robert Irwin's glowing disk *Untitled* (1970), a drawing by de Maria, and a small sculpture by Jesus Rafael Soto.

mily played a visual game with American patriotism in the guest bedroom in ladison by placing Tom Wesselmann's *Great American Nude* above a wood-burning ove, while on the wall she hung one of Warhol's soup cans.

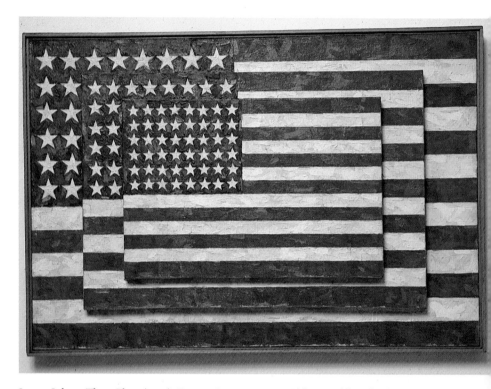

Jasper Johns. *Three Flags* (1958). Encaustic on canvas 30⅞" × 45 ½" × 5". The Tremaines acquired *Three Flags* in 1959 through Leo Castelli. In 1981, they sold it to the Whitney Museum of American Art for $1 million, which was the highest amount paid up until that time for the work of a living American artist. *Collection of Whitney Museum of American Art, 50th Anniversary Gift of the Gilman Foundation, Inc., The Lauder Foundation, A. Alfred Taubman, an anonymous donor, and purchase.* © *Jasper Johns/Licensed by VAGA, New York, NY.*

arnett Newman. *Euclidean Abyss* (1946–47). Gouache on canvas board 28″ × 22″. Newman dicated that this painting was a demonstration of the dangers of geometry, implying that the d concepts of art were at an end. *In private collection.*

Jasper Johns. *The Device Circle* (1959). Encaustic and collage on canvas with moveable arm 40″ ×
40″. Acquired by the Tremaines in 1960 from the Leo Castelli Gallery. *In the collection of Denise
and Andrew Saul.* © *Jasper Johns/Licensed by VAGA, New York, NY.*

collection. He felt more at home in Madison, partially because he was always interested in gadgets and in the latest electrical paraphernalia, and there he was able to tinker to his heart's delight. He set up lighting that, as twilight deepened, lit up the sculpture in a slow sequence, while classical music played from hidden loudspeakers. He especially loved kinetic sculpture that he could set going. A magazine reporter noted, "When a visitor approaches a mysterious Lucas Samaras box, Burton calls out, 'Wait! Let me get it started. I want to surprise you.' His long, lean frame loops over to the sculpture and he begins to tinker with the back of it. . . . When his preparations are over, Burton steps back and begins to unfold a series of progressively smaller and smaller doors each opening into the next, like a stack of Chinese boxes, until, at least a half a dozen doors later, we've arrived at its center, a tiny liquid whirligig of color, 'A tornado I caught in a box,' Mr. Tremaine announces gleefully."[30]

Among these pieces of art, the Tremaines lived easily, entertaining often in the 1950s and 1960s. There were small elegant dinner parties with fine wine and rare foods cooked to perfection by Sabine, their French housekeeper and chef. The china, table linen, and centerpiece were carefully coordinated so that the entire environment was harmonious, and Burton would have the lights and music choreographed to heighten the effect of the art. There were grand cocktail parties in the barn and in the New York apartment, where members of the International Council of the Museum of Modern Art, in which the Tremaines were very active, mingled with artists, dealers and other collectors. Showing visitors the collection was always a major pleasure. An interviewer who came to visit them in Madison one winter was struck by both the frigid temperature in the small farm building that the Tremaines used to store art and the warm joy the Tremaines took in their collection: "They are irrepressible enthusiasts, irrepressible adventurers. I will never forget a subzero morning in Connecticut when they showed a couple of guests part of their collection stored in a converted but unheated barn. Busy among the paintings, carting and lugging out giant works they had not seen in some time and exclaiming with delight, their breath coming in frozen plumes, they seemed entirely in their element — a couple of pioneers. While we blew on our stiffening fingers, they told us how this and that work had been found and decided upon. They were so forceful that, even in our congealing state, we relived moments of pure exuberance."[31]

There were also ordinary pleasures, such as throwing lively birthday parties for their grandchildren, who were always made to feel welcome in Madison. "I remember visiting as a child, and it was fun," said Janet. "There were things that moved, that were intriguing. It was sort of magical. Yet it all seemed to be a normal part of their lives. They didn't talk about what this painting meant or who this artist was. There were no mini-art lessons given to us grandchildren." Tony concurs: "Emily was always intrigued to know what others thought of her art. As they collected art, frequently there would be changes in the paintings at Madison. When we would arrive for a luncheon and a swim in the pool, she would say, 'Well kids, we've got a new piece of art, can you find it?' So we had to first know the collection well enough to identify the new piece and then we all had to study it carefully and then try to be the first back because she then wanted to know what we thought of it. We had to find it, evaluate it, and come back. Then there would be a discussion. Senior would be very interested at this point because they bought on consensus."

When she was little, Sarah, the youngest grandchild, once visited an art museum in Washington, D.C. with some friends. "I thought it was like my grandparents'. After all, didn't everyone's grandparents have wonderful art on their walls? To us grandchildren, it was natural."

Jesus loved little children because of their freedom from wrong and their receptiveness of right. While age is halting between two opinions or battling with false beliefs, youth makes easy and rapid strides towards Truth.
—*Mary Baker Eddy*

CHAPTER SEVEN

IMPERFECTIONS OF THE HEART

Jasper Johns tells a story about a painting by Franz Kline that hung in the Tremaines' New York apartment against the bank of curtained windows. Once when the apartment was to be repainted, all the art was taken down and the curtains were opened allowing the sunlight to stream in. The painting by Kline was leaning temporarily against a window when Burton entered and saw a pinprick of light through the canvas. He took a closer look and discovered a very small hole. Upset, he called Leo Castelli, the dealer from whom the painting had been purchased. Castelli suspected that the hole was probably made by Kline himself, who sometimes used heavy pressure in applying his dramatic brush strokes. At Castelli's request, Kline went to the Tremaines' apartment and confirmed that the little hole was not an accident caused by one of the workmen painting the apartment, but that he had made it himself. He turned the canvas over, circled the hole and wrote "OK, Franz Kline" on the back.[1]

Both Burton and Emily could be as demanding in their personal relationships as they were with their art. Emily, in particular, tended to assess a person rapidly and then was either exacting, if she expected much from the person, or lenient, if she expected little. As a result, people had very different impressions of her. Sporadically, Emily and Burton were very generous, but they could also withhold aid even when the need was obvious. As a result, they had many acquaintances and friends but few close friends of long standing. The people whose memories of Emily and Burton are the brightest and warmest are their four grandchildren, the children of Burton Jr. They had the pleasure of Emily and Burton's company and art and the benefit of their guidance, without feeling the heavy weight of dictatorial hands on their shoulders. They also were at ease with Emily's spiritual side, even if they did not come to share her belief in Christian Science; and, in their own ways, they all grew to love art because of her.

The word that is most commonly used by friends, family, and acquaintances in describing Emily is *reserved.* Whether someone was allowed to see beyond that reserve depended on Emily's assessment of their capabilities, not on their assessment of hers. To some she appeared very witty and lively while to others she seemed aloof and opinionated. Young people who loved her were also awed by her, a response that did not translate easily into feelings of personal warmth. "I was a little terrified of her," remembered Janet, Emily's step-granddaughter, "but I also worshiped her. When I was a teenager, she treated me as an adult, was interested in what was happening in my life and was always serious in the discussions that we had. But she wasn't funny or light. It took me a long time to realize she was shy and quiet. She was very strong in her personal beliefs and she had this reserve about her that put me off a bit. Once somebody got stung by a bee and my response was that it was nothing to worry about because there were two people that could take care of it—God and Aunt Emmie. Now, Daddy B., as we called our grandfather, was big and jolly, kind of a big bear."

Both Emily and Burton liked young people, especially their openness to new ideas and their vibrancy. As Emily grew older, she became increasingly impatient with those who were no longer willing to change. "My own age group frankly bores me," she told Paul Cummings in a 1973 interview. In talking about those interested in the arts, Emily said:

> My age group is still buying Matisses and things that don't exactly bore me but they are established, and we are curious. [When they see our collection] they're turned off. You have a tendency not to like what you don't understand, or to fear what you don't understand, or to reject it rather than to stop and see whether there's anything there worth knowing. But the younger people, they see it and don't reject it, and they don't get frightened. ... The young ones are really curious and they're really sincerely moved by them. ... I think that the young people today are just marvelous anyway

because they're making their own standards. "Why do I like this?" "Why do I do that?" It isn't because their grandfather did it. They don't reject but they make their own value judgements, and they do that with the art. I really think that it's very fortunate for me that 80 percent of my friends are in the twenty-five to thirty-five age group, and I'm just delighted.

"There is a notion held by a lot of people that you are daring when you are young and conservative when you are old. My grandparents were daring when they were young and stayed daring," remarked John Tremaine. John was impressed that, as he and his brother Tony entered their teenage years in the early 1960s, it was their step-grandmother who seemed to be most with the times. She wore miniskirts, hip-huggers, and go-go boots and had her hair in a severely short cut similar to the style worn by Edie Sedgewick, Warhol's protégée, whom she treated as if she were a daughter. Even though she was in her fifties, she sported a pair of heart-shaped glasses with blue lenses like those worn by Nabokov's Lolita. From the 1950s on, she refused to have her picture taken because she did not like to be reminded of her gradual decline. Friends and family were not surprised when she was one of the first people to get a facelift in the early 1960s and another one in the 1970s. "Her elixir, her fountain of youth was to surround herself with young artists who were on the cutting edge. It's how she dressed, how she cut and dyed her hair. I don't think she ever looked at herself as somebody that was growing old," said John, who recalled the first time he gained insight into Emily's avant-garde ways:

When Tony and I were young teenagers, in the heyday of Pop, we stayed at the farm for a weekend. We went up to the guest room and there hanging up high on the wall was this perfectly round painting by Tom Wesselmann called *Great American Nude* that left nothing to the imagination. While it might be a stretch to say that I had never seen a *Playboy* at that time in my life, the painting certainly wasn't something that I would associate being hung by my grandmother in her guest room. Tony and I discussed it and concluded that there was a greater life ahead of us than we could ever possibly imagine. We both thought that grandmothers, by virtue of the fact that they had "grand" in front of "mother," were almost over the hill. How could anybody of such advanced years put something so advanced visually in the guest room?

Many young adults felt that when Emily expressed an interest in them, she virtually adopted them, going out of her way to take them to museums and introduce them to important people in the art world. Pat Patterson, whose mother was a friend of Emily's from her California days, visited with the Tremaines often in the late 1940s and 1950s. "I remember saying that I didn't understand modern art that well. She told me to think of it as an artist who is expressing himself from the inside out, rather than from the outside in. Instead of painting the picture outside and copying something outside, [the artist is] expressing something from the inside." Because of Emily's influence, Pat took courses on contemporary art and eventually joined the International Council of the Museum of Modern Art, of which Emily was a very active member. "She really opened up a lot of worlds to me in terms of seeing things in a different way. She used to invite me for dinner all the time with people like Philip Johnson, fascinating people." [2]

Another young person who benefitted from Emily's guidance was Agnes Gund, who eventually became president of the Museum of Modern Art. Gund felt indebted to Emily for taking her to artists' studios, teaching her to look at art herself, and encouraging her to get to know the artists personally. In 1968, when Gund still was living in Cleveland, she visited the Tremaines' apartment while on a trip to New York. She told Emily how much she admired their painting by Rothko and remarked she wished she could acquire a Rothko. Without hesitation, Emily said, "Let's go to Rothko's studio." They went, saw several works, and Gund purchased a painting from the artist directly, who at that time was not yet represented by Marlborough Fine Art Gallery. It became one of her favorite paintings. "One day I fell asleep and when I woke up I saw the painting hanging on the wall and it looked beautiful yet different. So I wrote to Rothko telling him how beautiful the picture was. He called me and he said he had never gotten a letter that nice." Rothko also told her he was in despair because he was not getting the attention he thought he should, and he invited her to come for another visit. When Gund arrived, the paintings that Rothko was working on for a chapel in Houston were up on the high walls. "He had a wonderful parachute over the skylight that was on top which meant that you could see them better than they could eventually be seen in the chapel." Gund attributed these kinds of eye-opening experiences to Emily. "She really did care and know the artists. I think I would have never had the richness of my life without her example." [3]

After Gund was divorced, she was considering whether to move to New York City. Emily helped her to make the difficult transition from being a wife in Cleveland, with its strict Midwestern values, to being single in New York City, where the rules were much more relaxed. Emily invited her to a dinner at their apartment at which there were to be several couples. Initially Gund turned down the invitation, explaining that she would be uncomfortable attending without a male escort. Emily persisted:

> "I'm asking you. You don't have to have anybody," she said to me. I protested once again. This time her voice rose and she said "Look, why don't you just come to dinner? We are just having dinner. We are not having sex!" And the way she said it made me see the silliness of thinking of myself as half a couple, [that if I didn't have a man] I wasn't accepted. It was very amusing. I never asked her again if I needed to bring a man or could come by myself. She made me feel very comfortable. She helped me take the chance to come to New York.

Although she loved to encourage young people to collect art, Emily rarely pushed her religious beliefs onto them. Frequently, she sent them Christian Science reading material, but she did not pressure them to read it. This included giving her step-grandchildren subscriptions to the *Christian Science Monitor* while they were in school. Sarah, the youngest grandchild, felt that Emily had a quiet foundation and strength, while her brother John thought of his step-grandmother as a seed planter. "She would plant a seed and then she would wait to see if it took root. She would give you something to read and say very simply 'you may find this of interest.' While you might not have had time at that point in your life to pick it up, you didn't discard it either." Only one young relative ever experienced the Christian Science approach to healing directly, coming away with a lasting negative impression. When Katie Tremaine, Burton's niece, was about twelve, she came east from California to visit a friend and then to stay with her aunt and uncle in Madison. While at the friend's house, she came down with a terrible case of poison ivy. By the time she reached Connecticut, she was completely miserable. Her case was so bad there were even blisters in her mouth. Emily called Katie's mother in California, who told Emily to take her daughter to a doctor right away, or, at the least to get her some calamine lotion to relieve the itching. Emily did neither. "All she did was sit by my bed occasionally. She'd come into my room, because I was so sick I was in bed, read [Christian Science literature] to me, and then tell me I didn't have the right attitude because if I did, and I was really absorbing what she was reading to me the poison ivy would go away. Well, of course, it didn't."

John Tremaine was the beneficiary of much Christian Science reading material, although he never chose to follow up on it. Even so, he felt that Emily exuded spirituality. "Being with Emily, particularly sitting with her quietly and talking, was almost a religious event for me. You felt as though you had more than just her attention. Her soul was involved in some respect. She was absorbed in more than just your words, she was absorbed in your whole thought in some manner and she would reflect on it and then she would ask very interesting questions, then give you some very sage, nonjudgmental advice. You could never predict what you would receive from Emily in the way of advice. She was a deep thinker, and with my limited experience in deep thinking at my age, I was always amazed at what she would come up with. It was like she had been there and you couldn't shock her."

However, what seemed like sound advice to children often seemed like meddling to their parents, many of whom were not happy with Emily's assumption of surrogate motherhood. Katie Tremaine remembered that it caused strife between her mother and Emily. "I think they were in competition with each other. I would have a fight on the phone with my mother. I'd talk to Emmie and Burton about it and Emmie would always say 'Well, your mother reacts totally on her whimsical feminine emotions. Your mother never is able to really sit down, think things out and understand you the way you are.'" Part of this attitude arose from Emily's belief in Christian Science, for Mary Baker Eddy stated that when "promising children" are placed "in the arms of gross parents, often these beautiful children early droop and die, like tropical flowers born amid Alpine snows." By "gross parents," Eddy meant nonbelievers who accepted the existence of the material world and who did not direct their children to understand their "higher nature."[4]

In the late 1940s and the 1950s, Burton's daughter Dee spent time with the Tremaines in Madison on her vacations first from Westover School and then from Smith College. For Dee those were times of high society and glamour, good humor, and practicality. Only a teenager when her father remarried, Dee was deeply impressed by Emily's worldliness. "Once I asked her how many times she had been to Europe and she said she had lost count. Her wardrobe was the best French couturier and her jewelry was remarkable. Not long after they were married, when they were in London, my father bought her a cat's eye ring as a belated engagement ring. I think it was one of the largest stones ever mined. She wore it always." But it was not the abundance of precious gems, nor their size, that truly impressed Dee. For her, the most fascinating aspect of Emily's jewelry was the design. Often a single piece could be taken apart and reassembled for multiple uses; the jeweled clasp of a necklace, for instance, could be separated from the strands and used as a pin, or the strands themselves could be shortened into bracelets. One gold pin in an amorphous shape had a diamond center that could be unscrewed and put into a ring. Some of the jewelry had moving parts, much like Calder mobiles and Tinguely kinetic sculptures. A flower pin had petals that wiggled. In a gold fork-and-spoon pin, the fork dangled from the spoon. "It was all big, even gaudy by some standards, but I loved every piece," said Dee. "As a young woman when I was about to buy my first important piece of jewelry, Emily guided me to the jeweler Seaman Schepps, in New York City, who had designed many of her pieces. I wound up with a double strand of cultured baroque pearls with a clasp of cabochon rubies and diamonds. The clasp had initially been one of a pair of earrings that Seaman Schepps had designed for Helena Ruben-stein. She had found the earrings too heavy and returned them. That clasp could also be worn as a pin or set into a gold bangle bracelet. It also had an alternative clasp of pearls if the occasion were not up to rubies and diamonds. And as the pearls were all the same size, I could wear the necklace frontwards or backwards. It was a very beautiful piece, but also very practical. This was Emily's influence."

Some of Emily's jewelry came with stories. For example, there was the scarab ring from Max, who told Emily it had been stolen from an Egyptian tomb. There was also a diamond pavé heart pin with a ruby in the center — which could be removed and worn as a pin or on a chain as a necklace — that was thought to bring marital happiness. Emily told Janet that her father had given it to her mother prior to their marriage. She wore it for their wedding, and they had a happy marriage. Then she gave it to Emily, who wore it for her marriage to Max, which was very happy. "She had not worn it on her wedding day to Adolph, and they had a terrible marriage," explained Janet. "Then she wore it on her wedding day with Daddy B, which was also wonderful."

Just as Emily's jewelry was a mix of perfectionism and practicality dusted with a touch of romantic myth, so also was her approach to travel. Dee accompanied Emily and Burton to Europe several times after her graduation from Smith College. They traveled through the wine country in France, watched bull fights in Spain, toured through the Alps, went to see cave art, visited art galleries and museums, met legendary people, and bought couturier clothing from Balenciaga and Dior. Dee recalls, "They made sure I saw everything that I should see on a Grand Tour. We wandered around all the art galleries and it was fun because it turned out Alfred Barr was also visiting those same galleries with friends and we were asked constantly 'Where are we shopping? Where are we going?' We once ran into Picasso at one of the galleries and were introduced. My father was so thrilled he equated it to shaking the hand of the President. I also had dinner with them and J. Paul Getty at Maxim's. He didn't impress me particularly because I didn't know enough to be impressed. As far as I was concerned, he was just a rich friend of Emily's who was a bit grumpy, quiet, and difficult to talk to."

As was usual for Emily and Burton, there was often a pragmatic component to the trips, including tiny cars (with Dee squished in the back seat), tiny suitcases, and tiny hotel rooms.

Once my father came in with one of those little folding suitcases that was probably six inches deep and about fourteen by sixteen inches and he unfolded it and said "Here's your suitcase for the next ten days." And I replied, "That's it? How can I possibly fit?" He said "you'll work it out." They had just come out with Dacron. Emily and I had similar dresses purchased from the same store, so we wore them a great deal. We'd wash them out in the sink at night and hang them up to dry. She was a real camper on those trips. Even though I was always pushed in the back seat with the luggage, we had great trips, learned a lot and went many places. Emily was a good traveler and a good sport. She didn't have to have it all wine and roses. Maybe that was her Butte, Montana, life coming back to her. I also remember staying with them at Claridge's in London. They had a beautiful, huge room but my room was obviously a maid's or chauffeur's quarters. It had a single bed, an armoire, and a wash basin. It had one small window looking over garbage pails and one bare light bulb in the middle of the ceiling. The toilet and bath were across the hall. One day my father came down to check on my quarters. He said it seemed adequate to him. He wasn't going to upgrade me at all. Fortunately I was just out of college and was used to such Spartan conditions.

In 1957 Emily and Burton invited Burton Jr., his wife Sally, and three of their children (Tony, John, and Janet; Sarah was too young to go) to Austria over Christmas and New Year's for skiing. It was the high point of their relationship. The family flew twelve hours nonstop to Zurich where Emily and Burton were waiting with two Volkswagen vans to take everyone and their equipment through the mountains into Austria. "We were a little groggy, having flown for so long, and it was night, but none of us will ever forget driving over the pass," recalled Burton. "There was the valley below us in which nestled the town of Lech with its lights sparkling, surrounded by open slopes full of snow. Janet, only seven years old, exclaimed excitedly that it was just as she had pictured it in her mind." The family stayed in the beautiful old Post Hotel, which was decorated for the season with Christmas trees lighted by real candles. On Christmas eve Burton and Sally were in their room wrapping some small presents for the children.

The window was cracked open a little bit and we heard a crunch, crunch, crunch in the snow, because it was really cold. Looking out we saw all sorts of people streaming through the town towards the church that was lit from within by candlelight. Shortly thereafter, we heard the sound of one sole, lone clarinet playing Christmas music from the top of the church. It was a crystal clear night with a big moon out and it was hauntingly beautiful. So we got our ski clothes back on, bundled up and went outside to join the crowd on the way to the church. The church graveyard was filled with snow and on every grave there stood a little Christmas tree covered with glowing candles. The church was so packed, people were standing on the steps outside. When the service started we could hear the singing. That was glorious. We had a wonderful trip. My father and Emmie couldn't have been more gracious and cordial. They hired two ski instructors who went out with us every day. Why we never did it again, I'll never know.

When Janet became a young woman, Emily and Burton took her to Europe for a mini-version of the grand tour that they had given to Dee twenty years earlier. Once again the Paris fashion houses were on the itinerary, as was the home of J. Paul Getty, which left a lasting impression. "We sat clustered at one end of his long dining room in which the table seemed to extend forever," recalled Janet. "Everything was dark: dark room, dark woodwork on the walls, dark ceilings. But out back through the French doors I could see daffodils. And lions! Instead of dog kennels, there were lion kennels. After lunch we walked out there and saw them in their cages." On the same trip Burton and Emily took Janet to Summerhill, the country manor of the D'Avadeau-Goldschmidts, which was markedly different from Getty's. "We walked into their front hall and there were tennis rackets over on one side and dogs on the other. After those visits, we went to Paris and Emmie and I both got fitted for suits at Courrèges. It was grand."

At first, such attention from the Tremaines brought with it a wonderful feeling of privilege, but it could become stifling, and frequently young people who had initially been very close to the Tremaines found that they had to back away, at least for a while. It was even worse if a young person disappointed the Tremaines by, in their estimation, not living up to his or her potential.

"Any time Burton and Emmie disapproved of you or your actions, or where you lived or who you were seeing, or what you were doing, you were not welcome," said Dee. "You never quite knew how things stood. You might be welcomed with open arms, or you might get the cold shoulder. At one point in my life, after my divorce, when I was teaching skiing and not making very much money, it was a very frosty time for me in Madison. Once Emily asked me how much I made. When I told her, she said 'My God, I pay my maid more than that.' The atmosphere was so chilled, I couldn't wait to get out of there. When you were disapproved of, you could look forward to a long bleak time before you ever got back in their good graces." Although Dee did eventually become reaccepted by virtue of marrying someone they approved of, it left a residue of ill feelings, as did their unwillingness to help her out financially during hard times.

Many others—family, friends, even artists—similarly experienced rejection because of doing or saying something of which the Tremaines did not approve. Arnold Glimcher, an art dealer, tells a story that occurred in the early 1970s when he, his family, and the artist Lucas Samaras were invited to lunch in Madison one Sunday. Burton loved the box by Samaras that had what Burton called a "tornado" inside. Samaras himself was young, having emigrated from Greece in 1948 at the age of twelve. He was radical in a surrealistic way, forthright and ironic, but according to Glimcher, those characteristics got him into trouble on this particular visit to the Tremaines: "Burton had a penchant for gimmicks. Anything that had a kind of machine aspect to it he liked. He had gotten a salad making machine and he was thrilled with it. Well, what that machine did was shred all the vegetables and turn them into a sour vegetable dough. It was very funny. We were all trying to eat this salad and it was really awful. Lucas finally said to them, trying to be cute and direct, 'This is disgusting. You destroyed the salad with this.' He is scrupulously honest like that, and it is disarmingly funny, but the Tremaines were not amused. It was the last time they had anything to do with Lucas."[5]

There were also many instances where gifts were given with strings attached, or it would turn out that what a person thought was a gift was actually only a loan. Part of the motivation was the Tremaines' increasing focus on limiting their taxes, but this practice also was a way to exert control. For example, Emily sent Dee the painting *Picking Horses* to hang in her dining room. Dee thought it was a wonderful gift and wrote a note of thanks saying how much she loved it. But then Dee's first marriage fell apart, and she went to Aspen to teach skiing, none of which pleased the Tremaines. "It was then that I received a letter asking for the return of the painting. It turned out it was only a loan." A similar situation occurred with Burton, Jr., who was loaned a Tomasello painting. For seven years, it hung in the master bedroom in his summer home on Fishers Island. Then one December day, according to Burton:

after the Fishers Island house was closed for the season and the ferries weren't running very often anymore, and I was terribly busy with year-end work at the Miller Company, I got an urgent call from Kathy Mitchell, Emily's secretary. Emily wanted the Tomasello delivered to the Wadsworth Atheneum just as soon as I could get it there because she wanted to make a gift of the picture and take a tax deduction before the year ended. It was not an "oh, do you have?" or "would it be any inconvenience to do this?" type of call. It was just a message that I had to get the picture to the Wadsworth within the next two or three days. So I had to arrange to get myself over to the island, get the picture, and take it to the Wadsworth at great inconvenience to myself. The Wadsworth then put it in storage, which is where it stayed until I became president of the Wadsworth. Although it is no longer the case, at that time it was a tradition that the president could borrow a work from the Wadsworth that they didn't mind giving up for a while. When I became president I said I'd like to borrow the Tomasello; so it went right back on my wall. I was president for three years during which time it stayed there.

Burton and Emily always enjoyed each other's company, liked to travel together, were inseparable at art exhibitions and events, and consulted each other all the time on art and architecture, to the point that they finished sentences and stories for each other. Many people thought they were a perfect couple. However, Burton was a passionate man who also felt the weight of Emily's controlling hand. Just as she had attempted to get Max to give up his perpetual games of polo and his constant courting of death, so she also attempted to change Burton's partying ways. She did not succeed with Max, nor did she with Burton. All she succeeded in doing was forcing Burton into apologetic subterfuge — hiding alcohol in secret places so that he could grab a drink when she was not looking and setting up secret assignations with his mistresses under the guise of business meetings.

Everyone in the family was aware of this situation, probably including Emily herself, but Burton never wanted to hurt her and always made an effort to keep his activities hidden. Burton Jr.'s second wife, Catherine, had not been a member of the family for long when she became aware of this secret component of Burton Sr.'s life. Catherine was trying to make small talk with her father-in-law as they rode in the car together. She jokingly asked him what he thought of his new girlfriend — referring to Emily, who had just had a facelift. "He was sitting in the back seat. I looked over my shoulder as I asked him and he looked so startled, as if he were wondering how I knew he had a mistress." Perhaps indicative of Emily's awareness that Burton had affairs is her fondness for a story about another couple with whom they were friends. The man had a mistress who was hard of hearing. Every time he returned to his wife after being with the mistress, he would talk too loudly and the wife would say, "I know where you've been!"

Just as the family was accepting of Burton's weaknesses, they also were accepting of Emily's efforts to help him stay out of trouble. Without her, his life could easily have spun out of control, and he himself knew it. For example, Burton Jr., attributed the sale of the beachfront property in Santa Barbara, for which Niemeyer had designed the beach house, to Emily's attempts to keep his father from getting too wild. "Emily knew that Santa Barbara was a dangerous place for men," said Burton, Jr., "Too much money, not enough to do, nothing serious going on, cocktails for lunch and dinner, out every night; wealthy society with no vitality in it at all. Emily didn't want Burton to spend much time there, so she sold the property." Because she felt it was really just an excuse to party and drink, Emily was also nonplussed by Burton's ownership of a cabin cruiser, which he kept moored in Long Island Sound not far from their home in Madison. Another much more minor source of annoyance was his constant tinkering with the newest electrical gadgetry on board. Once when they had friends out for a short cruise in the evening, Burton was holding a flashlight when he fell overboard. Seeing him below the surface with the beam of the light glowing through the water, Emily said laconically, not at all concerned, "Burton will be delighted to know his flashlight is still working."

Burton had fallen in love with Emily when she herself was a hard-drinking, hard-living woman who was a good friend of Hollywood stars, to the point of having a torrid love affair with Johnny Weismuller, who could ride a horse, shoot a gun, and walk on an airplane wing. Burton had an equally steamy past. The only difference was that, as the years went by, Emily became more and more conservative morally, although not conservative at all in her hair, dress and taste in art, while Burton changed little. "For years my father kept a photo on his desk of Emily as a young woman in Montana," said Burton, Jr. "She held a shotgun under one arm and a brace of birds in her hand. She looked very natural, naive. That was his favorite photo of her. It was how he liked to think of her."

In the final analysis, art collecting was the glue in their marriage. "It brought them both joy, the fun of the hunt, getting up in the morning and having something to do together, to be all embroiled in what was going on in the art world and the intrigue with dealers," concluded John Tremaine. "That is what drove them. It kept them both young."

I believe that here in America, some of us, free from the weight of European culture, are finding the answer, by completely denying that art has any concern with the problem of beauty and where to find it. The question that now arises is how, if we are living in a time without a legend or mythos that can be called sublime, if we refuse to admit any exaltation in pure relations, if we refuse to live in the abstract, how can we be creating a sublime art?—Barnett Newman

CHAPTER EIGHT

THE ABSTRACT EXPRESSIONISTS

The renowned art dealer Leo Castelli once said that a real art collector is very rare. "There are many people who only buy paintings until they run out of wall space. The real collector goes on buying irrespective."[1] If wall space were the limiting factor in purchasing art, the Tremaines would have quit by the mid-1950s, at which point they had surpassed even the limits of their newly renovated barn. Via constant lending and moving paintings around, Emily managed to keep much of the collection out of storage, a condition she equated with nothingness and silence. On this point she was unyielding. For example, she was dismayed that the paintings of J. M. W. Turner for some time were considered of so little worth that they had been consigned to storage in the cellar of the Tate Gallery in London. "I don't know how many years the Turners were in the basement of the Tate. Had they been up a little bit, would our history have changed a little bit? Would that vision have come into it?"

Although the Tremaines would become best known for their assiduous collecting of Pop Art in the early 1960's, it was Abstract Expressionism that held their interest the longest. This partiality was evident in what the Tremaines kept until the end of their lives as compared to what they gave away, traded, or sold. The creators of the works they kept were among these characterized by art historian Roger Lipsey as artists-metaphysicians and by art critic Henry Geldzahler as a generation of rabbis: "That whole generation wanted to project the immanence of God, of divinity, in their work, without specificity. Rothko, Newman, Still, and Reinhardt — they were all about having an out-of-body experience, confected with the use of the physical pigment and of the eye, and without grounding you in anything specific that you could then dismiss. They wanted to lift you and keep you at that elevation. And they did it in different ways. So it's kind of a rabbinic tradition, a generation of rabbis."

While their collection was touring the country and various architects were bent over drawing boards struggling futilely to design ranches, beach houses, and visitor centers that would meet with their approval, Burton and Emily set out in search of that "generation of rabbis," especially those who were young and avant-garde. Increasingly, their pattern became the buying of art by unknown painters, moving on when the painters' reputations grew and the price of their art subsequently rose. Whenever the Tremaines, already highly regarded as very savvy collectors, purchased a work by an unknown artist, they helped to elevate the artist's status. In an interview with Aline Louchheim in 1947 in connection with the *Painting Toward Architecture* exhibition, Emily made clear their collecting philosophy, "We will get more of the 'older men' if important ones come our way, but we are primarily interested in the expression of this form today."[2] She and Burton were true to their word, buying the "older men" when the chance arose. For example, the Tremaines bought Giacometti's *Man Walking Quietly under the Rain* in 1949 and acquired his *Spoon Woman* (created in 1926) in 1971. However, it was the works of younger artists, particularly those who emerged in the period from the mid-1950s to the mid-1960s, that began to dominate the collection.

According to Tracy Atkinson, director of the Wadsworth Atheneum in the 1970s and 1980s, the Tremaines were ready for Abstract Expressionism by virtue both of their mutually reinforcing temperaments and their astute acquisitions of twentieth century masterpieces, including not only "the great Léger but also the magnificent Gris, the rare Le Corbusier and the five Paul Klees." He wrote, "The Tremaines were one of those couples who constantly and consistently reinforced each other in a very fundamental sense. Emily was clearly the 'explorer' who delighted in climbing the long stairways of three and more story walkups to artists' studios, but Burton was always there urging her on and from time to time making an even more foresighted acquisition than she. . . . They were thus attuned and ready for the great events which were about to swirl about them in the Abstract Expressionist movement and all that followed." [3]

Abstract Expressionism was not as hegemonic as it appeared. It included several subsets of artists, the principal two among them being the action painters (also called gesture painters), who were more instinctive, and the color field painters, who were more reflective. Neither group was particularly pleased with those labels or, for that matter, any labels.[4] A rich diversity really existed during this period. At precisely the same time that Pollock was splashing paint in a way he hoped would be non-referential to nature (although some critics interpreted it as organic), de Kooning was painting his series of transmogrified women. At the same time that Newman was using color metaphysically, Kline was evoking the coalfields in Pennsylvania via slashes of black paint. There also were many young artists who were beginning to experiment with new approaches to art. Among them was Robert Rauschenberg, who walked into Betty Parsons Gallery in 1951 with a series of abstract allegorical cartoons under his arm.[5] Another young artist, by the name of Jasper Johns, had the idea of painting the American flag.

The Tremaines began to shift their interest to what was happening on the edge of the art world, growing less and less conservative as the years went by. However, there were almost always precursors to the new works in their collection. For example, their interest in kinetic sculpture, which they started to collect in the 1950s, arose naturally from their pleasure in the Calder mobiles they had acquired in the 1940s. Eventually they would own kinetic works by Jean Tinguely, Vassilakis Takis, Jesus Raphael Soto, Pol Bury, and von Theinen — art which tinkled, zigged, and purred in the process of playing with the concepts of time and motion. Irene Rice Pereira's use of glass that caught light and cast shadows in her painting *Transfluent Lines* was but a flicker away from the light sculptures of Chryssa, Dan Flavin, James Seawright, and Robert Irwin that began to filter into the collection in the 1960s. In his introduction to *The Tremaine Collection,* the catalog for the 1984 exhibition at the Wadsworth Atheneum, art historian Robert Rosenblum was struck by this continuity:

> How many times, for instance, does one find in this collection not only Albers but artists of later generations paying homage to the square? We see it in, among other works, Stella's one-foot square exercises in primary patterns; in Noland's dissection of the potential vector thrust of a square corner tilted at 45 degrees; in LeWitt's architectonic dialogue of a cubic

void and solid; in Andre's checkerboard purity of six-times-six one-foot squares of two alternating metal elements, magnesium and aluminum, laid out like tiles for us to walk on; in Agnes Martin's exquisite, graph-paper plotting of the rectilinear surfaces of exactly square canvases; in Mangold's location of four squares of different but related sizes within a pure, circular field. And as for that circular field, it, too, with a shout of Eureka, has been rediscovered countless times in our century, not only by Delaunay, back in 1913, but in endless later themes and variations. Johns, in his *Device Circle,* rediscovers how to make one, as one might re-experience the invention of the wheel; and Wesselmann, in several of his *Great American Nudes,* mocks its iconic format, familiar from great Raphael Madonnas, by venerating within it, as Warhol was also to do in his *Head of Marilyn Monroe,* the deities of later, secular religions.[6]

It was as if the Tremaines had established a visual baseline that would serve them as a guide as they pursued the avant-garde. Once Emily was asked how living with art had affected her thinking and attitude toward life. She replied that even though she had found qualities in artists such as Mondrian that had made her more aware of certain values, the influence was principally the other way around, "My attitude towards life, my thinking and my philosophy have influenced the collection." As a result, the collection had an internal logic, and, for that reason, Leo Castelli felt that it was the best collection of twentieth century art outside of the Museum of Modern Art. In 1957 Castelli opened his gallery with his wife Ileana Sonnabend at 4 East 77th Street and began to show deKooning, Dubuffet, Léger, Delaunay, Smith, and younger artists including Johns, Rauschenberg, and Stella, and eventually Lichtenstein and Warhol. Although the Tremaines looked far and wide for the art they purchased, Castelli was their principal dealer for over two decades; even so, he felt that his influence on Emily's selections was slight.

I just went along and agreed with what she was doing. She was very happy about her choices. It's not that she would discuss them. It was she who initiated the choices and made her selections. In the 1960's there were some galleries like mine that had "the right stuff," and that's where she found them. There was general knowledge about who the good artists were and that at the time they were in my gallery. She was pretty reserved. She did not have a good sense of humor, but she was really wonderful to talk to and deal with because her taste and understanding were so good.[7]

Before he met Emily, Burton had dabbled in painting realistic landscapes in watercolor. However, his enthusiasm for abstract art increased steadily after his purchase of the painting by Perle Fine, the one that reminded him of how the brain of his chief engineer worked. During the early years of their married life, Burton had followed Emily's lead in art purchases, but, as his own knowledge grew and his eye sharpened, they began to consult each other and their collection became truly a joint endeavor. A note to Emily from Burton dated February 5, 1947, confirms the joint nature of their purchases:

Dear Emily, Under date of January 31, I sent my check in amount of $5500 to Samuel M. Kootz, of Samuel M. Kootz Gallery, in payment for "Jeune Fille au Chapeau" by Picasso. I wish to acknowledge receipt of your check in amount of $2250 as payment for one-half of this picture. The picture, therefore, becomes our joint property, each having paid half of the purchase price. With love Burton.[8]

Although Emily did most of the searching, she would ask Burton for his opinion, which she valued highly. They both admitted that her taste in art tended toward the intellectual, or, as Burton described it, "the Platonic absolute, the carefully constructed, and the mathematical." His taste tended toward the more playful, kinetic and feminine side of art. Emily described his taste as lyrical and hers as architectonic. Despite their differences, they usually agreed on purchases: "For Burton and myself, it's been very much a collaboration. I'm apt to go out and find new pieces because he's too busy, he just hasn't the time to go to exhibitions and studios. But when I see something interesting, he makes the time, usually on Saturdays. Once in a while I'll see something, or he will, and one of us will just say, 'I bought something today you'll love.' If it's important, we always do it together. He's more courageous than I am, much more courageous. In fact, it is his encouragement that has been my source of courage."

Once they were unable to attend an exhibition at the Museum of Modern Art together, so they decided to list on separate sheets of paper their first four picks of the best in the exhibition and then compare notes later. "When we got home and compared our comments, our top four pictures were the same, and Em's number one was my number two and vice versa," said Burton.[9] Over the years such agreement became commonplace, although occasionally they disagreed about how a work of art should be hung. They laughed about a ladder by Bruce Robbins with one side painted in pastel shades so light they looked metallic white and the other side painted black. "We don't know which side we prefer here [in Madison]," Burton said to a visitor, "but in New York we are quite firm as to who likes the painted side and who likes the black side." About placement in New York they concurred: it leaned against the wall near Mondrian's *Pier and Ocean, 1914,* but Burton was certain that the black side served the Mondrian better. "Nonsense. It's just the opposite," Emily retorted. As a compromise, they rotated the sides.

It was no surprise to Emily, although it may have been to his family, that Burton was the one to choose the Tremaines' first painting by Barnett Newman. In 1948 Emily and Burton went to Chicago by train to see an exhibition put on by the Chicago Art Institute titled "Abstract and Surrealist American Art." Having decided ahead of time to select works separately, Emily chose a watercolor by Cady Wells, and Burton chose Newman's *Euclidean Abyss.* He found it so powerful he could not get it out of his mind. Newman had been painting for years, but this was the first work he ever sold.[10] One of Abstract Expressionism's primary theoreticians and polemicists about the struggle to dematerialize painting, Newman relied financially on substitute teaching in the New York City schools, as well as on his wife's income as a teacher. Eventually his austere paintings would be highly regarded, first by other artists and then, slowly, by collectors and museums, but at this point Newman was not able to get gallery space. Resolute about the integrity of his artistic vision, he would not have his first one-man show until 1950. For Newman himself, *Euclidean Abyss* was a breakthrough painting, the first time that he used only a few simple lines:

> I would say that it began in 1946–47. In those years, whenever I did a painting with one or two elements in it, it did always have a sense of atmospheric background, I suppose — with the exception of a painting which I called *Euclidean Abyss,* where the background is black and has some of the white coming through, but there's no true atmosphere; and where I move to the edge, the edge has a yellow edge with a corner in it. For me, it's a historic painting in terms of my own history, because there for the first time I moved to the edge, and the edge becomes lighter than the central section. Ostensibly it should have ended where the dark part ends, but I moved further to the actual edge of the canvas, and I felt that I'd moved to the edge but hadn't fallen off . . . By "nature" I mean something very specific. I think that some abstractions — for example, Kandinsky's — are really nature paintings. The triangles and the spheres or circles could be bottles.

Burton and Emily Tremaine, late 1940s.

They could be trees, or buildings. I think in the painting *Euclidean Abyss* I removed myself from nature, but I did not remove myself from life.[11]

The Tremaines' interest in the art of Barnett Newman did not end with his death in 1970. They purchased *The Moment II* in 1978 from his widow, Annalee Newman, thirty years after acquiring *Euclidean Abyss*. A year later, they purchased *Outcry*, a stark, elongated black and white canvas only six inches wide and eighty-two inches high. Newman had suffered a severe heart attack in 1957. When he recovered from that soul-shaking experience, he began working on *Outcry*. "I was trying to call attention to that part of the Passion which I have always felt was ignored and which has always affected me and that was the cry of Lama Sabachthani. . . . . Why? Why did you forsake me? To what purpose? Why?" explained Newman. Annalee Newman remembered the sale of *Outcry* to the Tremaines, "Mrs. Tremaine kept calling me and calling me. She wanted that painting. But I did not want to sell it. It was full of tears for me, full of tears. She finally wore me down."[12]

After completing *Outcry* in 1958, Newman started work on the fourteen canvases that would constitute his magnum opus *The Stations of the Cross*, which he completed in 1966. *The Moment II,* painted three years later, was one of the last works Newman finished. Shortly thereafter, it was stored away. Following his death in 1970, it was misplaced. Eight years later, Annalee Newman, hoping for a sale, invited the Tremaines to look through her husband's paintings that were stored in a warehouse. Emily and Burton took a look at the paintings, but they could not find anything they wanted. They came upon an unopened crate, and, with Mrs. Newman's permission, they opened it up. When Mrs. Newman saw *The Moment II* inside, she gasped, "It's the lost painting, the one that follows *The Stations of the Cross*."[13] Although Newman had not included it in the *Stations of the Cross,* both Annalee Newman and the Tremaines viewed it as the final resolution of that series, the moment of atonement and ascension.

The Newman paintings were among the most difficult in the Tremaine collection for Emily to hang to her satisfaction, because they needed their own space. "We must listen to the immobility of the painting with the same terror that causes us to hear the silence of deserts and of glaciers," Newman once said.[14] Deserts and glaciers are usually perceived as vast, monochromatic, inhospitable places. Seekers after metaphysical truth often are drawn to the desert, sensing that from its visual poverty springs spiritual wealth, and Newman was a seeker even if he never left New York. The arid ground he contemplated was on his canvas.

Beginning in the late 1940s the Tremaines spent several months each year skiing in Europe, but this had its drawbacks when it came to collecting American art. "Obviously," Emily said, "we missed some of the greatest paintings that were ever done in the early 1950s because we were up there in the Alps breaking our legs. Of course there have been hundreds of things that have passed us by. I never walk through a museum without thinking of the lost opportunities, of what I could have done if I'd had more courage. As for private collections, someone often got there before I did. The world is full of those things, I just have to come home and count my blessings and be glad for those pieces I do have."

Emily's reference to "breaking our legs" was not merely a turn of phrase. She actually did break her leg, at which point she decided that Christian Science had no answer for cracked femurs. She went to a doctor and had the bone set. Emily's explanation about missing "some of the greatest paintings," however, was also a facile excuse given to interviewers who wondered why the Tremaines owned only two works by Pollock, the more major of which was painted at the end of his life. She told one interviewer that she and Burton had gone out to Long Island to see Pollock's work and "were so overcome with what we saw we could not make a decision." They chose to put some works on hold before leaving for Europe. However, this episode occurred at the end of Pollock's career. The work they eventually bought was one of the last that Pollock delivered to his dealer, Sidney Janis, right before his death in 1956. In fact, the Tremaines had had several opportunities to acquire Pollock's work and had declined. The first opportunity was when they attended the opening of Pollock's show at Betty Parsons Gallery on November 21, 1949. Pollock's previous shows had attracted little attention, and only Clement Greenberg gave them positive reviews, but this show was markedly different. In the previous August, *Life* had run a large article titled "Jackson Pollock: Is he the greatest living painter in the United States?" On the first page was a picture of Pollock looking disdainfully cool before his eighteen-foot-long painting *Summertime*. The lead-in copy was meant to be provocative: "Recently, a formidably high-brow New York critic hailed the brooding, puzzled-looking man shown above as a major artist of our time and a fine candidate to become 'the greatest American painter of the 20th century.' Others believe that Jackson Pollock produces nothing more than interesting, if inexplicable, decoration. Still others condemn his pictures as degenerate and find them as unpalatable as yesterday's macaroni."[15]

The tone of bemused consternation continued throughout the article. "To find out what he has been doing, he stops and contemplates the picture during what he calls his 'get acquainted' period . . . Finally, after days of brooding and doodling, Pollock decides the painting is finished, a deduction few others are equipped to make." The *Life* article fueled great interest in Pollock and when his show opened three months later at Betty Parsons Gallery, an overflow crowd packed the exhibition. This time it was not just curious artists and friends of Pollock's who attended but collectors and art cognoscenti, including Alfred Barr (who had previously expressed dislike for Pollock's work), Roy Neuberger, Sam Kootz, and the Tremaines. One of the other reasons that this particular show was a success was that the works were small and moderately priced. The Tremaines purchased *Number 6,* not for themselves, but as a gift for Burton's son, who picked it out. The recreation room in his home in West Hartford, Connecticut, had just been redesigned with the help of Philip Johnson, allowing for a better view of a waterfall and creek in the back. The redesign also provided a blank wall perfect for a large dramatic painting. According to Burton Jr.:

At Philip's suggestion, we used striated plywood which we painted white. Then we put black asphalt tile on the floor, so it was a black and white room—a wonderful space. My father and Emily had offered us a trip to Mexico as a gift but because of our children we could not go, so instead we said: "We're not sure that we are going to get to Mexico very soon, but we've got this wonderful wall in this new room. Could we exchange our Mexico tickets for a piece of art?" And they said "Of course." So we came down to New York and Burton and Emily took us around to all the current galleries. We saw a number of works and at Betty Parsons we chose a Jackson Pollock. We paid $649 for it.[16]

Burton Tremaine, Jr., owned the painting for thirteen years, until he sold it to the Museum of Fine Arts in Houston. He used the proceeds to purchase a summer home on Fishers Island in Long Island Sound.

In 1962 we rented a house for a month in the summer at Fishers Island. We had a chance to buy the house and we had to make a rapid decision in twenty-four hours, so we decided that it was going to be of greater importance and value to our family to have the house than to have the Jackson Pollock. So we set about trying to sell the Pollock. We went to Castelli and asked him to sell it. He had the picture for over a year and we didn't get any offers. Then Emily was walking down some avenue in New York with

Jim Sweeney, director of the Houston Museum of Fine Arts, and she said, "How would you like to have a pretty good Pollock?" and he replied "I'd love it." He came to see it, went back to Houston, passed the hat because they didn't have the money at the museum, got benefactors to put up the money, and bought it directly from me with no commission.

The Tremaines had another opportunity to purchase Pollock's work in 1950 when they seriously considered commissioning him to paint a mural for them. Pollock used a small notebook or sketchbook made of mulberry paper in which he drew and wrote notes. On page eight in pencil he wrote "Tremaine, Geller, Museum of Modern Art, May 22, 1950" among other doodles, numbers, and names. Bertram Geller was a shoe manufacturer who had commissioned a house by Marcel Breuer in Lawrence, Long Island, as well as a small mural by Pollock to go with it. The mural recently had been completed and would be installed in July 1950 on the back of the kitchen cabinets, facing the dining room. The seventy-two by ninety-six inch canvas "came folded up like wrapping paper," according to Giorgio Cavallon, the artist who handled the installation, and had to be ironed to get rid of the creases.[17] The Tremaines wished to see it before considering a similar commission. However, for some reason the commission never came about. To Pollock's dismay, neither did many other prospective mural commissions from other collectors. The murals were so large many collectors were intimidated by them.

Eventually Emily and Burton came to appreciate Pollock's work. Perhaps they were not so impressed by it at the beginning, because it was more emotional than intellectual, and Pollock's individualistic technique was not classical. Pollock used house paints directly out of cans lined up around the edges of the canvas, which was spread out on the floor of his workshop. Instead of brushes he used sticks to swirl, drip, and throw the paint. He maintained great control over these unusual tools, but it was an unusual kind of control, made up of unconscious rhythm and grace. To Betty Parsons, his compositions "were so complex, yet he never went overboard, always in perfect balance. . . . When Jackson would get lost, I think the unconscious took over, and that's marvelous."[18]

In the late painting titled *Frieze*, which the Tremaines eventually owned, Pollock incorporated thick impasto brush strokes with bold drippings. The unusual fact was not that Pollock slashed aluminum paint across primary colors until the canvas almost vibrated but that he resorted to brushes. To some critics this was a regression; others saw it as Pollock's attempt to fight his way out of the technique box that he himself had built. However, this may have been what attracted Burton and Emily who tended to like artists who used classical techniques, albeit in radical ways. Another reason for their initial reserve toward Pollock may have been that he was not overtly spiritual. Pollock, like Emily, had been born in Montana and had moved in his childhood to California, but that was where the similarity ended. He was a haunted alcoholic who did not care to spend time philosophizing about the nature of art, although when pressed he could be eloquently succinct. He was either very friendly, painfully shy, or violently antisocial, generally depending on how much he had drunk. He felt himself under enormous pressure to be constantly innovative, and it ate away at him. His death in a car crash in 1956, drunk, seemed more like suicide than an accident. As Parsons had said, he got lost—and he never found his way back.

Besides *Frieze*, the Tremaines also purchased *Silver and Black* from Sidney Janis in 1958. Janis had written on the invoice that *Silver and Black* was "achieved" by Pollock. Burton wrote back and asked him to change the invoice. "I suspect I should have looked up what Webster says the word 'achieve' means. My trouble is that I never heard a painter achieving a picture. I have heard of many painters having painted a picture." Janis did as he was told and the word "achieve" was replaced with "painted" on the corrected invoice.

There is a footnote to the story of the Tremaines and Pollock. Sam Green, a close friend of the Tremaines, recalls that years later they had a chance to acquire *Lavender Mist:* "We took a trip to East Hampton to visit the painter and art sponsor Alfonso Ossorio who was selling off his fantastic Pollock *Lavender Mist*. He had asked me if the Tremaines would be interested because they had such a good collection. He asked me to be the go-between to see if they wanted it for, I believe, $700,000, which was a great deal more than the Tremaines had ever spent on a painting. We drove out, saw the collection, had lunch with Alfonso amongst his Clyfford Stills and Pollocks and Dubuffets. On the drive back to the city Burton and Emily discussed the pros and cons of spending that amount of money and they concluded that they would further the collection better by not buying *Lavender Mist* and continuing to buy on the cutting edge instead of looking back." [19]

One of the Abstract Expressionists whose work Emily did appreciate was Mark Rothko. She especially liked his spiritual paintings of the 1950s. However, she did not consider Rothko a true Abstract Expressionist. "Of course, he was known as an Abstract Expressionist and certainly had the temperament of one, but somehow he wasn't quite," she said. Rothko was so visionary that he thought of his art, not as paintings, but as dramas that acted as doorways to a transcendent realm for the viewer.[20] Emily believed that his dynamic waves of color and light, both scintillating and serene, required an intuitive response. Recalling her purchase in 1953 of *Number 8,* Emily said: "I thought Rothko was absolutely marvelous and bought the second Rothko I ever saw. As a matter of fact it was interesting, the day I bought that Rothko, I'd been at the Nierendorf Gallery. I'd gone through a pile of Klees and put about ten aside and they were all marvelous. I went from Nierendorf to see a show of Rothko at Betty Parsons. I saw this Rothko and I knew we had to have it, but I didn't think I should be so extravagant and buy the Rothko and the Klees the same day. I made the choice and said no, I want the Rothko, I'll try to forget the Klees. I bought this one and I still think it's one of the most glorious things we own."

Besides the sublime quality in his work that appealed to the Tremaines, Rothko had high technical skill. His work required forethought, preparation, and patience. He was a colorist, who knew how to build up very thin layers of diluted paint in a manner used by Renaissance artists, although he tended to be indifferent about the durability of his paint and the permanence of his colors. In the painting *Maroon and Blue,* which the Tremaines owned, the edges of the canvas are feathered into an ethereal blue on which float three rectangular clouds in darker blues and maroon. The painting hung in the summer room in Madison. Placed in front of it, embodying the essence of tranquility, was a sixteenth century Siamese head of Buddha that the Tremaines had purchased on a trip to Asia. In their New York apartment, the scintillating yellow and red *Number 8* shared a wall with a tam-tam, an enormous Oceanic wooden sculpture, totemic in its power.[21]

Throughout the 1950s and into the early 1960s, the Tremaines were as assiduous in acquiring good European art as they were American art. When not skiing, they haunted the galleries, Iris Clert's being a favorite, and purchased the works of Yaacov Agam, Karel Appel, Asger Jorn, Jean-Paul Riopelle, Kenneth Armitage, Piero Manzoni, Jean Tinguely, Vasilaskia Takis, Yves Klein, and Michel Seuphor. Agam would become one of the first of the kinetic artists who wanted to involve the viewer as a participant, but the work that the Tremaines purchased was created in 1952, prior to his individual and group exhibitions. Karel Appel was born in Amsterdam but moved to Paris in 1950. He and Asger Jorn, who was Danish, were expressionists similar to the American action painters. Both used paint vehemently and emotionally. According to Appel, during that period, "My painting was a fight. I did not paint — I hit!" [22] In his early thirties, Jean-Paul Riopelle was a Canadian who, like Appel, had settled in Paris after the war. Swiss-born Jean Tinguely made "machines" that had a sense of aberrant playfulness about them. Yves Klein, who was exhibiting at the same time as Tinguely, was among the most unusual of the group. He became famous for his sponge paintings in which he used natural sponges to apply blue paint to naked women who then rolled themselves over unprimed canvas at his direction. Klein then mounted the paint-hardened sponges on wire and attached them to a base. He sold as art both the sponge forms (one of which the Tremaines owned) and the body-printed canvases.

Not only did Emily introduce several of these artists to American collectors, she helped mount an exhibition of their work in the spring of 1959 to give them greater exposure. Shortly thereafter she wrote to Iris Clert about the event:

The Museum of Modern Art helped me install everything and rearrange the program. Thursday, the day of the exhibition, poured down rain but even so, over two hundred people came and all were most enthusiastic. I had many, many inquiries about the different artists especially Takis who was a sensation. Please do me a big favor and find two or three more Takis's before he becomes famous. Send me photographs and measurements as soon as you can. Also, my brother-in-law tells me you are having a very small Soto made for him; I too would like one or two small Sotos for [my] mini-gallery.

I cannot remember how to hang [the painting by] Lora; does it go perpendicular with the little spots at the top or should I hang it horizontal? It seems to work both ways.

The day after the exhibition I had a large cocktail party. Philip Johnson was there as well as Alfred Barr, Leo Castelli, etc., etc. All were very enthused especially about my miniature gallery. You must keep a good eye out for me to add to this. Philip Johnson is very jealous about my Blue Sponge; he thinks it is far more beautiful than his.[23]

But the *Blue Sponge* by Yves Klein was causing Emily problems over and above Johnson's jealousy. Less than a month later she again wrote to Clert, inquiring if she could purchase a larger version:

Now about the Klein — the large picture is now installed after terrible trouble (it is so heavy), but it is very handsome hanging in a small gallery which

Philip Johnson built for us. In front of this large Klein I have placed a low antique Chinese Ming table in white lacquer, and on this I have placed the blue sponge. It is terrific, but the sponge is a little too small; in fact, quite a bit too small and detracts from the dramatic effect I had hoped to achieve. The big sponge is very tempting, but I have spent so much money this year and I have just had to pay over $50.00 to have a very handsome plastic base made for the sponge as it kept losing its balance and falling over. Do you think Klein would make a very, very special price for me of $500.00 for the big sponge? Remind him that it will be installed in a very prominent place where many of the art world will see it to its best advantage and that I have already bought from him the large picture and large sculpture besides the sponge.[24]

Apparently, Klein agreed to the price, because Emily did obtain the larger blue sponge, which measured forty-five inches high by twenty-one inches wide. Her argument that she should pay less for it because it would be to Klein's advantage to have his work showcased by the Tremaines was one she used many times over the years with artists who were not yet fully established. It was a convincing argument, but it often left the artists with mixed feelings toward the Tremaines. They were honored to have their work selected but at the same time felt a little miffed at having to accept less money for their efforts.

Emily also could be very encouraging. However, she never became a patron of any particular artist. The only artist whose career she could take a modicum of credit for launching was Belgium-born Michel Seuphor. An eminent critic and commentator on art, especially on the work of Mondrian, with whom he had been close friends, Seuphor did not consider his own artistic creations to be of much worth until Emily displayed an interest in them.

I think I was the first person who bought his drawings. I was talking to him about his Mondrian book. He had never been to New York and he wanted to be brought up to date on the New York period. This pile of drawings was on his desk and while he was out of the room, I looked through them. When he came back, I asked, "Who did these?" He replied "Oh, no one very important." I told him that I really liked them and [wanted to know] who did them. He said "I have insomnia and I do them when I can't sleep at night, but I'm a critic and a poet, not a [painter.] I said, "Well, sell me something." "Oh I'll give them to you." He gave me three or four and I said, "I will not accept these as a gift. If I were buying these at a gallery I'd pay so much for a drawing and you just must take it." After that he decided he would sell and he went to Denise René. I still like his things very much.

Frequently, the Tremaines sought out other collectors in Europe, just as they did in the United States. One individual whose collection struck Emily as particularly fine was Count Giuseppe Panza di Biumo, a lawyer and realtor who owned a country house in Varese in Tuscany. He eventually became a collector of Minimalist art, but at the time Emily and Burton first met him (probably in the early 1960s), he had amassed a fine selection of the works of Mark Rothko. Emily recalled:

> One evening in Milan will always be outstanding. We were on our way from San Moritz to Sestrierre and had gone to no end of wire-pulling to get seats for a gala performance at La Scala the one night we were to be in Milan. We arrived in Milan in the afternoon. As a compass needle is drawn to the North, we are drawn to painters and galleries. At curtain time we found ourselves the guests of a newly made friend, a Milanese count whose ancestral castle is filled with Rauschenbergs, Klines, and Rothkos. The setting gave more drama and mystery to the works of these artists than I had ever experienced before. And the duet from *Rigoletto* was sung without us. I have recently heard that this collector is now converting the large carriage house on his estate into a shrine to house a dozen more Rothko's.[25]

For all her careful attention to the works of European artists, Emily came to the conclusion that modern European art was not as strong as American. "When we were in Paris, the pictures we bought were very good quality, but we had forgotten the excitement of New York." When the Tremaines returned to the United States, they quickly made up for lost time. By the end of the decade, the Tremaines had acquired paintings by Pollock, Rothko, de Kooning, and Franz Kline. They also bought *The Chess Game* by Conrad Marca-Relli, a composition that incorporated sand, and Raoul Hague's sensuous sculpture carved out of a tree trunk called *Swamp Pepperwood 1956*.

The Tremaines were quick to admit that they made many mistakes of judgment in buying art, even if that was not obvious because they exhibited only the best, not the worst. Due to the fact that they did not wait for critical opinion to coalesce about a particular artist before purchasing, they sometimes decided ruefully that they had bought in haste and now had the time to repent in leisure. But they never repented for long; instead they donated works they did not consider first-rate to museums and art schools. Rarely did they lose money, because a donated painting that had appreciated in value might easily be worth more as a tax deduction than its original cost.

They also readily admitted to missing many opportunities, not only in the United States but in Europe. Speaking in 1965 at the 7th Selection of the Society for the Encouragement of Contemporary Art in San Francisco, Emily told about her greatest missed chance:

> I think it is only fair to confess that all is not triumph. We have had some shattering frustrations. A few years ago in Paris, Ellsworth Kelly told us he had been to Monet's place in the country. He had looked into a barn with a leaking roof and there appeared to be quite a number of large canvases leaning against the wall. He had not seen them very well and Monet's son was indifferent about them. Ellsworth begged us to go and look at them carefully, insisting the whole barn could be bought for $10,000. The weather was miserable, we were anxious to get on with our skiing, and we made plans to go to Monet's on our return. We did return to Paris some six weeks later to learn that a gentleman and scholar named Alfred Barr had taken care of the situation very adequately and had acquired all of Monet's last canvases, the now renowned water lily paintings.[26]

Around this time, Emily and Burton became involved with the International Council at the Museum of Modern Art, which had been formed in 1953 under the leadership of Blanchette H. Rockefeller (Mrs. John D. Rockefeller III). Its purpose was to support the international program of the museum and to increase understanding through the exchange of contemporary art. Prior to that time, very little American art was exhibited in European museums. "The Europeans thought that America was nothing but bubble gum and Cadillacs," said Elsa Parkinson Cobb, a museum trustee.[27] Elite, dedicated, and enthusiastic, the members of the Council became the nucleus of the Tremaines' social life. There were meetings at Blanchette Rockefeller's guest house, designed by Philip Johnson, with its atrium pool traversed by walking on three stepping-stones. There were symposiums held in the museum's penthouse on the state of art around the world. Members frequently traveled abroad together to see exhibitions, although the council itself did not hold its first official meeting out of the country until 1968, when as a group it went to South America. Emily served as the council's treasurer in 1958–59, the year that it supported two controversial exhibitions on American Abstract Expressionism: *The New American Painting,* which traveled to eight European cities, and *Jackson Pollock, 1912–56,* which was first exhibited at the São Paulo Bienal in 1957 and subsequently traveled to Europe. She was also involved in the council's Art in Embassies program in which contemporary art was loaned to American embassies around the world.

As the 1950s drew to a close, American and European Abstract Expressionists were well represented in the Tremaines' collection, but so also were artists heading in new directions, including Johns, Stella, and John Chamberlain. By then the major aesthetic questions posed by the Abstract Expressionists essentially had been answered. All that remained were little ones, refinements instead of revelations. There was no room left for big breakthroughs. What initially had been so frighteningly directionless now bordered on the formulaic. To get an idea of the Tremaines' ability to sense where art was heading, one need only look at what they purchased from 1958 to 1960 and from whom:

Jasper Johns *White Flag* (1955–58), *Three Flags* (1958), *Device Circle* (1959), Leo Castelli Gallery.

Jackson Pollock *Silver and Black* (1950), Sidney Janis Gallery.

Franz Kline *Lehigh* (1956), Sidney Janis Gallery.

Robert Motherwell *Spanish Elegy Number 17* (1953), Sidney Janis Gallery.

Louise Nevelson *Moon Garden Reflections* (1957), *Moon Garden Series* (1958), Grand Central Moderns Gallery and from the artist.

Robert Rauschenberg *Construction* (1958), *Flemish Blue* (1958), Leo Castelli Gallery.

Piero Manzoni *Petit Subject* (1958), Iris Clert Gallery.

Joan Miró *Makimono* (1952–1957), Hans Berggruen.

Karel Appel *Two Clowns* (1958), Iris Clert Gallery.

Asger Jorn *Bird* (1959), Iris Clert Gallery.

Jean Tinguely *Plate Sculpture* (1959), *Meta Mecamic* Iris Clert Gallery.

Vassilakis Takis *Signal* (1958), Iris Clert Gallery.

Yves Klein *Blue Sponge, Composition Monochrome Blue* (1959), Iris Clert Gallery.

Frank Stella *Untitled* (1959), Leo Castelli Gallery.

John Chamberlain *Gramm* (1960), *Greek Key* (1960), Leo Castelli Gallery.

Nassos Daphnis *S.7–60* (1960), Leo Castelli Gallery.

Ad Reinhardt *Blue Composition* (1959), Iris Clert Gallery.

Jésus Raphael Soto *Vibration,* Iris Clert Gallery.

Other works purchased during the same period (as noted in Emily's card file without complete titles or dealer names) were by Kalinovski, Lora, Tsingos, Gontcharova, and Kriche.

Emily's personal favorites were the *Moon Garden Series* and *Moon Garden Reflections* by Louise Nevelson. Although she had her first one-woman exhibition in 1941, Nevelson did not develop her distinctive style of monochromatic sculptures tucked into wooden boxes until the mid-1950s. Nearly sixty years old at the time of her Moon Garden exhibition at Grand Central Moderns in 1958, Nevelson had been fighting an uphill battle her entire life because she was a woman artist. Some critics found her constructions sinister, partially because they had a hidden, internal quality, but they also exuded an edgy tranquility. Like an abandoned elevator for a mine shaft is boarded over with broken planks, Nevelson's work conveyed the aura of a dark, dangerous past. In an undated letter, Emily wrote to Nevelson about a piece she was working on: "I am very excited to see what you create to support the Greek columns (it always makes me think a little of "Mourning Becomes Electra"). Philip Johnson, my husband, and I all love it, but we also love the pieces that give us a sense of the mystic emotionalism of the Gothic spirit. The macabre playfulness with grotesque angles, high vaulted shadows, nails, etc. We seem to remember the two original supporting boxes were in this mood, but none of us can quite remember them in detail. However, we all feel that each piece you do surpasses its predecessor so we are not worried." [28]

The paintings that would spiral upwards in value the most and that would guarantee the fame of the Tremaines' collection were those painted by a young man named Jasper Johns, who in the early 1950s was selling books and designing window displays to supplement his art income. His coolly intelligent and emotionally reserved paintings were as enigmatic as Nevelson's but more ironic. They were carefully thought out (like Barnett Newman's paintings) yet were physical (like Pollock's murals). As a result, Johns would be seen as the precursor for several nascent art movements, including Pop, Minimalism, Post-Minimalism and Conceptual Art. Yet Johns himself managed to slip through the net of labels that critics and art historians kept casting over him. For Johns, his use of the commonplace in his art never became commonplace. The most public of images, such as the flag, were reproduced innumerable times yet retained a sense of being private and one-of-a-kind. This was unlike what was to happen shortly in Pop, when mass-produced silkscreens took over.

At Johns's first show at the Leo Castelli Gallery in 1958, there was figurative art, even still life, in the form of flags and targets. There were also numerals and letters straining against the ambiguous geometry of the surface plane, about which Emily said, "When I look at Jasper's number and letter paintings, I think of a critique I once read on Sarah Bernhardt. It said she could recite the alphabet and bring tears to your eyes."[29]

According to Johns, the first paintings that the Tremaines acquired from his dealer Leo Castelli were *Tango* and *White Flag:* "Castelli told them that *Tango* was the only thing available after my show, which was true. . . . I remember they didn't believe him and subsequently came to my studio."[30] On that trip they saw the unfinished *Three Flags* and instantly wanted it. Recalled Emily, "I sensed immediately upon seeing *Three Flags* that it was a great new invention." She arranged to buy it through Castelli. These acquisitions were a bold move, because the paintings had stirred protest from people who felt Johns was vulgarizing a sacrosanct symbol.

Robert Rosenblum in his introduction to the catalog *The Tremaine Collection* drew a thoughtful parallel between *Three Flags* and the works of Mondrian and Delaunay that the Tremaines already owned. "Finally, the motion here, like the vibration of rectangles in the Mondrian or of arcs and circles in the Delaunay, has a frozen, deadlocked quality, almost embalmed or petrified in the taut precision that informs these austere vocabularies of elementary geometries and stepwise intervals." Initially Johns himself had seen no such connection. "When I first saw my paintings hung in their apartment next to the Delaunay and Mondrian, I was not so impressed with their works. Subsequently, of course, we all became impressed by Delaunay's work and realized his importance. I'm not sure that I really cared about the European things. [The American ones] were important to me. But the Delaunay and the Mondrian became extraordinary paintings."[31]

Ostensibly two-dimensional, *Three Flags* actually projects out of the picture toward the viewer, inverting in the process the concept of perspective, because the flag that is closest is the smallest and appears most distant. The art critic Leo Steinberg once said, "Whatever else it may be, all great art is about art," and in this respect Johns's work was the logical successor to the Abstract Expressionists.[32] Johns had painted his first flag in 1954. In 1962, reflecting on his choice of the flag as a symbol, Johns said, "Using the design of the American flag took care of a great deal for me because I didn't have to design it. So I went on to similar things like targets—things the mind already knows. That gave me room to work on other levels." *White Flag*, which hung in the Tremaines' New York bedroom, is one of the most radical works of the series because although the lineaments of the stars and stripes are there, it is almost as if the colors have bleached away. Yet the expressive brush strokes in encaustic paint on top of layers of newspaper convey a physicality quite different from that of a real flag.

Johns began making significant changes in his art after meeting Marcel Duchamp in 1959. In some respects, *Device Circle,* painted that year and purchased by the Tremaines in 1960 for $1,620, can be seen as a transitional work; it included a real object that projected three-dimensionally. Duchamp's influence and the principles of Dada can be seen in the inclusion of the title in the work and in the "found" element, which in this case is the device that draws the circle. Johns, however, used Dadaist principles for his own purposes. Here the device can actually move around the canvas, it *makes* art and *is* art at the same time, synthesizing symbol and gesture, which in the *Flags* series were at odds with each other.

Johns was an occasional guest at the Tremaines' home in Madison and at their apartment in New York. "The one event I remember was I went to a kind of cocktail party and Harry Abrams was there and Emily introduced Bob Rauschenberg to Harry Abrams. As a result, Abrams published [Rauschenberg's] *Dante's Inferno.* I had the idea that Emily had arranged this encounter deliberately to accomplish this." [33]

Emily did not like forcing artists and art into categories. "It really does not work. How can there be an empirical formula for art?" Even so, in her 1965 speech for the Society for the Encouragement of Contemporary Art, Emily talked about Abstract Expressionism and why she felt that the movement had worn itself out by the end of the previous decade.

About 1950, the creative tides were reaching an ebb in Europe and rising with great force in New York. The war was over, and the word freedom meant more to us than ever before. Jackson Pollock painted freedom as he cut through traditions and limitations, and others quickly followed. We called this Abstract Expressionism and action painting. For ten years it explored with emotion and vigor. Often it expressed anxiety. These painters were introspective and foreboding, perhaps fearing to lose the freedom they had suffered so deeply to preserve. Perhaps this angst was conditioned by the years of the Depression and the war, but a young generation was growing up and they had not been deeply involved in either and they were getting ready to show us a world we had not been seeing. In his recent book *The Anxious Object,* Harold Rosenberg disposes of Abstract Expressionism briefly when he says "Barney Newman closed the door, Rothko pulled down the blinds, and Reinhardt put out the lights."[34]

Among the younger artists getting ready to "show us a world we had not been seeing" was Andy Warhol. In 1962 the Tremaines purchased fifteen works from him before he even had a regular dealer. By so doing, they helped fuel his meteoric rise. Pop was not really new. It had many artistic antecedents. What was new was the speed at which it crossed the line to respectability. This was not brought about by dealers or museums. It was brought about by private collectors. And the Tremaines would be the leaders of the pack.

I was never embarrassed about asking someone, literally, "What should I paint?" because Pop comes from the outside, and how is asking someone for ideas any different from looking for them in a magazine?—Andy Warhol

CHAPTER NINE

THE POP DECADE

In January 1965, just three years after they had purchased their first work of Pop Art, Emily told the Society for Encouragement of Contemporary Art that Pop was dead. Had they been in the audience that day, Warhol, Oldenburg, and Lichtenstein would have been surprised by that pronouncement. The Tremaines were considered to be among the most important collectors of Pop, yet Emily was writing its epitaph before the paint was dry on Warhol's silkscreens.

About 1961 a comet flashed across this dark scene with a blazing light and we saw objects we really had not seen before, we were too busy looking within, but now we looked out and saw a yankee doodle world of pop bottles, trading stamps and comic strips. This was Pop Art and it painted the wonderful, vulgar, jazzy, free and crazy New York. It was not like Dada. The artists did not know one another. No one was angry. There was no manifesto. They just were aware of the same images, but they used them differently. Rosenquist and Oldenburg were somewhat surrealists; Lichtenstein seemed amicably iconoclastic; and Andy Warhol we thought was naive, a new douanier Rousseau—how wrong we were there. Now I think Andy may be the most complex of the lot. Anyway, Pop came and went and when that blazing comet veered away we were left with spots in front of our eyes.[1]

Why would two patrons of abstraction suddenly start buying paintings of soup cans and green stamps? Why after buying Pop so heavily would they suddenly quit? Because Pop was as much a cultural phenomenon as an art phenomenon, the answers are found not in the paintings, but in the turbulent times.

If the importance of something were determined by the size of the media event it generates, then Pop would be considered the most important art movement of the twentieth century. It appeared at a time when Marshall Mc-Luhan had just announced, "The medium is the message," referring to the powerful role of mass media. That was the new faith, and among the true believers were the handsome young president with a beautiful, young, and artistically savvy wife. (If there was a mantra for the early 1960s it was the word "young.") John F. Kennedy knew that the impact of his public image was as important as his beliefs. He understood that with the increasing dominance of television, a sound bite was more likely to be broadcast than lengthy analysis.

Pop Art exploded onto the cultural scene at the same time and, at least initially, embodied the same values. Its subjects came from advertising, newspaper and magazine stories, and consumer detritus, such as beer cans and lipstick. The artistic techniques employed mimicked those used in graphic design, a field in which several of the Pop artists had worked successfully. It smacked of mass production, even when the artist had to go to painstaking lengths to capture that feeling. For example, Roy Lichtenstein carefully painted large ben-day dots to convey the impression that his art had been printed on a gargantuan offset press. Before too long, Warhol began to use silkscreening, thereby reintroducing an actual mechanical process into the making of art.

Suddenly artists were not holed up in studios out at the end of Long Island in solitary and depressed communion with the muse of art. They were not writing angry manifestos on the nature of abstraction as a sublime art. Instead they were having fun at the center of a "happening," in Warhol's "Factory," or at Oldenburg's "Ray Gun Store," amidst strobe lights, rock-and-roll, glitz and, most of all, media coverage. Warhol was his own creation. He craved the pop of the flashbulb even if he had to upstage his art to get it. He was constantly aware of the impression he wanted to make, and he shaped his milieu accordingly. For example, he would play classical music in the Factory when he was working, but as soon as he knew a visitor or a collector was coming he would put on a single rock-and-roll record to play repeatedly ad nauseam at

One Christmas, Warhol left a small Head of Marilyn Monroe *by the Tremaines' door in gratitude for their support and encouragement.*

high volume. Emily remembered that, when she and Burton visited, sometimes Warhol would be playing both classical music and rock-and-roll at the same time, letting the two compete.

Because the Pop artists were not theorists about their work or themselves, the definition of Pop was unclear, at least at the beginning. Europeans saw it as an anti-capitalist statement, while the American artists themselves insisted it was statement-free. Warhol said over and over again that he loved the objects he was painting. Campbell's soup, he maintained, was his favorite food. He loved looking at pictures of movie stars in the fan magazines. He insisted that his work was a way to get people to see those things around them that were so commonplace they had become invisible. For example, when one looked closely at green stamps, handed out by the hundreds of thousands to consumers in supermarkets and gasoline stations every day, one discovered they were beautiful.

When they did write about their work, Pop artists could be maddeningly inconsistent. For example, at one point Robert Indiana insisted that the New Art (another name for Pop) was a "re-enlistment in the world. It is the American Dream, optimistic, generous and naive." Then he contradicted himself: the works conveyed that "modern man, with his loss of identity, submersion in mass culture, beset by mass destruction, is man's greatest problem, and that Art hardly provides the Solution—some optimistic, glowing, harmonious, humanitarian, plastically perfect Lost Chord of Life."[2]

Many of the Pop artists—most of whom were academically trained—realized that their work was not statement-free, at least in regard to Abstract Expressionism to which it related dialectically. For example, the use of silkscreening was a counter move to the personal brush strokes of the Abstract Expressionists. "I am anti-experimental, anti-contemplative, anti-nuance, anti-getting-away-from-the-tyranny-of-the-rectangle, anti-movement and light, anti-mystery, anti-paint quality, anti-Zen, and anti-all those brilliant ideas of preceding movements which everyone understands so thoroughly," declaimed Roy Lichtenstein.[3] And although Indiana was delighted that the new art "walks young for the moment without the weight of four thousand years of art history on its shoulders,"[4] Pop artists were quick to return to painting the still life, except that instead of fruits, they painted cans and hamburgers. They painted genre scenes, but instead of hearty Dutch peasants bringing in the wheat, they substituted cartoon detectives and superheroes. They focused heavily on portraits and the human figure, except that Wesselmann's nudes had no eyes, Oldenburg's arms had no body, and Warhol's faces were off-register.

Unaware and uncaring about how Pop fit into art history, young Americans almost literally ate it up (food images abounded in Pop), even if they were not the ones collecting it. Old abstract art was stultifying and elitist; Pop was liberating and democratic. Embracing dance, music, drama, and writing, it was decadent fun. In an all-too-brief time of incredible optimism, Pop seemed to bounce, explode, and roll out of the studios in New York City, shaping the images in the mass media, even as it was borrowing from them.

The late 1950s saw a period of demoralization, as the United States came to believe it was being bested on the cold war battlefield by the Russians. The U.S.S.R. had launched Sputnik while Americans were rock-and-rolling to Elvis. Then the nation was embarrassed by the U-2 spying incident, in which

Francis Gary Powers, an American pilot, was shot down over Soviet territory. The country needed a boost. Kennedy's election and the Camelot imagery that went along with it seemed to be the answer to the despondency. Yet in spite of Kennedy's stirring rhetoric, Soviet strength continued to build in Europe; the arms race heated up; Khrushchev ordered the construction of the Berlin wall; the rumbles from Vietnam became more ominous; and the ill-conceived invasion of Cuba at the Bay of Pigs failed miserably. When U.S. reconnaissance planes discovered Soviet missile and bomber bases in Cuba easily capable of striking at America's heartland, the initial euphoria that had bubbled up during the early days of Kennedy's incumbency began to evaporate. The subsequent U.S. blockade forced Soviet Premier Khrushchev to dismantle the bases and remove the missiles, but the euphoria was gone. It was "Blowin' in the Wind" as Bob Dylan's song of the era aptly put it. At the time that Kennedy was killed on November 22, 1963, the nation was already involved in Vietnam, and the Northern ghettoes were on the verge of riots. Forgotten in the subsequent process of making Kennedy into a fallen hero, was the fact that his Camelot, always more a figment of the imagination than a reality, was turning to ashes even before Lee Harvey Oswald pulled the trigger.

Many Pop artists reflected the tenor of the times in their work. For example, from 1962 to 1963, Warhol went from drawing bright, friendly Campbell's soup cans to silkscreening pictures of suicides and gruesome car crashes. Even his most famous image of Marilyn Monroe was conceived just after she died. Pop Art may have started out as an affirmation, even a glorification, of mass culture. But how was the repeated image of an electric chair affirmative? Where was the fun in the image of a dead man crushed beneath a tractor-trailer truck? Was the painting of a woman smiling provocatively at the viewer while holding a soda bottle to be taken at face value, or was it indicative of exploitation and brainwashing?

Outpacing the art critics, it was the collectors who were thinking about those questions. Emily felt strongly, however, that she was doing more thinking than were other collectors, especially Ethel and Robert Scull, the New York couple with whom the Tremaines were in frosty competition. Scull was a taxi tycoon whose blood was not as blue as Emily's, at least according to her color chart. He and his wife began buying Pop heavily at exactly the same time as the Tremaines, and the relationship between the couples was so antagonistic that if a dealer had the audacity to show a work to the Sculls before showing it to the Tremaines (or vice versa), he ran the risk of jeopardizing all future sales.

Historically, antagonism between collectors is common. One nineteenth century observer made the acerbic remark that the rarest thing he had ever seen among collectors was goodwill. This was true of the Pop collectors, who wanted to get there first, buy the best, and shut each other out.[5] When asked about other collectors of Pop, Emily veiled her antagonism with intellectual arguments. She said, for instance, "I think there was opportunism with some of the collectors of Pop Art. The very boldness of the work attracted early publicity and I think that some people who did not really think too deeply were attracted to it because it was new and they knew a soup can when they saw it. They felt more comfortable with things than with ideas; so they were willing to accept Pop Art as things even though the ideas, I think, often missed them."[6]

The ideas that Emily believed other collectors were missing had to do both with what Pop was attempting to say and with how it related to earlier aesthetic movements. Emily first thought that Pop artists were helping viewers to see "the good in the bad," as with Warhol's green stamps, which she considered "little poems." This distinguished Pop from Dada, which also used "found" objects, or "readymades" as Marcel Duchamp called them. Dada was ironic, even caustic, in its approach to the culture of which those objects were a part. A famous example is Duchamp's urinal, signed "R. Mutt 1917" and titled, euphemistically, *Fountain*. The two movements were similar in their longing to burn up "all aesthetics" (Duchamp's words), to break free of the restraints of traditional artistic technique and subject matter. The irony for the Pop artists was that exactly the same motivation had been shared by nearly every art movement from Cubism to Abstract Expressionism. Emily initially considered Pop markedly different from Dada because of its inherent optimism, but she came to believe that Pop was "putting on everything I despise about our own society" and that Pop artists were "concerned with some of the causes of the neuroses rather than the neuroses themselves."[7] There was a major shift from seeing Pop as a form of affirmation to seeing it as a form of accusation.

No matter how it came to be interpreted, Emily never considered Pop a new movement in art. She insisted that "taste must have suffered somewhat similar shocks when first presented with the subjects selected by Dutch genre painters and even by Chardain."[8] The Tremaines owned several earlier works that used detritus from popular culture in creative ways. For example, *Composition* by Stuart Davis, painted in 1930, showed the black outline of a factory filled in with a few colored areas, and the word *paint*. Warhol's paint-by-number series, of which the Tremaines owned *Do It Yourself (Violin),* bore a clear affinity to that work. In a collage by Kurt Schwitters, painted in 1922, a clipping from a German publication is inserted upside down, presaging Oldenburg's collages and Rauschenberg's "combine" art.

During 1961, the year in which the Tremaines first bought Pop art heavily, they purchased three *Great American Nude* paintings from Tom Wesselmann, four paintings and sculptures from Claes Oldenburg including *Street Head I,* which was made out of newspaper soaked in wheat paste over a wire frame, and three by James Rosenquist. Several of the Pop artists, including Warhol, did not yet have dealers, and few critics were taking the work seriously. In the 1940s when the Abstract Expressionists were struggling for recognition, they were championed by the critic Clement Greenberg before their works began to sell to collectors. He was joined by other critics, including James Sweeney and Thomas Hess, who served as translators of the arcane visual language of abstraction. However, the language of Pop did not need translators, leaving academically trained critics, as well as museum curators, befuddled and disgruntled. When the subject matter, as in Abstract Expressionism, was really art itself, critics and curators were needed to tell the uninformed viewer what principles of art a particular artist was attempting to surmount. Critics see themselves not only as interpreters, but as protectors of the barricades between culture and popular culture. No wonder they were at a dismaying loss for words when the subject matter shifted to beer cans, hamburgers, and portraits of Elvis.

Because critics were slow to comprehend what was happening in Pop, the movement was left to a small, bold group of collectors acting on their own. It therefore meant a great deal to the artists when the Tremaines paid them attention. Because of their reputation for spotting talented new artists, the Tremaines were watched closely by other collectors. When they began to buy Pop heavily, they started a trend. As much as the Pop artists said they were not interested in art history, to have one of their paintings sharing a wall with Mondrian in the Tremaines' apartment gave them a real sense of pride and reinforced the belief that they were in the avant-garde of the entire historical movement of art; they were not marginal. This meant their work was influential, and influence meant power.

Tom Wesselmann remembers when the art dealer Ivan Karp first brought the Tremaines to his studio and a subsequent trip he himself made to their apartment to deliver a painting. Karp was working at the Leo Castelli Gallery at the time, but Castelli himself was not interested in representing several of the Pop artists whom Karp admired, so Karp was attempting on his own to stir up collector interest and get dealer representation. Because the Tremaines had been major customers at the Castelli Gallery since it had opened only a few years before, Karp made certain to introduce them to several artists, Wesselmann among them. Their visit to Wesselmann's studio left a vivid impression:

I became an artist because I had to do it. I didn't know you could make a living at it. Then collectors came along. The Tremaines have a special place with me because they were the first ones who bought my paintings. Ivan Karp, a New York art dealer, brought them to my studio before I really sold my work. Until then, I didn't really know you could get money for painting. They chose one large work and a smaller one, which was one I liked very much. Back then I priced things according to the way I liked them, so the small one cost more than the big one. Ivan called me later and explained that art is fundamentally sold by size; the little work had to be priced dramatically lower than the big one. So the Tremaines were Lesson No.1 for me.

I remember once I was delivering a small painting and Emily invited me in to see the paintings in her New York apartment. She had one of my paintings hanging between a Jasper Johns and a Picasso. That felt nice. She compared my work to the European artist Enrico Baj. She said one is sardonic and one is satiric. I didn't know what she thought mine was, and I didn't ask. I usually don't want to know how people interpret my work.[9]

James Rosenquist also was positively affected by the Tremaines' early interest. They purchased *Come play with me/Hey, Let's Go for a Ride* as well as *Zone,* a very large canvas (96" by 96") that the Tremaines eventually sold to the Philadelphia Museum of Art. The introduction this time was made by Dick Bellamy of the Green Gallery, which along with the Stable Gallery, the Sidney Janis Gallery, and the Leo Castelli Gallery, was part of the emerging epicenter of the Pop movement. As had Wesselmann, Rosenquist found the introduction to the Tremaines and his subsequent visit to their apartment to be eye-opening experiences.

Dick Bellamy brought Burton and Emily to see my paintings in 1961. I was part of the beat generation at the time. I had clothes and food and a $31-a-month apartment on the Upper East Side, and I didn't think much about selling my art. Emily came in wearing those "Lolita" heart-shaped glasses and Burton was dressed in knickers, as I recall. She kept asking, "Oh Dick, how much is this painting?" and in one case he said, "You can't have that one, I sold it to Scull last week." [After they chose three paintings] I said, "Wait a minute, these paintings aren't for sale." Later, I decided I could either have three sales or I could have my paintings. So I sold them the paintings.

Emily asked me to bring one of the paintings over, and she invited me in for a drink and showed me where she wanted to hang my work. When she took down a Paul Klee, my stomach was dropping. I thought it was going to look awful, but it turned out it looked great. After she showed me Lichtenstein's *RotoBroiler* hanging in the bedroom and asked me whether she should buy it, I told her. "I don't know what it means; but you should buy it."[10]

Emily first began to comprehend what the Pop artists were doing when she saw Claes Oldenburg's *7-UP*, a relief in plaster and enamel paint, at the Green Gallery. It had reminded her of "the big 7-UP sign that blares across the river from the United Nations Building."[11] Intrigued, she decided she and Burton should visit Oldenburg's studio themselves. Dick Bellamy supplied them with the directions to the Ray Gun Store, as Oldenburg's store-front studio was called, but the taxi driver dropped them off at the wrong location.

We lost our way and looking for the address we walked through the wholesale district where brides' dresses are sold, and the windows were full of them. Then we turned a corner onto Second Avenue and as we walked up the avenue toward the street where Oldenburg had his store, we passed a mission on the roof of which was a cross and crown. We passed a restaurant with pies in the window. Just before we got to the store, there was a youngster with an improvised shoe shine stand. He had written out in pencil "fifteen cents." The first things we saw when we entered the Ray Gun Store was a bride made in the same plaster and enamel as the 7-UP we had seen at Dick Bellamy's Green Gallery. There were also plaster cakes, pies and things that were in the window of the restaurant and the cross and crown we had seen on top of the mission, and I immediately remembered a collage I had seen at the Green Gallery in which Oldenburg had used the 7-UP, a piece of cake and a fifteen cent sign. Of course, I bought this collage as soon as I got back to the Green Gallery and I also bought the 7-UP plaster relief. Having gotten lost was, I am sure, a great help in showing us at once what was going on. These artists were looking out, not in. They were not tormented introverts expressing their furies and their anxieties as were many of the Abstract Expressionists.

Soon after our trip to the Ray Gun Store, Ivan Karp told us of Andy Warhol, and we went to his house on Lexington Avenue. It was not hard to locate the house as it was among a group of highly colored houses: one green, one pink, etc. Across the street was a big supermarket. Here we found Andy was commenting, in a way not dissimilar to that of Oldenburg's, on the images in his environment. Here we saw the multiple soup cans, the multiple coke bottles, large single soup cans like great icons, and green trading stamps that looked like little poems. We made several visits to Andy's studio and came to think of both Andy and his work as perhaps the most enigmatic and complex of any of the artists we were beginning to know.

We saw Jimmy Dine's work and Tom Wesselmann's and Jim Rosenquist's and Lichtenstein's. Once or twice I invited these boys to our apartment and in several instances they had not yet met one another. I remember in particular that Rosenquist met Lichtenstein for the first time here.

I remember they did not like each other at first. They were criticizing each other. But a month or two later they saw each other in the right way. I remember Rosenquist saying "I don't see why you bought that Lichtenstein." I said "you're missing the point," because, of course, Rosenquist was more romantic. Then about a week later I saw him on the street and he said, "You're right about that man. He's a genius. He's brilliant."

So it seemed to me quite clear that this was not a group movement influencing each other but a general sensitivity that occurred simultaneously. Each artist was commenting on our visual environment in a very individual way, but none of them with approval as far as I could see.[12]

To Emily it was all "a great, kind of fun release. Art stopped being so intellectual, so introspective." Because there were only a few collectors interested at this early stage, the work also was dirt-cheap, and the Tremaines were not running any financial risk in buying it. For example, in 1962 Warhol was so desperate for attention and so flattered that the Tremaines were interested in him, that he practically gave them the paintings. Some of the small paintings the Tremaines bought that year cost only $60. At that point, making money was not a major concern for Warhol, because he had a lucrative commercial art business; what he wanted was recognition, which the Tremaines provided.

In 1962 the Tremaines bought fifteen works by Warhol including: *Do It*

Yourself (Violin), Close Cover Before Striking (Pepsi-Cola), A Boy for Meg, Round Marilyn, 12 S & H Green Stamps, 70 S & H Green Stamps, 7 Cent Air mail, Campbell's Soup Can with Can Opener, Little Campbell's Soup Can (Minestrone), Little Campbell's Soup Can (Pepper Pot), Printed Dollar Bill, Small Blue Flowers, and the *Marilyn Monroe Diptych,* which was exhibited in Warhol's show at the Stable Gallery in November. Warhol first showed the Tremaines the *Marilyn Monroe Diptych* as two separate canvases — one colored and one black and white. Emily suggested that they be put together, and Warhol concurred. However, Warhol habitually asked visitors for their advice, as if taking a poll, and Emily was not the only one to make the suggestion. According to David Bourdon, a friend of Warhol's and his biographer:

> For the *Marilyn Diptych,* also known as *100 Marilyns,* Warhol painted fifty black-and-white faces of Monroe on one area of canvas and an equal number of colored faces on another. He was ambivalent about the relationship, if any, between the two versions. In the black-and-white section, Marilyn's face varies from a crisp photographic image to a black blue, suggesting smudged newsprint; the faces are either clotted with too much pigment or dryly rendered with too little pigment. In the brightly colored panel, which is relatively garish because of the intense hues, each face appears to be variously off-register. Initially, Warhol debated with himself whether to present the canvases as two separate pictures. But the visitors he polled liked the tension set up between the two contrasting versions, so he abutted the two panels.[13]

Also in 1962, the Tremaines acquired six works by Jim Dine and five by Roy Lichtenstein, including *Aloha* and *Femme au Chapeau,* his satirical version of a Picasso that the Tremaines owned. They had purchased *I Can See the Whole Room . . . and There's Nobody in It!* in 1961 before Lichtenstein had a dealer. Perfectly square, as if it were a box from a comic strip, this painting is satirically nihilistic. The cartoon figure peers through a hole toward the viewer and concludes that no one is there. Dine incorporated actual tools into his paintings. *A Little Scissors and a Little Screwdriver* and *The Small Black Screwdriver* had the named objects embedded in paint in a format only 5½" by 5½". In the much larger work titled *The Hammer Acts,* a real hammer jutted from the edge of the canvas, while a shadow of the hammer floated above a board and three nails at the bottom, as if to show where the hammer had been or where it was going. Dine's interest in banal objects, such as hammers, wrenches and scissors, was genuine, not sarcastic, which gave his work staying power.[14]

Besides paintings, the Tremaines also continued to buy sculpture, taking a special interest in the "crush" sculptures of John Chamberlain. In 1962 they acquired from the Leo Castelli Gallery two of his works *Sinclair* and *Arch Brown*. These were composed primarily of used car parts that were punched, compressed, twisted, and welded into tight shapes. Body paint, including rust, was retained. *Sinclair*, only six inches in size, brought the Tremaines a good laugh. When the two delivery men, charged with the responsibility of handing it over, showed up at the Tremaines' door, they immediately began to apologize, asserting strenuously that they had not broken it. It wasn't broken, it just looked that way.

Part of the attraction of the Pop artists for Burton and Emily was their crazy lifestyle. They were not just painting on the edge, they were living on the edge, with a "seize the day" mentality. The Abstract Expressionists had begun to drift toward middle-class respectability, whereas the Pop artists wanted life to be a "happening." Even though the Tremaines were members in good standing in "culture," "counter-culture"and the young people who were making it happen amused them, and when the opportunity arose, they enjoyed mixing the two. For one of the parties at which they entertained a large group of collectors, they borrowed from Warhol his "silver clouds," helium-filled aluminum "pillows" that floated in mid-air. The clouds bumped in a friendly way the guests, who often could not resist bumping them back. A reporter at the event remarked that one of the maids had to brush one aside to get through with the hors d'oeuvres. Another maid had to dodge a Calder mobile as she carried a tray of drinks through the living room. When the reporter was finally able to take his eyes from the silver clouds, he was bedazzled by finding eleven works of art in the entrance foyer alone.

There were 25 more in the living-dining room, 20 in the master bedroom, 29 in the study. No, we didn't have to go around counting to find out. The Tremaine apartment is visited so often by groups (frequently as a benefit) that a list of the art is given to each arrival . . . Quite a few of New York's young artists were there, and so were gallery heads. Andy was missing. He's out in California, running his traveling show in the South. You might expect the hostess in such an avant-garde setting to dress a bit on the far-out side. Not at all. Gracious Mrs. Tremaine wore an elegantly simple off-white sheath and handsome jewelry, and her silvery blonde hair was conservatively coifed. Her husband laughed off questions about why they have collected so much modern art with: "There's really no motive, other than that we like it." A genial host, he set to working several kinetic sculptures in the study. For one, the motor turned on air pressure that bounced a blue and a red ball in a white machine. "One of them always flies out," he predicted only a short time before he was down on his hands and knees retrieving the red ball.[15]

Notwithstanding that they felt out of their element at such parties, Pop artists appreciated the Tremaines' support, especially the exposure of their work to other collectors. Warhol was so thankful that one Christmas morning he left leaning against their door a small gold *Marilyn Monroe* as a present. Emily also tried to make artists feel at ease by using humor. "Emily was sometimes a real cutup," said James Rosenquist. "I remember somebody walked into the bedroom where they had . . . Wesselmann's nude, and he pointed at it and said, "What's that hanging over there?" And Emily quickly asked, "Why? Does it remind you of your mother?"[16]

Claes Oldenburg also was a little awed by the Tremaines, given their reputation for owning twentieth century masterpieces. He felt honored to have his works in their collection. Dick Bellamy remembers that after the Tremaines bought his work, Oldenburg "prepared for the Tremaines a couple of jars of color and a small brush that was attached to the colors with a rubber band asking me to deliver this to them for repairs, to touch up in case [the art] got nicked. It was as though Claes were saying, 'I really want you to take care of my objects,' as if they were his progeny."[17]

Among the Tremaines' new acquaintances during this period was a young man named Samuel Adams Green.[18] Only in his twenties, Sam loved art but was not an artist, nor was he academically trained. As a result, he was perfectly suited to serve as a go-between for the Tremaines. "I was a good liaison officer between the artists and the Tremaines because the artists were somewhat scared of them for two reasons: they were patrons, and they lived on Park Avenue and served hors d'oeuvres. They didn't know what to wear or how to behave. So I would tell them to relax and not to wear their motorcycle boots, sort of smooth everybody. A little bit of diplomacy was needed." Sam was to remain a close friend of the Tremaines until the end of their lives. He frequently accompanied them on trips to galleries and artists' studios, introduced them to emerging artists he had discovered, and occasionally handled art trades.

A pivotal event that indicated Pop was beginning to be recognized as serious art was the group show titled *New Realists* on October 31, 1962 at the

Sidney Janis Gallery. Although it was only three days after the Cuban missile crisis, the younger artists included in the show were totally upbeat, even exuberant. To be shown together in a gallery that heretofore had been a bastion of Abstract Expressionism seemed to them an artistic coup, a sure sign that they were in the ascendency. However, the older abstract painters — including Motherwell, Gottlieb, Rothko and de Kooning — who found themselves sitting on the sidelines, were furious at Janis for mounting an exhibition that they considered no better than kitsch. Accusing Janis of aesthetic treachery, they left his gallery en masse. An incident at the Tremaines' apartment immediately afterward alerted James Rosenquist to the fact that a change was taking place in American art: "After the opening, Burton and Emily Tremaine, well-known collectors, invited me over to their house on Park Avenue. I went and was surprised to find Andy Warhol, Bob Indiana, Roy Lichtenstein and Tom Wesselmann there. Maids with little white hats were serving drinks and my painting *Hey, Let's Go for a Ride!* and Warhol's *Marilyn Diptych* were hanging on the wall next to fantastic Picassos and de Koonings. Right in the middle of our party, de Kooning came through the door with Larry Rivers. Burton Tremaine stopped them in their tracks and said, 'Oh, so nice to see you. But please, at any other time.' I was very surprised and so was de Kooning. He and the others with him soon left. . . . At that moment I thought, something in the art world has definitely changed." [19]

Despite Burton's actions toward de Kooning and fellow artist Larry Rivers, the Tremaines in no way shut the door on the Abstract Expressionists. Nor would they have agreed completely with Rosenquist's assessment of the change. Regardless of the amount of attention that was suddenly being paid to Pop, it was never the only game in town for the Tremaines; it was merely the most hyped. They continued to acquire a very broad range of art, most of it concerned with issues far different than those with which the Pop artists were dealing. The Tremaines, in fact, never collected art solely of one particular movement, era, or artist. They collected new art that they believed bore a relationship to the other art in their collection; that is why their collection had coherence. In the year following the show at Sidney Janis, they purchased more works by Jasper Johns and Robert Rauschenberg and added a large painting by Larry Poons. In 1964 one of the works they purchased was *The Fisherman* by Richard Tuttle, who told Emily that it was difficult for him to put into words what he was seeking in his art because it had never existed before. Emily thought that "his hands look like Botticelli's drawings" and equated the ideas behind his search to Brancusi's *Bird in Space*. [20]

Another painting they purchased in that year was *Homage to the Square: Arrival* by Josef Albers, whose art they had first acquired in 1945. By the middle of the decade, the work of artists experimenting with new forms of abstraction, Minimalism, Op, and Color Field began to enter the collection, including works by Sol LeWitt, Agnes Martin, Walter de Maria, and Richard Artschwager. As always, the Tremaines refused to limit the acquisitions to only Americans, or only the young. In 1965 they bought their first painting by seventy-five-year-old Man Ray *Ce Qui Manque a Nous Tous*. On acquiring the painting *Uomo Di Schiena* by the Italian artist Michelangelo Pistoletto, the Tremaines hung it in the front hall. Because it showed the back of a man (who looked disarmingly like Burton) on a metal reflective surface, it mirrored the Tremaines' black-and white tiled floor and their front door; as a result, it functioned as a visual pun for their departing guests. Bridget Riley's *Turn* and Marjorie Strider's *Red Lilies* also were given space on the increasingly crowded walls. At the time that the Tremaines first purchased her work, Riley, a British artist, was having a terrible time getting serious attention in the United States. "I think Riley handles this work with intelligence and skill," said Emily, but she added that she did not find her paintings as beautiful as those of Larry Poons. Using categories she often evoked in regard to the works in the collection, she concluded that Riley was Apollonian and Poons Dionysian.[21]

Among the young artists whose art they found fascinating was Christo. Their purchase of *Double Store Front* at a time when few people were buying his work was of great importance to him. "*Double Store Front* was about urban architectural spaces, and it preceded my work with covering things." To him, Emily's approach to collecting was not about art as a commodity, but about "taste, education and sensitivity." He elaborated: "Mrs. Tremaine was not a fashionable collector, she was a fine collector. She bought what she liked. She was a passionate collector, and passionately collecting art is an extremely private business. It's like making love. Making and consuming art is a very exclusive affair; it is a unique and irreplaceable experience. And the artists benefit from this kind of collector—passionate collectors who see and share the exclusivity of their work.[22]

Although they continued to search for artists working in new areas, the Tremaines began in this period to collect primitive and native art, specifically, African, Oceanic, and Indian work. This new interest was ignited at an exhibition of Oceanic figures at the Galerie Jean Boucher in Paris. While wandering around the gallery, the Tremaines suddenly heard a very eerie sound and turned to see two men beating a large tam-tam (a hollowed-out log in which slits are cut) with a wooden club. The men turned out to be Max Ernst and Alberto Giacometti, whose works had long graced the Tremaines' collection. The Tremaines were interested in acquiring the drum but learned that it had been sold already to the Kroller Müller Museum. With the help of Samuel Wagstaff, then chief curator at the Wadsworth Atheneum, they located a similar tam-tam. It stood an imposing nine feet high and had huge elongated eyes. Probably used to accompany ceremonial dances, a tam-tam such as this one was a consecrated object and was thought to possess great spiritual power. The Tremaines had found the search for this piece so fascinating that they launched upon a full-scale hunt for more primitive art, resulting in the purchase of ten more pieces over the next two years. Both in New York and Madison, Emily intermixed these pieces with her modern and contemporary art in compelling ways. For a while the tam-tam stood next to Léger's *Le Petit Déjeuner* in the New York dining room, while from under the glass-topped dining table peeked two Austrian Baroque putti. On the mantel in the living room, a Senufo female form from the Upper Volta contemplated Delaunay's *Premier Disque*. Although Emily moved the art around a great deal, as old works were loaned and new works acquired, her goal always was to achieve resonance across time, space, and style. Asked once what it was like to live in the midst of such visual intensity, Emily said simply that it was like living with books. "I never sit in front of art that I don't get ideas. It's a catalyst."[23]

In the same vein, the Tremaines acquired fifteen Kachina dolls made by a man whom Emily considered the Picasso of Kachina makers. The last purchase was made in 1985 when Emily added a very unusual and powerful war god figure to the collection. The following story of how the Tremaines came to own it was printed in *Connecticut Home & Garden*.

The Tremaines have a long-standing and deep respect for the Southwest Indians. Not too long ago, Mrs. Tremaine was walking on Madison Avenue when her attuned eyes caught sight of a Zuni war god in the window of a gallery. In asking about the god, she learned that it came from a distinguished Indian art collection in France formed about 50 years ago. Mrs. Tremaine requested a picture of the god so she could study it, presumably for future purchase. But she knew exactly what she was doing. The photograph traveled with her to Arizona, where she found a Zuni priest. The old priest instantly recognized the war god. It was stolen by a Frenchman 50 years ago near Gallup, New Mexico. The Frenchman came upon the Indians, befriended them and lived with them. "He was very good to our people and they loved him," relayed the priest. "Then one night he disappeared and took many of our treasures, including the war god." This god is particularly sacred. It must never be shown publicly. Some museums, such as the one in Flagstaff, have their gods in their collections, but dare not show them. It is a taboo. After Mrs. Tremaine was satisfied that she had cleared up the identity of the god, she asked the priest if he would mind if she bought it from the Madison Avenue gallery. He gave permission, saying he knew it would be in good hands. The Zuni war god now stands in the Tremaines' New York apartment. Mrs. Tremaine vows that he will never travel again.[24]

Their interest in modern painting and sculpture extended as well to those works that had a primitive quality. As was so often the case with their collection, they had purchased two works many years earlier that presaged this new interest, Picasso's *New Hebrides Mask* and Hilary Heron's *Girl with Pigtails*. When Giacometti's *Spoon Woman,* owned previously by Nelson Rockefeller, came on the market in the early 1970s through the art dealer Harold Diamond, Emily wanted it enough to trade Georgia O'Keeffe's *New York Night* and Charles Sheeler's *On a Theme of Farm Buildings. Spoon Woman* was based on the shape of a ceremonial spoon from the Dan tribe in Africa. "I wanted that Giacometti very badly and it was very expensive. I didn't think I should pay that much. . . . And so I made a trade on that and I was very happy to get it because it is such an early one and not easy to find."

There is no better way to determine just how far the Tremaines had moved from Pop than to look at the artists Emily selected to showcase for other collectors. In 1965 she was asked to put together an exhibition for the Society for the Encouragement of Contemporary Art in San Francisco, to be called *A New York Collector Selects.* From Pop, Emily selected works by Warhol, Lichtenstein, Rosenquist, and Oldenburg. In her accompanying speech she said, "I have brought you a few recent pictures by artists who were classified in the Pop movement, but just as the Dada painters moved on to their own individual paths, so are the Pop artists moving on. Andy, who painted the multiple soup cans, this year brought us a flower garden. True, they are rather aggressive, evil, fleurs de mal, but they are also strangely beautiful." She also chose Gerald Laing, Stella, Neil Williams, Leo Vallador, Richard Smith, Charles Hinman (whose work she found exciting because "his colors smash together like a jazz band and the tensions are wonderful"), Toni Maĝar, Dan Basen, Pistoletto, and Christo. She selected a single pastel from George Segal. It was a medium that she felt he handled with "exceptional skill and beauty," but she apologized to the audience for including so small a piece, which was not representative of his work as a whole. "I would have loved to bring a Segal environment of two life-size figures embracing at the foot of a real tenement stairway; it will always haunt me, but to bring it would present as difficult a problem as Mark di Suvero did last week when he wanted us to install a new piece of his work that includes a 24-foot beam." Emily also chose to include calligraphy by Charles Simon, and Norman Ives. From the new field of Op art she selected works by Richard Anuszkiewicz, Riley, Diter Rot, and Poons. She explained to the audience that William Seitz at the Museum of Modern Art was preparing an exhibition of Op, called *The Responsive Eye,* which was to open the following month. "I have seen many of his selections for the exhibition. He seems to be choosing the strongest and toughest, almost brutal examples of this kind of work. Burton is negotiating now to get the Dramamine concession at the Museum for the duration of the exhibition." In contrast, Emily selected the work of Agnes Martin, which she considered more serene. She also chose Tuttle, whose work she felt had great sensitivity. "I am strongly attracted to this kind of art," she concluded. "Perhaps it is because I am so much in the city with billboards and store windows and traffic and neon lights. I like work that invites tranquility and contemplation, like the Zen wall."

Some of the reasons why Emily considered Pop dead by 1965 are apparent in her exhibition speech, but there are several others. The first is that Pop had become popular with collectors and as a result had soared in value. The collectors were investors, not patrons, primarily acquiring precisely because the values were rising so rapidly. Pop had kicked the art world into a new economic level, elevating the incomes of artists and dealers alike, but in the process it had also destabilized the art world. The value of a painting was determined by what it could be sold for today, not by a careful analysis — a give-and-take between critics, dealers, collectors, and curators — achieved over time. Emily was nonplussed by this change that was making the art market a raucous place. She began to feel that too much economic success was flowing too rapidly to Pop artists.

Pop Art also carried within itself the germ of its own obsolescence, because it presupposed a body of shared cultural knowledge on the part of the viewer. The person standing in front of one of Warhol's green stamp images in the 1960s could have had a perforated strip of green stamps in her pocket at that very moment, having obtained them from the supermarket. Once stores stopped distributing green stamps, younger viewers had no idea of the painting's cultural context. One of the criteria for a work eventually being judged a masterpiece is its ability to transcend cultural context, and although some Pop Art undeniably possessed that ability, much did not.

From Emily's personal standpoint, the most powerful reason that Pop had died so soon was that it had turned from playful to sardonic; it had moved from aesthetic comment to social criticism. When James Elliott, at that time director of the Wadsworth Atheneum, consulted with Emily about the wisdom of buying one of Warhol's electric-chair paintings for the museum, she was adamantly opposed; the painting was altogether too dismal.[25] Similarly, John Tremaine got a strong reaction when he asked for her opinion of a painting by Rauschenberg that he was considering buying.

The painting reflected the anguish of the country at the time particularly related to the Vietnam War, Civil Rights issues, even space exploration. It was a collage of numerous images, a very strong piece, and I showed it to Emily. When she really got into studying something, she lifted her eyebrows up and looked at it intently. She was sort of like a computer scanning a document: all her emotions and her sensitivities and her intellect were being passed through quickly. In this case, her judgement was negative. When I asked why, she replied, "You know these images are just so disturbing that I couldn't live with it." She said that the art that she really wanted for herself was art that she could enjoy and live with and that it should evoke pleasant emotions, something that you were secure being with, spiritually uplifting. When I went back and looked at their collection with that in mind, I found the collection to be a joy, always a joy. If you were to have art in your life, to be surrounded by art, you can understand her thinking. If you go to a museum and see paintings that are emotionally charged and take from the experience what you need, you can remove yourself as you walk out the door, but to have that in your bedroom or living room would be pretty tough, day in and day out.

In marked contrast to the painting that John Tremaine had considered acquiring was Rauschenberg's earlier work *Windward,* which was filled with positive images of freedom, including the American bald eagle, the Statue of Liberty, even a photo of an Ecumenical Council meeting in the Sistine Chapel. Emily loved it, and for many years it hung over the fireplace in the barn in Madison.

Over and over in Emily's little notebooks, in which she kept quotes by and about artists interspersed with Christian Science material, appear Brancusi's words "I give you pure joy." When asked in an interview for the Archives of American Art in 1973 why she had not acquired the works of any of the photo-realists, she said flatly, "They're marvelous, they're mordant, they bring things into focus, and in a sense they are the folk art of America. They are important, there is no question about it, but I just personally have to have things I can live with—with joy. I just can't live with them with joy." When the joy went out of Pop, the Tremaines stopped collecting it.

[Collecting] is not a pastime but a passion and often so violent that it is only inferior to love or ambition in the pettiness of its aims. —*La Bruyère*

CHAPTER TEN

DISEASE AND DISENCHANTMENT

In the late 1960s, Emily suffered a major recurrence of tuberculosis. She recovered enough to continue to tramp up dark stairways into artists' studios and to look at hundreds of paintings in search of the one that cried out to be purchased. However, during the last twenty years of her life she lacked energy and was very frail. When she died in 1987, the precipitating factor was a broken hip, but the real cause was tuberculosis. During her final months, her lungs were so deeply scarred from the disease that she could not breathe without oxygen. Because Emily was a Christian Scientist, her illness presented not merely a physical crisis but also a wrenching spiritual dilemma. One of the tenets of Christian Science is the maintenance of health via spiritual purity and unity with the divine mind. Illness can put a peculiar strain on an adherent because it is a sign of disunity, hence spiritual failure. This belief leads to guilt, which only exacerbates the problem.

One of the characteristics of tuberculosis is that it can lie dormant for years and then suddenly recur. Over the centuries, it has been known by many names, including scrofula, the king's evil, phthisis, the white plague, and consumption. It can kill rapidly, a course often described in prior eras as "galloping," or with exquisite slowness. Before the discovery of streptomycin and other effective drugs, those with the disease wasted away, their voices softening to a whisper, their frames becoming skeletal, and their energy level dropping toward zero. Before the First World War, the disease was rampant. Places such as Butte, with its crowded conditions and unhealthy air, had especially high rates, and most children were exposed to the tuberculosis bacillus. Many developed a resistance to the disease, but others fell prey to it when they reached their teenage or young adult years. As discussed earlier, Emily's first bout probably occurred in the mid-1930s when she was in her late twenties.

Some religions require a leap of faith as the very first step to belief, a radical reshuffling of how the material and spiritual worlds are perceived. Christian Science is one such belief system. To an outsider such a system can appear incredible, although to the insider it makes perfect sense. Emily was an insider who believed that sickness and death were illusions. Burton was a tolerant outsider, who often went to church with her on Sunday mornings simply to keep her company. Family members and friends were bemused by the odd balance struck between a man who was very physical and not at all spiritual and a woman who was very spiritual and who saw herself as not at all physical. As far as he was able, Burton was supportive, but their beliefs eventually came into conflict. As one Christian Scientist has written, "This is not a faith one can successfully embrace in name only. It is not a religion in which, like a sponge, one can soak things up without much effort. It calls for daily effort and self-immolation."[1] When Emily was healthy, Burton was sympathetic to her belief that doctors and medicine were unwarranted, but when she became ill and began to suffer, it tormented him. He longed to get her medical help, but she would have none of it.

The first indication that the disease had recurred came in 1968 when Emily started to lose weight and became exhausted. The slightest exertion was an effort. Because they were in Madison at the time, they were able to go into seclusion, so that friends and family were not aware of Emily's decline. Burton watched her wither away, unable to help. In desperation he invited a doctor to dinner in hopes he could talk her into getting treatment, but when Emily found out who the dinner guest was, she was so angry she refused to come down from her room. Burton Jr., remembers that during this time his father "was beside himself that Emily was feeling so dreadful. He really got down in the dumps about what was going to happen to her." Finally he took to shaking his head and saying, "you cannot tell someone else how to die." Emily took to heart Mary Baker Eddy's writings specifically about tuberculosis and was determined to rid herself of the error of thinking the disease was real:

Show that it is not inherited; that inflammation, tubercles, hemorrhage, and decomposition are beliefs, images of mortal thought superimposed upon the body; that they are not the truth of man; that they should be treated as error and put out of thought. Then these ills will disappear. If the body is diseased, this is but one of the beliefs of mortal mind. Mortal man will be less mortal when he learns that matter never sustained existence and can never destroy God, who is man's Life. When this is understood, mankind will be more spiritual and know that there is nothing to consume, since Spirit, God, is All-in-All.[2]

In spite of her own efforts and those of her Christian Science practitioner, Emily's illness advanced. Finally, too weak to get out of bed, she asked Burton for the name of the doctor he had invited to dinner. She was taken by ambulance to Yale-New Haven Hospital and then transferred to Gaylord Hospital in Wallingford, which though primarily a rehabilitation hospital, still operated as a sanatorium for tuberculosis patients. The drugs she was given forced the disease into remission but did not cure her completely, as tuberculosis already had caused irreversible damage to her lungs.

To make matters far worse, Emily's sister Jane developed cancer. She also sought treatment at Yale-New Haven Hospital, but doctors were unable to stop the spread of the disease. During this ordeal, Burton almost became ill himself from the strain of trying to look after both women. Jane died in February 1969. Her funeral was conducted by the Presbyterian minister of the Montecito Presbyterian Church, located not far from Glen Oaks and Brunninghausen.

With Jane's death, Emily lost not only a sister but a spiritual mainstay. Via her long letters, Jane ardently had encouraged Emily to remain true to the faith. Emily also had lost the support of her practitioner. In Christian Science, when an adherent seeks medical aid, the practitioner withdraws under the principle that it is not possible to walk down two paths to healing at the same time. Emily had made a choice, and having made it, could not retrace her steps. From then on, she accepted—but did not seek—medical help when needed. In the late 1970s, while the Tremaines were staying at their vacation home on the island of St. Martin, Emily suddenly developed an intestinal blockage and was in critical condition. She was airlifted to Puerto Rico, where emergency surgery was performed. During her last year of life, she was in the hospital for months at a time on a respirator that helped pump air into her deteriorating lungs. Even so, Emily stayed an ardent believer in Christian

Science to the end of her life. However, her belief was tinged by a sense of her own failure to unite fully with the mind of God and thereby rid herself of tuberculosis.

Perhaps this is what led the Tremaines to experiment with Transcendental Meditation in the 1970s. Like Christian Science, Transcendental Meditation propounds the belief that the physical world is an illusion. This leads to a mind-over-body orientation, the necessity of mental concentration (for Christian Science, "working;" for Transcendental Meditation, repeating a mantra), and an emphasis on individual enlightenment instead of social justice. Another similarity is that both beliefs call for the utilization of a more enlightened person (called a practitioner in Christian Science and a facilitator in Transcendental Meditation) to guide and encourage the neophyte. After a few years, the Tremaines stopped practicing Transcendental Meditation, but Emily never stopped practicing Christian Science.

Emily managed to return to the things she loved, including going to galleries and artists' studios and traveling abroad with the Museum of Modern Art's International Council, but she did so more slowly and in a more remote way. People who came to know Emily for the first time in the 1970s recall her fierce artistic intelligence, but had no experience of her sense of humor or her pleasure in entertaining. Instead they describe her as withdrawn and quiet, occasionally sullen, and reported that she and Burton tended to keep to themselves when attending social events. There were no more soirées at which silver balloons bumped amicably into visitors, and artists by the fistful tried uncomfortably to make small talk with wealthy collectors. When their fine housekeeper and chef Sabine Weber retired in the 1970s after many years of service, gourmet dinners were replaced with Stouffer's French bread pizza and vintage wine by cheap jug brands. Only the art—and the drive to collect it—stayed incomparable.

Sam Green was incredulous at Emily's determination to continue the hunt even when she was not feeling well: "She didn't mind where she went. She'd go even when she was sick. She'd walk up six flights of stairs into an artist's loft under the worst conditions. I remember once Agnes Martin, who was disgruntled with the art world but not with me, gave me the keys to her warehouse where she had twenty or thirty paintings on rolls on the canvas. She hadn't even stretched them. She said 'sell these, all of these for me, I want $20,000 each for them and I want them in the best collections.' Which is what I did. But Emily and I had to go to this warehouse and unroll the paintings on the floor."[3]

Paradoxically, the art world in the early 1970s was itself suffering from creative exhaustion. Some artists had simply turned their backs on the entire scene. These included Agnes Martin, who decamped from New York in 1967 and took up residence in an adobe hut in New Mexico, and Jim Dine, who fled to London before finally settling in Vermont. Some of the former Pop artists began to reveal touches of abstraction in their work. For example, Warhol was cranking out portraits of the "me" generation that were almost painterly in their use of color. Meanwhile, the Minimalists were struggling with the dilemma that austerity could be boring visually. For the Tremaines, it was becoming more and more difficult to tell what, if anything, was really avant-garde. Even the word itself seemed passé. "I feel there is just a rehash, maybe very well done, but not saying anything new, so more or less I am [too] bored to buy them," Emily said. "Once in a while there will be [a painting] that I think is very beautiful and worth living with. I think to a degree I've had it, I've had the most beautiful things in the world and it is hard to keep up that standard."

There was a small group of artists in whom the Tremaines remained interested. They added more works by Agnes Martin and Frank Stella, both of whom were in the elite circle of artists whose work the Tremaines acquired over many years. In 1970, they purchased a work which was to become one of Emily's favorites, Robert Irwin's *Untitled, 1970*. They already owned two of Irwin's paintings, but this new work was entirely different, a disk made of plastic on cast acrylic. *Untitled* was meant to be positioned a few feet from the wall by a pole and then cross-lighted by four low-intensity bulbs located on the ceiling and floor. The effect was to make the edges of the disk recede and disappear into the surrounding shadows. As described in *The Tremaine Collection*, "Through the use of light, Irwin has dematerialized our perception of the work itself to the point that the viewer perceives what cannot be possible, that solid and void have reversed their apparent structural roles."[4]

Emily found this luminescent golden orb so serenely magnificent that she rearranged the entryway in their house in Madison to exhibit it with maximum effectiveness. A more prosaic reason for giving the orb its own space was that the Tremaines had a few years before hung another work by Irwin, also composed of light, in their New York living room, only to find that it haughtily negated everything else there, "like a nun at a cocktail party," concluded Emily. Reluctantly, they had taken it down. Although J. Carter Brown, then assistant director at the National Gallery of Art in Washington, considered him to be one of the most talented artists since Rothko, Irwin was very discouraged because, with the exception of the Tremaines, most critics and

Emily Hall Tremaine and Steingrim Laursen of Copenhagen, Denmark, at the Kimbell Art Museum, Fort Worth, spring meeting of the International Council of the Museum of Modern Art, 1976. Printed with permission of The International Council of the Museum of Modern Art.

collectors ignored him. "The disks were the last of my non-site works. No one wanted to buy them. I guess they were too theatrical, not Greenbergian enough. The New York criticism was very negative. But the Tremaines didn't wait for a ground swell or to become part of a position. Like all the greatest collectors, they were willing to trust their own eye. They bought early, in the beginning, on faith."[5]

In the 1970s and 1980s, the number of paintings the Tremaines acquired dropped off, but the works that they did buy were rigorous and demanding. No one could accuse them of becoming conservative. Many were more to Emily's taste than to Burton's. He freely admitted that he couldn't "see yet" what she admired in some of these austere works. He preferred the tactile pleasure of the swaying antennas of *Signal* by Vassilakis Takis or the jigsaw-puzzle pieces of Michael Heizer's *Circle*. As pleased as he was with owning raw silk scrolls by Joan Miró and Jean Dubuffet, he was equally pleased with the plexiglass case he had designed so that they could be displayed and unrolled without damage.

In 1974, they added to their collection art by Dan Flavin *Monument 7 to V. Tatlin,* Carl Andre *Aluminum-Magnesium Plain,* Robert Mangold *Four Squares within a Circle,* Michael Heizer *Russian Constructivist Painting, No. 1,* and Dorothea Rockburne *Indication Drawing.* Eventually works by Barbara Valenta, Brice Marden, and Mel Kendrick also joined the collection. The Tremaines took great pleasure in all of them. However, Burton left it to Emily to keep artists, periods, and influences straight. Showing a visitor a wood sculpture by Kendrick, Burton affectionately patted it on the head. "It's so cubist," he said, while Emily quietly interjected, "I think it's so Brancusi."[6]

Emily also continued to add to her collection of very small art works, several of which were displayed as a group on a shelf in the apartment, while others served as tiny counterpoints to larger works. Accumulated over many years, some were gifts from appreciative artists. In this category was the little *Gold Marilyn* that Warhol had left at their door as a Christmas present and *Grey Numbers,* a diminutive (5¾" by 4¼,") painting by Jasper Johns for Emily. Other tiny works included Jim Dine's *A Little Scissors and a Little Screwdriver* (5½" square), and Lichtenstein's *Ceramic Sculpture* (9½" high) and *Small Landscape* (4½" square). Size had nothing to do with visual impact, however, as made evident by de Kooning's *Yellow Woman* (8½" by 5½") and Motherwell's *Spanish Elegy* (9" by 12"), two paintings that demanded attention regardless of size.

Only two works shared the entry hall in Madison with Irwin's orb: a small sculpture by Jésus Rafael Soto and a drawing by Walter de Maria, which he had given to the Tremaines as a thank-you gift for permitting him to use the Bar T Bar Ranch as a testing ground for his Earth Work *The Lightning Field*. He and the Tremaines had hoped to install that work permanently, but the ranch was a corporation, and the board of directors did not approve the idea of hundreds of steel poles cemented into a piece of desert nearly one mile square to attract lightning. Ernest Chilson, a rancher through and through and a member of the Bar T Bar board of directors, said pragmatically, "We were afraid the lightning might kill some cattle."

The *Lightning Field* was art at its most extreme, using the forces of nature as canvas and paint, eschewing museum walls, and making the very idea of ownership absurd. In a way, it was Barnett Newman's work writ large—the earth and sky perceived as sacred artistic space, free of artificial aesthetic constraints. Even the most savvy of New York critics were uncertain what to make of Earth Work art. Just to see it required expensive trips to out-of-the-way places. Otherwise, viewers had to settle for photographs to gauge its attributes, hardly an adequate substitute for first-hand experience.[7]

While waiting for the Bar T Bar board to make its final decisions, de Maria became impatient and the prototype started to fall apart. In a letter to Emily and Burton in 1977, de Maria wrote that it had been three years since the start of the project and that, although he appreciated their loan of the land because it had helped him "determine what qualities were necessary for the construction of a work such as this," the temporary foundations of the steel poles were no longer holding the elements vertical:

> The location of the work was perfect, however, I see no way that it can remain there. Emily and Burton, the reason that it can't work is, how shall I say, political, not technical. As we know there were four or five people or groups who would impinge on the ownership and use of this work. They are: Virginia Dwan, yourselves, the Meteor Crater Enterprises, Chilson and the Ranch, and myself. After many conversations with Virginia Dwan and you, and remembering the reaction of your board of directors, etc., I have just come to the conclusion that there are just too many people to please to make this joint venture work. It's just too god damn complex. I'm sorry about this. . . . As a token of my appreciation I am working on a special work which I would like to give to you soon.[8]

Shortly thereafter, he sent Burton and Emily the picture that they hung in the entryway next to Irwin's orb. On receiving it, Emily wrote back, "Burton and I are both overwhelmed by your gift. It is as beautifully expressed as an idea could be. It recalls so much of the wonder we experience when we are in Arizona. Thank you very deeply." The people at the Bar T Bar felt toward the *Lightning Field* a different kind of wonder summed up in a book written about the ranch. "So the de Maria project, which had locals scratching their heads in wonder, was abandoned. Bar T Bar cowboys helped dismantle the array, no doubt marveling all the while at the crazy people who would spend good money to put up such a strange display."[9] Yet, within the year, Virginia Dwan, the art dealer who actually owned de Maria's concept for the *Lightning Field,* donated it to the DIA Arts Foundation, a tract of land was purchased in New Mexico, and de Maria finally had the satisfaction of overseeing the installation of four hundred permanent steel rods.

At the same time as de Maria's prototype was waiting for a thunderstorm, the Tremaines made the acquaintance of Charles Ross, a young artist who was becoming interested in Earth Works and who shared with them his ideas about the role that art should play in the discovery and exploration of the universe. To Emily, this tied in perfectly with what was taking place at the ranch. Because impact craters are common on the moon, NASA had decided that Meteor Crater was a perfect location for moon-landing simulations. The space agency began to use the crater to train astronauts destined for the Apollo missions, including Neil Armstrong, Charles Conrad, James Lovell, and Frank Borman. Ross perceived of people as "beings of the stars" and said that art "has the ability to create windows, to view larger layers of the natural order and to connect them with your senses . . . giving you a feeling that you don't get from science."[10] The Tremaines invited him out to the Bar T Bar to take a look at the crater. They hoped that he could develop an Earth Work which, in Ross's own words, would extend one's concept of being in the cosmos: "They had possession of one of the great environmental wonders of the world and they were thinking of doing a museum that dealt with ecology or forces. I looked at the crater and proposed a piece that had to do with the spectrum and the sound of the solar system." Ross envisioned a horizontal stack of acrylic prisms, eight feet wide, which would be turned to the sun in such a way as to cast a spectrum on the wall of the crater. On the rim of the crater, a radio telescope antenna would track the sun and broadcast its sounds live. As Ross explained it, the observer would be listening to the sun's sound and looking at the colors simultaneously. "The sun sounds a bit like the ocean. During times of sunspot activity, the sound rises and falls like waves, so for the most part it would be like a gentle hissing coming out of the ground, but when there were sunspots there would be a sudden crescendo."

Ross believed that the Tremaines were excited about the idea, so he was surprised and deeply disappointed when "the whole project sort of faded away. We never got as far as a model." Ross got the feeling that the Tremaines were constrained organizationally from following through on his plan, as had been the case with de Maria's *Lightning Field.*

Never one to give up easily, Emily later tried to interest the artist Peter Erskine (through whom she had become interested in Transcendental Meditation) in planning a work for the crater. "She was interested not necessarily in an Earth Work but in art that she felt related to these larger forces of nature, the sun, the planets, the solar system," said Erskine. "I realized that was why she had been interested in the *Lightning Field* and that her interest in meditation was an extension of that. The reasons she was interested in my work was because it was always involved with light." Erskine was one of the few artists to whom Emily revealed her spiritual side, and, in spite of the fact that he also was to be disappointed in the Meteor Crater project, he nevertheless appreciated her support. As a result, he came to believe that "I really had the right to do the things that I thought I should be doing, instead of being told by somebody else what to do. Maybe I never would be where I am now, doing things like the *Secrets of the Sun.* I followed my own daemon and I think that is something I learned from her. She did it in her life." [11] Erskine was the last artist that Emily approached about the crater. In the end, it stayed as it had been — a cosmic earthwork, devoid of steel poles, prisms, and radio telescopes.

Far removed from the vast scope of the Earth Works were the paintings of Neil Jenney, a self-taught artist whose figurative work was edgy and ironic. Agnes Gund remembers accompanying Emily to Jenney's studio at the time of her first purchase in 1975: "Emily really started me going and looking at studios. We went to Neil Jenney's and considered the paintings *Cat and Dog* and *Husband and Wife.* It was just a toss up. Finally she said "which do you want?" and I said "No, which do you want?" She chose *Husband and Wife* and I chose, and love, *Cat and Dog.*"

To Jenney, that visit summarized what he had hoped the business side of the art world would be like: Emily showed up at the studio, looked at all the paintings, picked out the one she wanted, and bought it. "Emily wasn't afraid to spend her money on a nobody. She didn't need the judgement of other collectors to know the value of an artist's work. I was a relative nobody when she came to my place the first time. She came with a friend one day to my small gallery space. I left them alone to look at the paintings, hoping they'd write out a check. When I came out and saw what she had chosen, I remember thinking, 'My God, Emily always chooses the best paintings.'" [12]

Emily was just as direct when she did not like something. Asked once why there were no works by Color Field painters, such as Jules Olitski or Helen Frankenthaler, in the collection, she said bluntly, "I find it terribly boring, verging on the decorative. Really I feel it's just more of the same, not saying anything new."[13] The Tremaines acquired *No. 133* by Morris Louis and *Stack* by Kenneth Noland, then turned around and donated the first to the National Gallery of Art and the second to the Wadsworth Atheneum. They collected few of the Op artists, none of the photo-realists, and none of the politically involved artists, such as Hans Haacke. Nor could they find room on their walls for the works of Francis Bacon.

Besides what she perceived as a diminishment of artistic creativity by the 1970s, Emily also was perturbed by the dislocations in the entire art market caused by the rapid inflation of prices. Big money had knocked everything out of kilter. There were more art institutions and more funding; the number and size of corporate collections had increased; there were far more galleries and one-artist exhibitions; there was a large pool of artists and an even larger pool of collectors. The Tremaines could not have been leaders of the pack no matter how superior their ability to pick quality, for there wasn't any pack; it was more like a horde.

The inflation in the price of art also upset the traditional collector and museum route for the acquisition and donation of paintings. Formerly, it was the role of dealers to spot new artists and then to bring their work to the attention of collectors, who were able to take the financial risk of buying a painting of uncertain worth. Museums held back to see how critics reacted, allowing a certain amount of time to enter into the process of forming a judgement. Meanwhile, they kept up good relations with collectors, in hopes of persuading them to donate, or include in their wills, works of art. The problem was that, with the inflation of prices of contemporary art, it no longer made sense for a museum to take a wait-and-see position, because by the time it got around to purchasing a "new" work, the price may have surpassed their entire acquisitions budget for the year. A museum might as well enter the ring with collectors at the beginning and run the risks of buying works by unknown artists. If a purchase seemed to have been a mistake, the museum could mark it for de-accession, a polite term for *sale*.

To Emily, this indicated that museums were losing objectivity in making acquisitions. "They are so badly motivated," she said. "I suppose it happens when things become successful or grow too big." In her opinion, for a museum to purchase paintings by new artists was to give them an imprimatur that they had not yet earned. Undeserved accolades could lead to the creation of inferior art, because artists would begin to respond to the opinion of critics and viewers instead of harkening to their own inner aesthetic voice. In Emily's opinion, it also negatively affected collectors. "Because so many people depend on the museum's approval to direct their collecting, they have no right to approve of something that they have only seen themselves 24 hours before."

Even the Museum of Modern Art, to which Emily had been loyal throughout the 1950s and 1960s, had fallen in her estimation by the 1970s. "When I think of the early days of the Modern, the dedication of the first trustees, the lengths they went to get the things they wanted to own — it was a kind of thinking that leads to great, honest collecting." She concluded that too much social and commercial prestige had become involved in making acquisitions.

The rising prices also began to warp the relationship between dealers and collectors. Formerly when there were fewer collectors, dealers had known the tastes and proclivities of each. They went out of their way to show works (even before exhibitions) to those collectors who were most likely to buy them. It was a delicate dance because every major collector wanted to have first choice and became incensed when he or she discovered another collector had been shown a work first, but it was a risk dealers had to run. At the same time as they attempted to keep their regular collectors happy, dealers had to cultivate new collectors or eventually they would go out of business because new forms of art appealed to different tastes. Emily and Burton, for example, had purchased several works from Ivan Karp during the 1960s, but when he began to represent the photo-realists, whose work Emily disliked, they no longer dealt with him.

Emily and Burton had worked out the following sliding commission scale for dealers who handled the sale of their art: 10% commission on the first $100,000 of purchase price, 8% on the next $2.4 million of the purchase price, and 5% on the remainder. This personal commission scale tended to alienate some dealers, who saw it as yet another indication of the Tremaines' highhandedness. Furthermore, the Tremaines rarely bought very expensive pieces at this point. When they did acquire a high-priced work, they were more likely to trade for it, as they did with Newman's *The Moment II,* for which they traded Jasper Johns's *Tango,* and Giacometti's *Spoon Woman* for which they traded both O'Keeffe's *New York Night* and Sheeler's *On the Theme of Farm Buildings.* As a result, as the decade advanced, the Tremaines were not receiving the kind of solicitous attention they thought they deserved, in light of the years they had collected. By the late 1970s even their relationships with dealers such as Leo Castelli, from whom they had bought heavily, had begun to fray.

The general rise in prices also changed the way artists themselves lived. They were no longer trying to cobble together an income by designing store windows, teaching part-time, or doing graphic design. Their art was bringing them enough money so that they could lead respectable middle-class, or even upper-class, lives. Some had crossed the line and were collecting art themselves, thereby blurring the distinction between dealer, artist, and collector. For example, on the island of St. Martin, where the Tremaines had purchased property in 1961, they numbered among their neighbors both Betty Parsons and Jasper Johns—collector, dealer/artist, and artist living the same lifestyle, dropping in to share lunch, inviting each other over for cocktails in what resembled a little tropical art community. "I often joined Betty on scavenger hunts, gathering flotsam and jetsam to which she applied her magic and which she made into art," recalled Emily.

For some of the older Abstract Expressionists, this new-found success created a spiritual crisis as profound as that brought about by Emily's failure to overcome tuberculosis. It is Henry Geldzahler's theory that Mark Rothko committed suicide in 1970 "because he found the success to be so misguided, so obscene, so much concentrated on the wrong level of appreciation of what he was doing. . . . Rothko just couldn't deal with the fact that these paintings were coming up to be worth a million dollars but were unappreciated for their spiritual value. That he was disillusioned is hardly the word for it."[14]

The meteoric rise in prices led to a very active resale market. Collectors who bought art specifically as an investment had no qualms about selling when they calculated the work's value had increased sufficiently to bring them a hefty profit. Simultaneously, auctions became more common, eventually taking on the aura of media events. Because the records of auction sales were obtainable, unlike those of private sales in the back rooms of galleries, the news that a painting had sold for a certain astronomical amount spread and tended to advance the price of all art. There is an old nautical expression that a rising tide lifts all boats. So it was for art. Not only did the price of Pop go way up, so did the price of Abstract Expressionism, as evidenced by the sale of Blue Poles by Pollock to the National Gallery in Canberra, Australia, for a whopping $2.2 million, bringing collector Ben Heller an equally whopping profit.

The Tremaines were not immune to the financial fever. As the value of their paintings continued to escalate, Emily admitted to a sense of satisfaction that went beyond aesthetics: "I recall *Esquire* magazine once suggested that a collector has one of three motives for collecting. A genuine love of art; the investment possibilities; or its social promises. I have never known a collector who was not stimulated by all three. For the full joy and reward, the dominant motivation must be the love of art; but I would question the integrity of any collector who denied an interest in the valuation the market place puts on his pictures and he cannot help but feel a satisfaction with his own acumen and with the approbation of his peers when he was perhaps one of those who were perspicacious enough to buy, say a Jackson Pollock in 1948, or a Jasper Johns in 1958."

The first newsworthy auction was of Robert Scull's collection of Pop art on October 18, 1973, necessitated by his acrimonious divorce from his wife and co-collector, Ethel. The auctioneer was Sotheby's, the prestigious London-based firm that was just beginning to expand into the field of contemporary art. It had purchased the Parke-Bernet auction house in the mid-1960s, and it was under that name (more acceptable to Americans, who were still chafing about the takeover) that the Scull auction was to be held. The day of the auction the weather was miserable, a cold rain mixed with sleet, but that did not deter a large crowd of spectators and journalists from showing up at what was sure to be a theatrical event. For an added bit of dramatic effect, several of the cabbies who worked for Scull marched outside of Sotheby's, waving placards that accused him of not paying them decent wages. The Tremaines made it through the crowd, as did Philip Johnson, several celebrities, and many dealers. Even Rauschenberg, whose works were in the Scull collection and hence up for auction, was there, although he was visibly upset with the idea that his art was going to be sold as if it were a slab of prime rib. "All the intimacy of the work is gone," he complained. From a sheer economic point of view, the auction was good news: if Rauschenberg's work fetched a high price, all the art he was then producing would likewise increase in value, to his benefit. But that was not the way he perceived it.[15] Auctions were not psychologically healthy places for artists, because they were not about art but about money. Of course, the back rooms of galleries, where the re-sale of art was carried on routinely, were also about money, but the scenario was not as blatant and certainly not as raucous. At this auction, money of a kind never before seen at such an event changed hands. Jasper Johns's *Double White Maps* was bought by Ben Heller for $240,000, setting a record for the highest amount ever paid for the work of a living American artist. *White Fire* by Barnett Newman fetched $155,000. Rauschenberg's works went for $85,000 and $90,000, leaving him fuming. The final tally was $2,242,900.

With higher-quality examples of art by the same artists in their collection, the Tremaines sat throughout the auction mentally tabulating the worth of their own collection. Over the years Emily had insistently, almost truculently, told reporters that she and Burton never bought paintings for investment only, but with these stratospheric values, the Tremaines could not help but be affected. For Emily, it was an affirmation of her aesthetic prescience. "I remember when I first bought a picture from Rosenquist. I asked him how much it was and he said that he hadn't sold a painting before but he thought he should get so much per square foot. It was eight-foot square and I paid him $800. I think that was a fair price at the time because I was taking a gamble. It gave him an opportunity not to have to paint street signs and to do his work. [Recently I saw one of his works at auction] and I think it went for about $16,000. Well, I thought, my eye's okay. Somebody else likes him that much. It's a great satisfaction."

Despite the affirmation, the astronomical increase in value also created a huge dilemma about what to do with the collection following their deaths, because to pass the art on to Burton's children would be to saddle them with an enormous tax burden. However, the Tremaines were not at ease with willing it to a museum with the possible exception of the National Gallery of Art, with which they had an ongoing and, at this point, amicable relationship. The nature of that relationship and the reasons why it eventually soured is a story that began in 1966, when Emily decided to do something about her pet peeve — art that was put in storage by museums. In defense of the museums, there was no way that everything donated could permanently be exhibited. There was only so much wall space available, and to agree to show everything all the time was highly impractical, if not impossible. Essentially, it would turn a museum into a mausoleum. Even when a major benefactor gave, not only an entire collection, but also the money to build a new wing and sufficient endowment to maintain and staff it properly, the stipulation that all of a collection be shown all of the time imposed a terrible burden.

The problem arose from the belief common among collectors that their artistic taste was impeccable and that they always chose wisely. No collector wanted to be told that he or she had paid dearly for second-rate work by second-string artists. But the risk that the taste of collectors of contemporary art would be questioned or completely derided as time passed was far greater than it was for collectors of Baroque, for example, on which generations of art historians already had passed judgment. Collectors also felt, quite rightly, that their largesse toward a museum was an extremely valuable cultural gift and that they were owed a high level of recognition and affirmation. Museum staffs routinely devoted a significant amount of time to handing out accolades to their benefactors to pump up their sense of worth. It was a normal part of their job. However, they could not accede to impossible demands that would undermine a museum's ability to grow and change with the cultural community in which it was situated.

Uneasy with the prospect of any painting going into storage, Emily came up with a novel idea. She proposed the formation of an arts foundation to which they would donate a portion of their collection. The foundation would then loan the paintings to museums throughout the country that did not have large quality collections. The aim was to keep the paintings exhibited all the time. According to Burton Tremaine Jr., "The thought of the foundation was to have all these pictures and to lend them out to various museums that might want them: not a short-term loan, nor on a forever basis, but sort of a long-term basis. In other words, if Kansas City didn't have a Jackson Pollock, then that would be a good place for the foundation's Pollock to go until Kansas City got one of their own, at which time the Pollock would go to another museum which didn't have one at all."

The second component of the idea was that the Tremaines would convince other collectors to donate their art to the foundation in return for substantial tax deductions, in effect forming a very large national lending library of artwork. Because Emily knew her concern about paintings not being exhibited was shared by many other collectors, she believed that the idea of an arts foundation would appeal to them. As Emily explained it, besides museums requesting paintings, collectors who donated their art to the foundation could stipulate that certain works be sent to specific cities or museums. For example, in her case she would stipulate that the *Victory Boogie-Woogie* stay in a musuem in New York City because that was where Mondrian found his inspiration, but since the Pasadena Museum already had a good collection of paintings by Paul Klee, "the Klees could go to Pasadena which would become a pilgrimage point for Klees." If the day came that the Pasadena Museum hired a new director who hated the art of Klee, the paintings would be returned to the foundation, which would then send them out to the second or third choices designated by the donor. The only hard and fast rule was that if a loaned painting were not hung for at least six months of the year, it had to be returned to the foundation.

However, not everyone was in agreement with the idea. Traditionally, patrons often bequeath their collections to the regional museum that is nearest their ancestral home, thereby conferring a touch of artistic immortality on the family name while enriching the local culture. As a result, the idea of museum patrons being solicited by a national foundation to give their collections to them instead of to the regional museums rankled many regional directors. Often in an uncertain economic state with very small acquisitions budgets, the regional museums did not want their donor pipeline cut off by the foundation, nor did they want to have to pay the costs attendant to borrowing a painting that might have been given to them outright had the foundation not existed.

Despite the opposition, the Tremaines decided to go ahead with the idea. They formed a board of directors composed of Thomas Hoving, director of the Metropolitan Museum of Art; James Elliott and Samuel Wagstaff, director and curator of the Wadsworth Atheneum; John Walker, trustee of the National Gallery, and Ralph Colin, head of the New York Art Dealers Association. They entered into an agreement with the Wadsworth Atheneum to manage the lending process, including shipping and security, in return for which the Wadsworth would get a donation from the Tremaines to offset the administrative costs.

Hardly had the lending program gotten underway when the Tax Act of 1969 was passed. Up until then, foundations were not required to give away anything each year, but now they had to give away five percent of their assets annually. That sounded the death knell to the concept of the foundation actually owning the art outright. Discouraged by the sudden turn of events, the Tremaines reconsidered the structure of the foundation and decided to approach the Museum of Modern Art to see if they would accept a donation earmarked not for the museum's walls but for the lending library. Basically, the museum would serve as owner/administrator.

It was Emily's dream that the museum's International Council, of which she and Burton were very active members, might be able to take the idea to a higher level. Under their aegis, paintings could be lent to museums around the world, which is why she decided to name the new body the International Art Foundation. "We can borrow a Van Gogh from the Kroller-Müller Museum and loan them one of our Mondrians for three or four years, not short loans," she explained. "This is going to be the most ecumenical thing that has ever happened in art." Emily invited several directors of European museums, including the director of the Tate Gallery in London, to the United

States to talk about the idea. Their response was very favorable. However, René d'Harnoncourt, director of the Museum of Modern Art, was unconvinced. Blanchette Rockefeller, who had been head of the International Council and who liked the idea, told Emily she would attempt to change his mind, but her support was to no avail and, as a result, the plan was doomed.

Discouraged but not defeated, the Tremaines decided to turn to the National Gallery and its young director J. Carter Brown. The National Gallery was Emily's second choice, after the Museum of Modern Art, for several reasons. The first was that she had great respect for John Walker, its former and longtime director, currently one of its trustees, and, conveniently, a member of the board of directors of the International Art Foundation. Walker was attempting to push the gallery in the direction of collecting modern and contemporary art, which pleased Emily: "I've known John a number of years. He's one of my best friends. I like him. I love to be with him and I agree with him. We read the same books. Carter Brown seems to me to be exactly the same type of man. I like his thinking. He has a marvelous historical background. He is an art historian, which is terribly important for anybody directing the twentieth century collections [so that they] know what came first."

Emily was also impressed by Andrew Mellon's altruism not only in starting the gallery in 1937 but in resisting the temptation to stick his name on it. She admitted to what she called "a terrible prejudice" against people who "hang their names on museum buildings" but who were not concerned about the quality of art inside or whether the museum had enough money to keep going. "I'd rather give my support to the Modern or the Metropolitan or the National Gallery than to some family."

After long discussion with the board of trustees and Carter Brown, the Tremaines decided to transfer to the National Gallery all the foundation's assets, and then disband it. The thirty-seven works that the Tremaines had donated already to the foundation were given to the gallery in 1969. These were followed over the next eight years by fifty-three others.[16] However, several snags soon developed. Burton Jr., explained: "The understanding was that the National Gallery would administer those assets just the way the International Art Foundation wished them to be administered. But the director of the National Gallery said that he could not make a contractual agreement that would tie the hands of future boards of directors. So the family went ahead on the basis of a gentlemen's agreement, that if the family or the Foundation transferred the assets to the National Gallery, it would indeed be administered in this fashion. Well, it all happened, the pictures went to the National Gallery and after about a year the National Gallery stuck them in the basement instead of lending them. That's what turned Emily and Burton off."

To be fair, the failure was not all the National Gallery's fault. Emily and Burton had to share some of the responsibility. First, the program turned out to be difficult and expensive to administer and the National Gallery ran into troubles almost from the beginning. Although Brown had backed the idea, and in 1972 had received Congressional approval to accept the contents of the International Art Foundation, he belatedly became aware of how difficult it was going to be to run the lending program. According to Brown, the Tremaines, "were always after us to promote it more. But we had this bad experience where the brochure that we had done to announce the National Lending Service was for cost reasons printed by the government printing office. Without our permission, they distributed it throughout their normal distribution channels all over the country. So we had this avalanche of requests for loans and we didn't have enough staffing to answer the mail. We had not wanted to go public with the Service until we had space to store everything, process it, and the staff to do it, which eventually we got from Congress." [17]

Another problem was that, according to several knowledgeable people, including Brown himself, the Tremaines had given the gallery second-rate paintings—in effect, Emily had culled the weaker work from her collection. "Emily would ask us statistically at the end of the year how many of the things that they had given us had been lent," said Brown. "Some had, but a lot hadn't and the reason was the one that we couldn't explain to her: that the paintings were her castoffs and they were not things museums were interested in borrowing."

The Tremaines felt otherwise; certainly there were weaker paintings and sculptures in the donated group, but there were also strong works. Nor could it be expected that while the lending service was in its formative, noncontractual stage that the Tremaines would donate works of the stature of the *Victory Boogie-Woogie* or *Premier Disque*. Artists included among the donated works were Miró, Baj, Bell, Callery, Crawford, de Rivera, Hartung, Irwin, Kline, Lipchitz, Louis, Matisse, Matta, Millares, Pereira, Picasso, Poons, Reinhardt, Riley, Smith, Soulages, Trova, and Warhol.

Thomas Armstrong, former director of the Whitney Museum, contended that the Tremaines had asked too much of the National Gallery.

Amongst my museum peers it was thought that to some extent they had exceeded the demands they could pose on the National Gallery. They represented that category of collector that has very high quality work and makes

great demands for the privilege of the network, in other words, the constant travel, the constant exhibition. The situation was unfortunate because
they were being watched by collectors, kind of as a trial balloon, to see
how far they could go with the museum. The National Gallery was not involved that sincerely in contemporary art and it would have been great if
the Tremaines had made an impact, but it didn't work. Then through con-
versations with others, I began to realize that Emily had reached that stage
of life where her relationships with dealers had turned somewhat sour. She
wasn't as tolerant of the machinations of the art world as she probably once
was. She wasn't the queen bee anymore. Lots of people had entered the
game.

Emily also had held out, like a carrot on a stick, the possibility that she
would will the National Gallery her share of the collection if the gallery followed through on the lending program. In 1973 Emily told Paul Cummings,
"If I die tomorrow the National Gallery gets my share of the collection," but
then she added that in order for that to happen they had to "keep shaping
up." She still had great faith in Walker, but she was cautious about Brown. "I
like Carter, I respect him, but he's very young, and I don't really know him. If
Carter keeps on the way he has, okay, but if he doesn't or if he drops dead, I'm
perfectly free to change my will until the day I die." In fact, that is just what
she did, cutting off the National Gallery when the lending program failed.[18]
This was not the first relationship that had turned sour because Emily wanted
to exert too much influence and alternately advanced and retracted offers of
art as a means of control. In this case, Brown readily admitted that her actions
hurt the gallery: "Like other museums that have been injured in the same way,
we tended to collect around what we had any reason to expect. Why spend
our pennies to buy something when a better example of it was in the Tremaine
collection and would be on its way to us eventually? So it was painful and
injurious. But it wasn't without injury to the Tremaines for there is a certain
satisfaction to having these objects memorialized, to having that fabulous art,
and the great collecting prowess it showed placed in as visual and permanent
a place as you can imagine—the National Gallery."[19]

Brown also believed that one of the unacknowledged reasons the Tremaines
became negative on the lending program and stopped donating works was
the escalation in the value of the entire collection. "It becomes a fascinating
game. You get mesmerized by the numbers when they start going up in such a
giddy way. It was beyond Emily's wildest expectations." Donating a painting

that was worth $100,000 was one thing; donating a painting that was worth $1,000,000 was another. Yet the only way to determine value was to sell. Brown continued: "She had been so put upon by people who thought this stuff was so far out that when it got expensive, it was a justification that she was right and they were wrong. But without selling it, she couldn't establish the degree to which this monetary value was indexed and how right she was. That is the way I psych it out, that she just had to have the reward of thumbing her nose at all those critics and tormentors, to be able to say 'I've been saying all along that, like the Velasquez at the Met, this Mondrian is way up there.' She was asking for applause, and she was bound and determined that she was going to get a number that would prove her correct." [20]

An unspoken dilemma for the Tremaines was that Burton was worried that they had too much of their net worth tied up in art, and that they needed more diversification. This dilemma did not douse Emily's pleasure in the collection, but it certainly made deciding what to do with the art far more complicated than it would have been in the 1940s and 1950s. Economics was crushing aesthetics, and Emily was not at all happy with the change, even though it was making her richer by the minute.

After the failure of the International Art Foundation, Emily and Burton were certain that only when a painting sold for a high value did anyone really appreciate it. This point of view had taken root earlier when the Museum of Modern Art failed to keep the *Victory Boogie-Woogie* constantly on view during the many years that it was on loan to them. "Emily and Burton became absolutely convinced that if you give something to an institution, it will wind up in the basement. Only if the institution buys it, will it go on the wall," said Burton, Jr. "So Emily and Burton decided that they would not give the pictures to anybody; they would sell them."

On and off through the late 1970s and 1980s, the Tremaines entertained envoys from museums seeking to be willed the collection. The Tremaines were invariably polite, but they never gave these representatives serious consideration. "We poured a mountain of calories into them, wining and dining them in the hope of getting it," confessed Thomas Hoving, who was at that time director of the Metropolitan Museum of Art. "They were will danglers." [21]

"They fought with all the museums at this point and they made the lives of many museum directors and board members and chairmen very difficult because all the museums wanted the collection and they felt that the Tremaines should be loyal to one institution," explained Sam Green. "Since it was American art they were collecting, it should go to the Whitney Museum. Since they were in Connecticut, it should go to the Wadsworth Atheneum. Since Burton's family came from Cleveland, it should go to the Cleveland Museum, and since they themselves had a long association with the Museum of Modern Art, it should go there. And nobody was getting anything unless they wanted to pay top dollar for it!"[22]

In one of the last articles written about their collection published by *House & Garden* in 1984, Emily said that she had no plans to keep it together, because she couldn't bear the idea of the work being shut up in some museum storage area. To her it was a living thing; better a life on the walls of a private collector than death in storage. According to Tracy Atkinson, who was director of the Wadsworth Atheneum, Emily "looked on the paintings as her children." It was time for some of the children to leave home.

Reality only appears to us tragical because of the disequilibrium and confusion of its appearances. It is our subjective vision and determined position which make us suffer. . . . But we can escape the tragical oppression through a clear vision of true reality, which exists, but which is veiled. If we cannot free ourselves, we can free our vision.
—*Piet Mondrian*

CHAPTER ELEVEN

THROUGH MONDRIAN'S WINDOW

In 1979 and early 1980, the Tremaines sold paintings by van Doesburg, Yves Klein, Arp, Rauschenberg, Kandinsky, and El Lissitzky through the art dealer Harold Diamond. In July of 1980 they sold Warhol's *Marilyn Monroe Diptych* for $270,000 to the Tate Gallery in London. These sales whetted the Tremaines' appetite for more. They scanned their walls again. This time their eyes settled on *Three Flags* by Jasper Johns. For all the enormous inflation in prices, no work by a living American artist had yet broken through the invisible barrier of $1,000,000. The Tremaines decided that *Three Flags* might be the painting to achieve this feat. Emily was proud that she and Burton had purchased *Three Flags* and *White Flag* in the late 1950s when Johns was just beginning to be recognized. If *Three Flags* were to sell for $1,000,000, it would bring to Emily not only great renown but also absolute proof of her collecting acumen.

Having made the decision to sell, the Tremaines had to consider who should handle the sale and what, if any, restrictions they should place on the purchase. They could put the painting up for auction at Christie's or Sotheby's, but they wanted to maintain control over the selection of the purchaser and the price. Emily felt that this painting should remain in the United States; she did not want it to go to a European collector or museum. It was acceptable for the Tate Gallery to own *Marilyn Monroe,* of which there were many variants, but Old Glory (in triple beat) should stay stateside. She had also made strong statements in the past that American museums should have the right of first refusal over European collectors and museums on American art. So the Tremaines rejected the auction route and decided to sell the painting through a dealer. Leo Castelli was Johns's primary dealer (meaning he sold Johns's new works), and he certainly would have been willing to serve as the secondary dealer for such a momentous resale. But perhaps because Castelli took a proprietary approach to all Johns's art, assuming such a sale would by rights be his to handle, the Tremaines chose to be contrary and approached Arnold Glimcher of the Pace Gallery, who just months before had handled the sale of both the *Marilyn Monroe Diptych* and Oldenburg's *7-UP.* The Tremaines did not specify an asking price or the type of buyer that they preferred, but they implied both in a way that Glimcher could not miss. "She said 'make me an offer that is not refusable,' and so I knew that it was a million dollars, that $800,000 or $900,000 would not buy the picture. It was very important to her that a museum pay a million dollars because if they paid a million dollars, they would have this obligation to continue to exhibit the picture. If they didn't pay a million dollars, they would put it in the basement." [1] Glimcher also agreed with the Tremaines that the painting should stay in America and that ideally it should go to a museum. "My feeling was that if there was one painting that said the Whitney Museum of American Art, it was this painting," said Glimcher.

In the late 1970s, Thomas Armstrong, director of the Whitney Museum, had begun to build up the Whitney's collection of paintings by Jasper Johns. Hoping that the Tremaines would become patrons of the museum, Armstrong had started to court them assiduously. Occasionally they had loaned art to the Whitney. However, Armstrong knew their loyalty was still strong to the Museum of Modern Art, even if they were not happy with all aspects of that relationship. He knew as well that the Whitney could not offer the Tremaines the social-intellectual network that the International Council at the Museum of Modern Art provided. Furthermore, besides her dislike of any museum that carried a family name, Emily was openly critical of the quality of the Whitney's acquisitions: "To me, they haven't, overall, hit the high ones, which they should, being right here in New York where it's happening. Of course, that's completely a personal judgement. Maybe my idea of the best isn't theirs. But I never get the boom when I go in there. Obviously they do have some fine ones, but they'll compromise. If they don't get the best, they'll take the second best. If I were the director, if I missed the best, I'd wait. Or if I'd bought something and a better one came along I'd make every effort to make the switch. But they seem to be perfectly willing to accept anything, and that doesn't impress me very much, and so I haven't been much interested in them."

Despite these substantial negative factors, Armstrong was hopeful that the Whitney's increasing attention to the art of Jasper Johns opened a unique window of opportunity. Therefore, he wrote letters to the Tremaines, arranged for them to see the exhibition of Johns's work during times when it wasn't open to the public, and finally visited them in their apartment. It was there that he asked them whether they would consider donating *Three Flags* to the Whitney. "They were very gracious and showed us around. It was an amazing experience to see the European and American art enjoyed simultaneously and respected equally. You had a sense of their eye, a sense of their judgment and the way they lived with art. I thought it was very eccentric because it was the dominant experience of the space. I will never forget the small works that artists had made especially for them or that they had collected. The visit was all very cordial but finally they said they weren't going to give *Three Flags* to us. Still I was hopeful."[2]

Armstrong received a call from Glimcher on June 11, 1980. "He told me that the Tremaines were selling and that he was aware that the Whitney Museum was interested in *Three Flags* and he wanted to give me first refusal." A million dollars was a great deal of money for the Whitney to raise, but with the encouragement of Leonard Lauder, head of the board of directors, Armstrong was determined to try. He was sensitive about dealing with Glimcher without Castelli's knowledge, and so decided to pay Castelli a visit. After talking casually to Castelli's wife, who was a friend of Armstrong's, and admiring the paintings in their apartment, he told her that he wanted to talk to Leo personally. "Do not talk business. Not in the apartment," she insisted, but then she left them alone. Armstrong got right to the point:

> "Leo, the *Three Flags* has been offered to us through Arnold and I'm going to try to buy it for the Whitney Museum." He said, "You'll never be able to do that. The Japanese will be able to buy it," from which I inferred that he had a Japanese client for it. I was sort of hurt because he didn't think I could accomplish the purchase and because he didn't thank me for telling him that it was on the market. His attitude was kind of "forget it, whipper snapper, I've got other plans for the picture."

After his discussion with Castelli, Armstrong told Glimcher that the Whitney was going to buy the painting. Then he set about raising the money in earnest. The price of $1,000,000 was paid in installments over three years. The Tremaines donated a part of the proceeds to Planned Parenthood, one of their favorite charities. Looking back, Armstrong recalled that he was very grateful to Glimcher. "He could have consummated this sale much quicker elsewhere. He brought it to us realizing that it would be an enormous struggle and that it was a big dare whether or not I could pull it off. Then he accepted terms for three years without interest."

Immediately the news got out that the $1 million barrier had been broken. It catalyzed the art world, and prices began to escalate. From then until the end of 1990, records would be set and broken repeatedly. Tracy Atkinson, director of the Wadsworth Atheneum during the 1980s, recalled that Emily told him she was embarrassed by both the price and the attention it was bringing, even though she and Burton had intentionally held out for a million dollars and had wanted the sale publicized. "She said to me that she was astonished and ashamed of that price. She thought it was outrageous."[3]

When Jasper Johns was asked several years later how he felt about the record-breaking sale, he said laconically, "I would have preferred to have sold the painting for $1,000,000 myself. In my childhood during the Depression, $1,000,000 was a constant reference to being a millionaire. From that point of view, it was incredible. But one adjusts very quickly to such things. One is uncertain about the relationship between money and the value of work because one knows too many things that sell for a lot of money."[4]

About Emily's motivation for the sale, Armstrong concluded, "I honestly think that Emily had reached the stage in her life where there was some bitterness about developments in the art community in terms of marketplace and perhaps not enough recognition of her role in recognizing these artists long before the public was aware of them. [It had to do with] the nature of her immortality and how she, Emily Tremaine, was going to go into history. She wanted the sale of *Three Flags* to prove her judgement about quality in art."

The sale provided the Tremaines a brief moment of fame, although the emphasis in the press was not on their perceptiveness in having first purchased the painting but on the sale price. To her discomfiture, Emily discovered that what she had gained from the sale was short-term notoriety, not long lasting respect. As a result, Emily had serious second thoughts after selling *Three Flags*. Two years later, she wrote apologetically to Johns, implying that she had been pressured to sell the painting:

Dear Jasper: Ever since "Flag Day" I've started several times to write you but kept postponing until it didn't make sense anymore. . . . When the

Whitney made us that offer, I really did not want to accept it. The picture meant more than that to me, but everyone else seemed to think that by re-fusing, I was doing everyone — you, the rest of the contemporary painters, the Whitney, even the United States — a disservice. I was still grieving that the National Gallery had not executed their agreement (that nothing would be relegated to storage — if not hung at the Gallery, then placed in other museums). The Whitney offer implied the picture would be displayed, per-haps even prominently. This was the strongest reason for my decision. Stu-pidly I just assumed you would approve of the transaction and I have always regretted I did not discuss it with you. Burton and I have invested the money and donate the income it produces to social causes, preeminently population control, so in retrospect it seems that it was a good decision. I was the only loser — I still love the picture as much as I did that first moment in your studio. . . . Emily Hall Tremaine [5]

By 1984 most of the major American museums had resigned themselves to the fact that they would not be the beneficiaries of the Tremaines' largesse. Already private collectors were eyeing the collection, and dealers were spar-ring with one another, goaded on by the Tremaines themselves, to see into whose hand the plum would eventually drop. Only the Wadsworth Atheneum was still hopeful that the Tremaines would change their minds and either sell or donate to them at least part of Emily's share of the collection. There were many reasons for their steadfast optimism. The first was Emily's long asso-ciation with Chick Austin, whose influence at the Wadsworth had been so profound during the 1930s and 1940s that it was hard to think of that mu-seum without conjuring up his name. The second was that Sam Wagstaff, the museum's chief curator during the 1960s, also had been of great assistance to Emily on numerous occasions, principal among them her 1965 presentation before the Society for the Encouragement of Contemporary Art. He likewise had assisted her in organizing an exhibition called *Connecticut Collects* for the Washington Gallery of Modern Art. Furthermore, the Wadsworth had been the initial repository and administrator for the Tremaines' International Art Foundation.

Despite the reasons for being hopeful, the museum was pragmatic about its chances. The Tremaines had always donated to the Wadsworth, yet there had been something perfunctory about their patronage. "They felt Hartford was a provincial town," admitted Gregory Hedberg, then chief curator. Even so, it was worth another try to see if they would either sell at a low price or donate. However, a special event was needed to broach the subject. Fortunately, a most propitious one was at hand. Avery Memorial Hall, built under Chick Austin's guidance, was about to celebrate its fiftieth anniversary in 1984, and the Wadsworth wanted to mount a major exhibition to mark the occasion. What could be better than to show the very best art in the Tremaine collection? It had not been shown publicly since *Painting Toward Architecture,* which had opened, providentially, in Avery Hall thirty-seven years before.

Emily said that when Gregory Hedberg and Tracy Atkinson brought up the idea of the exhibition, their principal argument was that the Tremaines' collecting activities spanned the same period as Avery Memorial Hall. "As our involvement with the Atheneum had much to do with abetting our enthusiasms, and as we already knew how beautiful our pictures appear in the superb space and light of the Avery Memorial, we came to be persuaded to participate in this celebration and we are so glad we did."[6]

For this exhibition, titled *The Tremaine Collection: 20th Century Masters, The Spirit of Modernism,* the Tremaines loaned virtually every major piece they had, including seventy-one pieces from their New York apartment and fifty-two pieces from their home in Madison. Furthermore, the Whitney agreed to lend *Three Flags.* A large-format catalog featured the *Victory Boogie-Woogie* on the cover. It contained an essay about the cohesiveness of the collection by art critic Robert Rosenblum, an article about the Tremaines by Gregory Hedberg, and an extensive interview with Emily. There were four-color reproductions of all the art on exhibition and photographs of the huge site sculptures at Madison. Because the exhibition was of a private collection, the Wadsworth could not use Federal grant money to pay for the printing of the expensive catalog, so the Tremaines picked up the tab themselves.

Coincidentally, the Museum of Modern Art was undergoing renovations at the time, so the exhibition was able to steal from New York City the claim to be the center of the art world and bestowed it on Hartford, albeit briefly. Not since the era of Chick Austin had the Wadsworth Atheneum received such attention. The Tremaines themselves were overwhelmed with the articles, reviews and letters. The ones that meant the most to them spoke of the changes in perception created by powerful juxtapositions. "To see the Mondrian *Victory Boogie-Woogie* at right angles to the Delaunay is an experience I will never forget. The rhythms that both of them achieve in such different ways with solid places of color are quite fantastic," wrote Nicolas Fox Weber, executive director of the Josef and Anni Albers Foundation:

Your Braque has the luxuriance of only his greatest still lives. The Hélion is loaded with motion; the Nicholsons are works of vast subtlety and finesse.

And that Pollock is absolutely unique; it has a depth of Monet's late *Water Lilies* and a power all of its own. What I found perhaps the most remarkable about your collection is that it made me consider works by artists I have never particularly liked in a new way. The general quality level, and the particular pieces that you have selected by some artists who have always been rather difficult for me, made me totally receptive to some new and rather startling pleasures. It is your creativity and eye as collectors that makes this sort of thing happen. Congratulations.[7]

Philip Johnson gave the lecture at the exhibition's opening on February 25, 1984. He spoke at length about Chick Austin and his influence on the art world and then explained his own relationship with the Tremaines, which he freely admitted was tinged with malice. "I'm very familiar with this collection. I'm also familiar with my jealousy and envy of it so if I start saying nasty things, you put that down to where they belong." Turning to address Emily directly, Johnson said that the only time he ever purchased a masterpiece before she did was in 1929 when he bought "a Paul Klee all by myself."

The gala dinner was considered by some people to represent the height of the Tremaines' entire collecting career, the moment when they finally received publicly the recognition they deserved. Important people from all segments of the art world were in attendance, among them the artists John Chamberlain, Dan Flavin, Dorothea Rockburne, Richard Tuttle, and Robert Zakanitch. Philip Johnson sat at the head table next to Emily, chatting with her about art and old times throughout the dinner. Dee Tremaine Hildt remembers that Emily was the perfect picture of understated elegance that evening. "She wore a pleated dress by designer Mary McFadden. It was mauve with a navy blue insert, quite somber, adorned simply with a stunning gold and diamond pin in an abstract shape. At the time I wondered why on earth she had not worn her fabulous diamond necklace and her very wide diamond cuff bracelet. After all, it was a glittering evening and such things would have been very appropriate. Then I realized that she was intentionally presenting a very minimalist image. Most people under similar circumstance would have gone for the diamonds. Instead, Emily's approach was true chic."

To some attendees, however, the dinner was a more complex affair. "There was always a kind of edginess about these events, because they were never a celebration of gifts. They were a kind of celebration in anticipation of celebration," said Tom Armstrong. "Let's put it this way: the cheers were muffled."

Only a few months prior to the show, the Wadsworth's board of directors had passed a resolution "to negotiate in all good faith with Mr. and Mrs.

Philip Johnson delivered the lecture at the opening night of The Tremaine Collection: 20th Century Masters *at the Wadsworth Atheneum February 25, 1984.*

Burton Tremaine, Sr., for the purchase of their collection of 20th-Century art, specifically the works belonging to them to be shown at the museum in the forthcoming exhibition."[8] Because those paintings constituted the heart of the collection, the museum was aware that the $3,000,000 they were prepared to offer was a woefully low price. However, a year earlier, Hedberg had come up with a possible solution when Burton had approached him about selling *Sinjerli Variation I* by Frank Stella to the Wadsworth for $250,000. Hedberg suggested that if Burton could get it appraised for that amount, then he should consider donating one-half and selling one-half. "Burton loved the idea. We bought it for $125,000, which meant he got both a capital gain and a tax deduction . . . I think it could have been a model for future acquisitions: a half-price sale." Possibly the board of directors was hoping a similar arrangement could be set up for the purchase of the entire collection, thereby at least doubling the $3,000,000. The difficulty (which turned out to be insurmountable) was to get appraisals high enough to satisfy the Tremaines yet which the Internal Revenue Service would accept as valid.

Short on cash but long on determination, the board of directors added several other resolutions to make the offer more enticing. In light of Emily's insistence that art be exhibited all the time, they resolved that the collection was to be utilized to its maximum, "keeping as many works on view as possible and making works that cannot be shown available for long-term loan to other institutions." They offered to renovate part of the museum, which would then be designated as the Tremaine Gallery, headed by a special curator of twentieth century art. They committed themselves to an expansion of the museum "in the not too distant future" to accommodate growth in the contemporary segment of the permanent collection. But the most unusual resolution was the seventh:

> Be it further resolved that subject to an agreement that the Tremaine Collection would come to the Wadsworth Atheneum under these or certain other conditions, the Trustees would also attempt in all good faith to enhance and complement the Tremaine Collection by the acquisition of Barnett Newman's series of canvases, the *Stations of the Cross,* presently the property of his widow.

According to Hedberg, this was proposed because Emily had indicated that if she did decide to bequeath her portion of the collection, she "didn't want it to be alone at the Wadsworth. So she introduced me to Mrs. Barnett Newman who was looking for a place for her husband's *Stations of the Cross.* Emily felt that if we could get Mrs. Newman to donate the *Stations* to Hartford, she would match them. She really felt that *The Moment II* was part of the *Stations,* and that *Outcry* was the ultimate." The idea was to make the Wadsworth a kind of pilgrimage point for Newman.[9]

None of these things came about. The Tremaines did not donate their collection. The *Stations of the Cross* went to the National Gallery. There would be no more supplications from museums. But the Wadsworth Atheneum did receive one very valuable gift. Following her death, the Tremaine family donated $1,000,000 to endow the position of Curator of Twentieth Century Art in Emily's honor.

From here on, the Tremaines became fixated on the collection's value—how to get the best price for each piece and how to lower their taxes. In essence, they wanted a dealer to peddle the paintings to various collectors in search of the highest offer. That was not the way prominent dealers worked, except for one — a new secondary dealer who had just arrived in New York City from Southern California trailing an uncertain past and mysterious financial backing. His name was Larry Gagosian, and the New York art world was instantly awash with rumors about him, none of them good, which Gagosian claimed were scurrilous. In his book *True Colors: The Real Life of the Art World,* Anthony Haden-Guest gives a description of how Gagosian and the Tremaines met.

> Gagosian opened up in 1985 in the street-level loading dock he had spotted in Sandro Chia's building on West Twenty-third Street. This location was off the art world's normal trade routes, but Gagosian quickly commanded attention with his first show, a tranche of the famous collection of Burton and Emily Tremaine. He had gotten hold of this through good ears and a lot of gall. "The Tremaines didn't like Leo," Jeffrey Deitch says. "Everybody likes Leo. But the Tremaines didn't." Castelli simply had not made the Tremaines feel sufficiently important. Gagosian said, "I got their number from Connecticut information. I offered a lot of money for a Brice Marden painting. Mrs. Tremaine liked me on the phone. She thought I was funny. Or maybe she liked the money I offered for the painting." [10]

The Tremaines had heard all the rumors about Gagosian and chose to discount them. In September 1984, when his gallery was still located in Los Angeles, they had purchased from him *Venus* by the "graffiti artist" Jean-Michel Basquiat.[11] Emily insisted that Gagosian was honorable and always dealt fairly with them, that if he said he could get a certain price for a piece, that is what he got. Gagosian also appealed to Burton's business sense as his focus was on money. He was fast, effective, and bottom-line oriented. However, Sam Green was convinced that the Tremaines picked him as their dealer at this point to tweak the art world. "I called this component of the Tremaines' life 'torturing the dealers,' and it was a sport that both of them enjoyed with great relish. That is why they chose Larry Gagosian, a person who couldn't have been more wounding to the art world."

Perhaps the biggest difference between Gagosian and the other resale dealers was his audacity. As was implied by his nickname "Go-Go," Gagosian went after what he wanted relentlessly, and when he got it he hyped it. He exemplified the hyperbolic American culture in the mid-1980s. His arrival on the New York art scene marked a sea-change in its way of doing business. He moved

Burton G. Tremaine, Sr. and Emily Hall Tremaine in the early 1980s.

resale out of the hushed back room and onto the raucous loading dock. The first painting he sold for the Tremaines was *Ideal Spot* by Robert Irwin in the fall of 1984. From then until Emily's death, he sold numerous works including *Spoon Woman* by Giacometti, *Strong Arm* by Oldenburg, *Departure of the Ghost* by Klee, and *Euclidean Abyss* by Newman.[12]

In spite of all these sales to different collectors and galleries, it was clear to the Tremaines that Gagosian was principally interested in their collection for one collector — S. I. Newhouse, the publishing magnate and multimillionaire who was trying to put together a collection of contemporary art that would surpass that of the Tremaines. In the mid-1980s, he had been a dinner guest, along with Gregory Hedberg and Jasper Johns, at the Tremaines' New York apartment, at which time he had shown intense interest in the collection. The Tremaines were not ready to sell in toto, but they were ready to part with some very valuable pieces for the right price, and Newhouse was able to meet that price. As a result, they sold him *Luis Miguel Dominquin* by Stella in the fall of 1984 for $1,350,000. This was followed in January of 1985 by Lichtenstein's *Aloha* for $1,000,000. Newhouse most wanted the center of the collection— the *Victory Boogie-Woogie*—which Emily was not about to part with while she was alive. Newhouse would have to wait—but not for long.

In May 1987, Emily fell in the living room in Madison and broke her hip. She was taken to Middlesex Hospital, where the doctors discovered that the break was a minor problem compared to the total devastation in her lungs. Put on a respirator, she stayed in Middlesex until midsummer, when she was transferred to Gaylord Hospital in Wallingford, the place where she had been treated successfully during the recurrence of tuberculosis in 1968. She rallied a little, but the damage could not be reversed. There was barely any healthy lung tissue left. Early in December she came home to Madison to die amidst the art works that had provided her more solace than anything else in her life. They were her friends, her family, her children, her high priests, her shamans.

A touchstone is a stone that indicates the purity of gold that is brought into contact with it. The *Victory Boogie-Woogie* was the touchstone of the Tremaine collection. Against it, every other work of art was assayed. If it was pure, it stayed; if it was impure, it was donated or sold. Emily believed that in the *Victory* Mondrian had "opened every window," but, cut short by death, he had not been able to go further. Paradoxically, the tragedy of its incompleteness, even its fragility, became a kind of blessing, goading others to seek beyond. "Mondrian felt that nothing is ever finished—always processing from the material to the spiritual, just as high as you are able to go with it," said Emily. "There is no beginning and no end." For forty-three years, after the *Victory's* purchase in 1944, Emily searched for the art beyond Mondrian's window. Repeatedly, she glimpsed the sublime out of the corner of her eye: it shimmered from Rothko's *Number 8,* emanated from Irwin's disk, whispered from Martin's *Desert.* Were glimpses enough? "If we cannot free ourselves, we can free our vision," Mondrian had said.

In her last week of life, Emily's step-grandson John brought his family to say good-bye. While the adults were upstairs, the children played outside. Hearing their voices, Emily asked John to open the blinds. Through the vertical frame of the window, beyond the grid formed by its panes, she watched the children running up the hill toward the sculpture that stood at the crest. As the sound of their laughter rose up and reached her, the light coming in through the window grew dim. On December 17, 1987, Emily Hall Tremaine died at the age of seventy-nine. On March 23, 1991, Burton Gad Tremaine, Sr., died at the age of eighty-nine.

THE AUCTIONS

There were two auctions: the first after Emily's death, the second after Burton's. Drama and intrigue swirled around both of them because the decision to sell at auction was controversial.

In the winter of 1988, shortly after Emily's passing, Burton Jr., accompanied his father to an important meeting in New York City with Larry Gagosian, about which he recalled, "Larry wanted permission to get Newhouse over to see *Outcry* by Barnett Newman and the *Victory*. Of course that was the one that Sr. was the most nervous about. It was the Crown Jewel because it had the greatest value. Larry said to Sr., 'I think I could get you $11,000,000 or $12,000,000 for the *Victory Boogie-Woogie*.' Sr. vacillated. What Larry really wanted to do was to negotiate a deal for the entire collection, bankrolled by Newhouse."

To get Burton Sr., away from Madison and New York for a while, Burton Jr., and his wife, Catherine, took him with them to Palm Springs where the warmth and change of scenery did him good. Still gregarious in temperament and distinguished in appearance, he enjoyed the camaraderie of family and friends during his last few years, but he was also a little lost without Emily on whom he had relied to jog his memory. "When he was alive, he would ask her questions, such as, 'Em, what's my favorite thing? Em, what's the name of that artist?' " explained Catherine. "Sometimes he would start a sentence and she would finish it."

While Burton Sr., was in California, negotiations continued with Gagosian. According to Burton Jr., "Almost immediately we sold *Outcry* to Newhouse for $1,000,000. And then along came an offer from Newhouse on the *Victory Boogie-Woogie* for $11,000,000. Back and forth, phone calls, terms, conditions. What about Perle Fine's two copies? Should they be included? And so we reached a decision to sell the *Victory Boogie-Woogie*. Under the terms of the deal, Newhouse got one of Fine's copies and we got the second, the one that was an interpretation. The understanding is that we get to keep it as long as we want it. If we ever want to get rid of it, he has the right of first refusal for a dollar."

That spring, the family hired Tracy Atkinson, who had recently retired from the Wadsworth Atheneum, to serve as the curator to catalog the collection. Beginning in 1979, when Burton and Emily had begun to reduce the size of the collection, paintings exceeding a market value of $12 million had been sold; however, what remained still was of prime quality. Atkinson divided the art into various categories, including those that were most likely to sell and those that the family wanted to keep. At his suggestion, Martha Baer, director of twentieth century fine art at Christie's, was hired to appraise the paintings. "Tracy made one of the greatest contributions to the family," said Burton Jr. "At a meeting in Madison, Tracy advised us to sell the contemporary paintings as soon as possible because he felt the market was peaking and there was a change coming. He thought that the earlier, prewar paintings would hold their value better than the contemporary paintings."

Shortly thereafter, Burton Jr., received a telephone call from Christopher Burge, president of Christie's, who asked for the opportunity to make a proposition to sell the contemporary paintings. At a subsequent meeting in Meriden, Burge, Baer, and Steven Lash, a member of Christie's estates and appraisals department, met with several members of the Tremaine family, including Burton Sr. "They argued for an auction, rather than private sale," said Burton, Jr. "They talked about the volatile market that was going up. They talked about recent sales." The dilemma was that, just prior to this meeting, Gagosian had made an astounding offer for the contemporary works on Newhouse's behalf. The Tremaines had to decide to close the deal with Gagosian or take the financial risk of going to auction. Burge's argument in favor of auction was that the art market was still very strong. The stock market had crashed the year before, but instead of the art market falling off, it had continued to surge as savvy investors turned to art.

Despite the fact that Christie's did not offer a guarantee, a practice that would later become standard, the family decided to take the risk. "They were very persuasive," said Burton Jr. "So it fell to me to break the news to Gagosian that Christie's was going to handle the sale. He couldn't believe it. He thought he had the inside track on the collection. He had made us an incredible offer, just incredible. We were on the verge of concluding the deal with him when Christie's came along."

The timing of the first sale was perfect, occurring at the peak of a strong speculative surge. On the evening of November 9, 1988, records for the art of fifteen artists were set on the thirty-two items that were sold. "While the group of paintings was of impeccable quality by major 20th century artists, the sale was a greater success than we dared to imagine," said Christopher Burge.[1] The total reached $25,824,000, a worldwide record for an auction of contemporary art. Among individual record prices were $7.04 million for Johns's *White Flag*, $5.72 million for Pollock's *Frieze* (a record both for that artist and for any Abstract Expressionist painting), $2.75 million for Rothko's *Number 8*, $2.31 million for Kline's *Lehigh*, and $2.09 million for Lichtenstein's *I Can See the Whole Room*. The gamble the Tremaines had taken in going to auction instead of accepting Newhouse's offer had paid off.

Martha Baer was astounded by the figures. "Looking back a decade to when we were creating a contemporary art department in New York, we would never have even contemplated the possibility of handling such a great sale. De Kooning's *Yellow Woman*, which sold tonight for $715,000, brought in more money than the $562,000 my first sale brought in 1978."[2]

The rest of the art world was not impressed by the auction and the sales figures. As Anthony Haden-Guest described the evening, after Christopher Burge had auctioned off the first piece, *Frieze*, he brought out *White Flag*:

Burge opened the bidding at $3 million. It rose to $6.4-$7 million, with commissions factored in—but stuck there, as if in mud. The clapping was muted. An Arshile Gorky soared to $3.2 million, a salesroom record for this artist. The seller had set an even higher estimate, though, and there was an odd whooshing sound, an exhalation of surprise, when the work was withdrawn. A Lichtenstein went for $1.9 million, $700,000 above its high estimate, and a Rauschenberg went for a fat sum, but elicited only a single clap. "Thank you," Burge told the zealot. A Tom Wesselmann reached $420,000, a record for that second-string Pop artist, but the crowd was quiet as they left the auction house, and the air of disappointment was strong enough to be bottled. "It did not seem to be a very lively sale," Castelli observed on his way out of the auction house. The prices had been high, but the expectations had been higher. The $10 million contemporary-art painting still shimmered unreachable overhead, like a grail or a chimera.[3]

The following evening, Sotheby's offered twelve paintings from the collection of Sally and Victor Ganz, among them Johns's *False Start.* Gagosian sat in the audience. So did Newhouse. Both Hans Thulin, the Swedish real estate investor who had purchased *White Flag* the night before, and Charles Saatchi, a New York businessman and contemporary art collector, were ready to bid by phone. The bidding for *False Start* began at $3 million and headed up steadily, soon surpassing $10 million. At that point Saatchi dropped out and a duel began between Thulin and Newhouse. Thulin conceded at $17,000,000. Newhouse had won. Some of the records set at the Tremaine auction had lasted barely twenty-four hours. Was *False Start* worth $10 million more than *White Flag*? The figures had nothing to do with value and everything to do with bidding fever. The headline on the front page of the *Wall Street Journal* on November 28, 1988, said it all: "Manic Market: Prices of Hottest Art Reach Stunning Levels as Boom Keeps Going; Some Still Say It Has to End, but Smart-Money Crowd Is Paying Little Attention."

The Tremaines themselves had another explanation for why *White Flag* had sold for so much less than *False Start.* It had nothing to do with either quality or buying frenzy; it had to do with getting even. "Larry Gagosian was very angry at us for turning down the offer Newhouse had made and for accepting Christie's instead. He was just steamed, so I think that he advised Newhouse not to buy *White Flag.* Then at the Ganz sale, he advised him to bid on *False Start.* It was Larry's way of getting back at us a little," explained Burton Jr.

Whereas the timing of the first auction had been perfect, the timing of the second was terrible. By November 1991 the art market had peaked. In contrast to the frenzy of 1988, the mood was very somber. The Japanese collectors who had helped to fuel the spectacular rise in prices in the late 1980s had fled the market, due in part to the ongoing recession. Even collectors who had the capacity to buy were being cagey because they expected the prices of art to fall further. Although the spring auctions had been disastrous, Christie's was hopeful that the market had begun to stabilize and that the eighteen works in the Tremaine collection were of such stellar quality that they would bring reluctant bidders out of hiding.

Sotheby's had never approached the Tremaine family about selling their paintings after Emily's death. However, the art remaining in the collection in 1991 was so fine that they decided to challenge Christie's. "When the second sale came around and Sotheby's expressed an interest, I asked John Marion, Sotheby's president, why they hadn't made a proposition on the first sale," said Burton Jr. "He said, 'Well, we thought it was a Gagosian done-deal.'" Sotheby's offered a guarantee on the sale, but so did Christie's. "We chose Christie's again because their guarantee was much higher than Sotheby's and we had been pleased with how they had handled the first auction," explained Burton Jr.

The works were to be auctioned in two separate groups on three evenings. On November 5, the paintings of the pre-World War II period were to be put on the block, including those paintings by Mondrian, Braque, Gris, Delaunay, Klee, Schwitters, Tauber-Arp, van Doesburg, and Le Corbusier. On November 12 and 13 the contemporary works were to be offered, including those by Miró, Léger, Calder, de Kooning and Johns.

During the first evening, Christie's withdrew some paintings from the auction when the bids were too low. These included Mondrian's *Composition* (valued by Christie's at $4 to $6 million) and Miro's *Le Chat Blanc,* also called *Tête* (valued at $1.5 to $2.5 million). Léger's *Le Petit Déjeuner* had been valued at $8 to $12 million but went for $7 million. Only *Premier Disque* by Delaunay went for more than its estimated value, selling for $4,700,000. The total for the entire auction was $25,145,000. Because of the guarantee, the Tremaine family did very well, despite what was from Christie's standpoint a disappointing auction. The unsold paintings became Christie's property.

Tracy Atkinson had considered being the curator of such an extraordinary collection a rare privilege, but, when the gavel fell for the final time, he felt a tinge of sadness. Prior to the auction, he had written for Christie's catalog what amounted to a benediction for the paintings:

> They formed a wonderful ensemble which will not be seen again, but that is in the nature of things and indeed it has been very much in the nature of this collection which has waxed and waned in both size and scope over the years as new developments came along in the art world, and as the [Tremaines] "traded up" towards that extraordinary standard of quality which they set for themselves from the very first . . . Now their collection, so carefully and devotedly assembled over so many decades, enters its final transformation—it goes out into the world to new owners to continue the stream of life of the individual works in ever new ways. The Tremaines expected that the collection would thus add to the richness of the world's cultural life rather than remaining a static monument fixed in time and space.

The Board of Directors of the Emily Hall Tremaine Foundation (l. to r.): Burton G. Tremaine III, Sarah C. Tremaine, Arthur J. Bulger, Jr., Sally Bowles, president of the foundation, Atwood Collins, III, Burton G. Tremaine, Jr., John M. Tremaine, Dee Tremaine Hildt, Janet Tremaine Stanley, and Kenneth Bryant Wick, Jr.

Prior to her death, Emily had established a charitable foundation. Members of the Tremaine family were to serve on its board of directors and to determine its focus areas. Besides resolving the issue of inheritance taxes, the foundation provided Emily with the satisfaction of knowing that the sale of her share of the collection would yield a great philanthropic benefit. Following her death, the board of directors decided that the foundation should seek to reflect in its grant-making philosophy Emily's distinctive foresight, imagination, and willingness to take risks. They chose to focus on learning disabilities, the environment, and the arts. Due to the huge success of the auctions, the Emily Hall Tremaine Foundation found itself in a far more favorable financial position to make an impact in these areas than Emily had anticipated.

Thanks in part to the guarantee provision of the second auction, the two auctions totaled more than $60 million. Sales of art from 1979 to 1987 had topped $12 million. The sale of the *Victory Boogie-Woogie* and *Outcry* totaled yet another $12,000,000. The art that had cost Emily and Burton approximately $500,000 to acquire had sold for more than $84 million. "My father could not get over just how much the art had escalated in value. He always said that the art collection was a better investment than all his oil deals, drilling, manufacturing, everything," explained Burton Jr. "But the greatest escalation was in the last ten years of their lives. If Emily and Burton had died in 1980, what would the collection have brought? $20 million? So it's a fantastic story, and it all began with Emily's purchase of *The Black Rose*."

NOTES

PROLOGUE: EYES LIKE GIMLETS

Unnumbered quote, Giedion-Welcker, *Constantin Brancusi*, 220.

1. Lecture at the opening of the *Tremaine Collection: Twentieth Century Masters, the Spirit of Modernism*, Wadsworth Atheneum, 25 February 1984. The Wadsworth Atheneum Archives (WAA), the Emily Hall Tremaine Foundation Archives (EHTF).

2. *Tremaine Collection*, 14.

3. All quotes from Emily Hall Tremaine, unless indicated otherwise, are from an interview conducted by Paul Cummings for the Oral History Program, Archives of American Art (AAA), Smithsonian Institution, 1973. There are two versions of this interview, the original and the edited version that appeared in the *Tremaine Collection*.

4. According to Rosenblum, the name *Premier Disque* was misspelled as *Premiere Disque* in the *Tremaine Collection*. Recent scholarship on the painting has resulted in a date change from 1912 to 1913–14. *Tremaine Collection*, 10–11.

5. Baro, "Decisive Art Collection," *Vogue*, 15 February 1969, 135.

6. Quoted in Hoffmann, "Emily Tremaine and Friends," *The Hartford Courant Northeast Magazine*, 6 November 1988, 13.

7. Cited in Lipsey, *An Art of Our Own*, 88.

8. Interview, 1997, EHTF Archives.

CHAPTER 1: BUTTE

Unnumbered quote, Pruitt, *Tender Darkness*, 16.

1. Howard, *Montana*.

2. Horace was forced to return to Illinois after a severe bout of "fever." He enrolled

in Northwestern University College of Medicine in Chicago and became a doctor, eventually joining his brother to practice in Butte. Hall, "Horace M. Hall's Letters from Gillespie County, Texas, 1871–1873, offprint from *The Southwestern Historical Quarterly,* 621:3 (1959).

3. *History of Montana.*

4. *Butte Blue Book of 1901.*

5. By the late 1890s Clark decided to buy himself a seat in the U.S. Senate, build a mansion on Fifth Avenue, and gain admittance into New York City's illustrious "400." He easily achieved the first two goals (although he initially was denied his seat in the Senate because it was discovered that he had paid Montana state legislators for their votes), but he never gained entry into high society. See Glasscock, *War of the Copper Kings.*

6. EHTF Archives.

7. The Smiths had six children: Charles, Stephen, Beauchamp, Sarah Purdon, Susan, and Mary.

8. Born in North Carolina on February 1, 1839, to a family of Methodist ministers and farmers, Stephen chose to become a minister in the Moravian church, of which his mother was a member. The only denominational college and seminary was in Bethlehem, Pennsylvania. He graduated from the school in 1861 and became pastor of the First Moravian Church in York, Pennsylvania. He married Emma Rebecca Fahs on April 9, 1862. Unpublished biography, EHTF Archives. See also "S. Morgan Smith Dead at Los Angeles," *New York Dispatch,* 13 April 1903.

9. *Butte Miner,* 23 March 1905, Butte-Silver Bow Archives.

10. Although there are birth certificates for both twins, only Adeline's birth was mentioned in the newspaper.

11. Butte-Silver Bow Archives.

12. Because there are no ministers in Christian Science, it is customary for Scientists to turn to other denominations for the performance of rituals. Emily's wedding ceremony and funeral were held in Episcopal churches, while Jane's funeral was held in a Presbyterian church.

13. Pruitt, *Tender Darkness,* 18.

14. In a disagreement that presaged Emily's battles with museums late in her life, Clark announced his intention to leave his collection, worth $4 to $5 million in 1925, to the Metropolitan Museum of Art if they would promise to display all the paintings all of the time, but the Metropolitan declined. Instead, most of the paintings went to the Corcoran Gallery, Washington, D.C., which, with an additional gift of $700,000 from the Clark family, built a wing for the collection.

15. EHTF Archives.

16. Baro, "Decisive Art Collection," 150.

17. Among the letters that Emily kept from her childhood were two postcards from the Uffizi Gallery in Florence of works of art by Botticelli. On one she had written her name very neatly, as if it were the signature of the artist himself. EHTF Archives.

18. EHTF Archives.
19. Myrick, *Montecito and Santa Barbara,* 358–361.
20. EHTF Archives.
21. Undated newspaper clipping. EHTF Archives.

CHAPTER 2: THE GERMAN BARON

Unnumbered quote, Lindbergh, *The Spirit of St. Louis,* 403.

1. Von Romberg genealogy, EHTF Archives. Antoinette Converse's father was one of the founders of the Bankers Trust Company.
2. The city was never in danger because trench warfare froze the front line of battle in place. It would not waiver more than thirty miles from 1914 until 1918.
3. EHTF Archives.
4. *New York Times,* 15 April 1928.
5. *Santa Barbara Morning Press,* 17 June 1928.
6. Ibid., 24 July 1928.
7. Lindbergh, *The Spirit of St. Louis,* 262.
8. *Santa Barbara Morning Press,* 14 September 1928.
9. Undated clipping, EHTF Archives.
10. Undated clipping, EHTF Archives.
11. All quotes from members of the Tremaine family are from interviews conducted by Sam Green, 1996, EHTF Archives.
12. Undated clipping, EHTF Archives.
13. *Los Angeles Examiner,* 20 March 1935.
14. "Love Trumps Jinx Card of Death!" *Santa Barbara Morning Press,* undated clipping, EHTF Archives.
15. Five issues of *Apéritif* are in the archives of the Santa Barbara Historical Society. One issue is in the EHTF Archives.
16. *San Francisco Chronicle,* 1 March 1936.
17. Ibid.
18. *Sunday Mirror,* 1 March 1936.
19. *Santa Barbara Morning Press,* 29 August 1936.
20. Ibid., 26 January 1937.
21. *Los Angeles Times,* 8 March 1939.
22. Ibid.
23. A subsequent owner said that the central tower was heavily wired. He likened the wine cellar to a holding room with escape routes and bars on the windows.
24. Because Riggs also functioned as general contractor, she kept lists of the firms and contractors. German and Northern European names predominate, lending credence to the rumor. Names include Shugart, Frankl, Hess, Hamlin, Dannenfelzer, and Haberlitz. Architectural Drawings Collection, the University of California at Santa Barbara.

25. The wedding was of the Countess Eleanora Colloredo-Mannsfeld and F.W. von Meister, a German official on the Graf Zeppelin II.
26. The *New York Times*, 5 June 1938.

CHAPTER 3: THE DARK YEARS

Unnumbered quote, Lipsey, *An Art of Our Own*, 44.
1. "In Santa Barbara," undated clipping, EHTF Archives.
2. "Sugar Heir Weds Fourth Wife in Reno," undated clipping, EHTF Archives.
3. "All His Sugar Millions Couldn't Sweeten That Swastika," undated newspaper clipping. Printed at the bottom is "Copyright 1940, American Weekly, Inc." EHTF Archives.
4. *New York Times* 28 December 1933, 22 February 1936, 14 March 1936, 4 April 1936, August 1936, 18 November 1938. There is also an article dated 11 April 1934 about Sibyl Esme Spreckels winning a final decree of divorce from Adolph B. Spreckels. If this is the same Adolph B. Spreckels, he must have been married to two women at the same time. However, the Spreckels family was very large, and newspaper reporters sometimes made errors.
5. *New York Times*, 15 June 1936: 1.
6. Spreckels had tried to destroy the evidence by throwing the marijuana into the ocean. *New York Times*, 11 January 1933: 15.
7. Clipping dated 27 January 1939, no publication name, EHTF Archives.
8. *Los Angeles Examiner*, 13 November 1940.
9. *New York Times*, 7 September 1940.
10. Undated clipping, EHTF Archives.
11. *New York Times*, 7 September 1940.
12. According to one source, the German flag flew outside of Brunninghausen until December 7, 1941.
13. Rubinstein, *American Women Artists*, 241.
14. *Santa Barbara Morning Press*, n.d. EHTF Archives.
15. *New York Times*, 1 April 1945.
16. *New York Times*, 27 December 1941.
17. The idea of wearing a mink coat to conceal an outrageous outfit occurs in a story that Emily told John Tremaine. "Once she went to a costume party that had the theme *Neptune of the Sea*. She wore a flesh-toned bathing suit over which she wrapped fishnet to which she attached live lobsters. Then she put her mink coat on to hide what she was wearing until the right moment of unveiling. Just before she left for the party, a man from the Internal Revenue Service came to the door to audit her personal income tax. He was so startled by her attire, he left and never came back."
18. Burton G. Tremaine founded the Fostoria Incandescent Lamp Company in Ohio. Then, with Franklin S. Terry, his business partner, he formed a holding company, the National Electric Lamp Association, which other lamp manufac-

turers joined in order to compete successfully against General Electric. However, Tremaine and Terry failed to disclose that their investment capital was supplied by General Electric. In 1910, Terry and Tremaine built an industrial complex, named NELA Park, near Cleveland. In the book *The Miller Company: The First 150 Years*, Marguerite T. Scheips relates what happened next: "In 1911 just as the planning for NELA Park was getting under way, the bubble of secrecy regarding the tie between the National Electric Lamp Association and GE burst. The federal government filed an anti-trust suit against the 35-member Association of Licensed Manufacturers of Incandescent Lamps, in which both NELA and GE were members. It forced the disclosure of the relationship between the two, and ruled that GE could do business in the future only in its own name. So GE exercised its option to purchase the remaining 25% share of NELA's common stock, dissolved it as a separate entity, and made it a division of GE with the name National Quality Lamp Division of GE. Terry and Tremaine became the division's officers."

19. EHTF Archives.

CHAPTER 4: THE GENESIS OF THE COLLECTION

Unnumbered quote, Lipsey, *An Art of Our Own*, 59.

1. Austin's uncle was Carey Etnier who was married to Emily's aunt Susan Smith Etnier. For an in-depth discussion of Austin and his influence, see Weber, *Patron Saints*.

2. A. Everett Austin, Jr., *A Director's Taste and Achievement*, 43.

3. EHT, interview with Fondlier, undated, WAA.

4. *Tremaine Collection*, 25–26.

5. Saarinen, *Proud Possessors*, 346.

6. Fondlier interview, WAA.

7. November 19, 1937, EHTF Archives.

8. The portrait was exhibited at the Chicago Art Club and the Grand Central Galleries in New York City in 1938. *Town & Country* printed it in November 1938.

9. Goodrich, *Yasuo Kuniyoshi*, 26. Receipt for *Picking Horses*, EHTF Archives.

10. Emily did not purchase the Derain painting. EHTF Archives.

11. See "Etnier: Remoter Realism," *Art News*, undated article in EHTF Archives.

12. EHTF Archives.

13. From an interview with a friend of Emily's, Pat Patterson, 1996. EHTF Archives.

14. EHT, "A New York Collector Selects," EHTF Archives.

15. Quoted in Geldzahler, *American Painting in the Twentieth Century*, 183.

16. *Tremaine Collection*, 27.

17. Hitchcock, *Painting Toward Architecture*, 82.

18. This painting came to be known as *New York–New York City*.

19. The exhibition also included Léger's *Les Plongeurs Circulaires*, which Emily purchased in 1945.

20. Seuphor, *Piet Mondrian,* 178.
21. Blotkamp, *Mondrian,* 240.
22. Interview with James Elliott, former director of the Wadsworth Atheneum, 1996, EHTF Archives.
23. In the *Tremaine Collection,* the purchase date is listed as 1942, but there is a receipt dated November 20, 1944 from the Valentine Gallery, EHTF Archives.
24. Lipsey, *An Art of Our Own,* 3.
25. Eddy, *Science and Health,* 284.
26. Lipsey, *An Art of Our Own,* 47, 87.

CHAPTER 5: THE VICTORY BOOGIE-WOOGIE

Unnumbered quote, Lipsey, *An Art of Our Own,* 69.
1. Rembert, *Mondrian,* 307. Rembert conducted two interviews with Emily in 1967 for her doctoral thesis. In her monograph, she writes that the only bad advice Chick Austin ever gave Emily was "not to meet the artist whose work she was collecting, so she would not be influenced by subjective feelings. Mrs. Tremaine regrets this because, as a result of it, she did not meet Mondrian, although she was very much aware of his presence in New York."
2. Von Wiegand, EHTF Archives.
3. Von Wiegand, "Mondrian's Latest Picture," 10 December 1942. Unpublished manuscript, EHTF Archives.
4. Sidney Janis interview by Rembert, quoted in *Mondrian,* 103.
5. Cited in Rembert, *Mondrian,* 139, 146.
6. Ibid.
7. Bradley, "Piet Mondrian, 1872–1944: Greatest Dutch Painter of Our Time," *Knickerbocker Weekly,* 14 February 1944: 16–23. *Knickerbocker Weekly* was published by the Dutch community in exile during World War II. Because this is the last interview with Mondrian, it is very important to understanding his late works. EHTF Archives.
8. According to Michel Seuphor in an interview conducted by Christiane Germain and Paul Haim, Emily hired a detective to find out Dudensing's tastes. She learned that his dream was to spend his last years in a small chateau in the Dordogne in France. So she found one and exchanged it for *Victory Boogie-Woogie.* Although it may be true that she hired a detective, she paid for the painting outright.
9. Rembert, *Mondrian,* 110–11, 308.
10. Ibid.
11. Letter to Naysmith, the Miller Company, dated 22 May 1945, EHTF Archives.
12. Letter, EHTF Archives.
13. Ibid.
14. Perle Fine was president of the Association of American Abstractionists.
15. Letter, EHTF Archives.

16. Ibid.
17. All the charts and the annotated notes are in the EHTF Archives.
18. Willy Kock completed an interpretation for the Stedelijk Museum in Amsterdam in 1946. EHTF Archives.
19. Rembert, *Mondrian,* 309.
20. Fine to EHT, EHTF Archives.
21. Rembert, *Mondrian,* 309.
22. Ibid.
23. Ibid.
24. Letter, EHTF Archives.
25. In a letter dated May 3, 1949, Caroline Keck wrote to Emily: "We fitted back all the loose pieces thanks to the very excellent copy. Did you know that at some point two additional pieces of black tape have been added? We spotted them first because the tape was so different from the rest and the wrong color, then we checked with the copy and they're not on it. Do you wish them removed? Also one strip which must have come off before the plexiglass protection was incorrectly replaced and we have changed it to the correct spot." EHTF Archives.
26. *Tremaine Collection,* 33. At the time they purchased the painting, it was called *Rhythm Circulaire.* See Seuphor to Emily, EHTF Archives.
27. Mary Ann Tighe, "Art at its Best," *House and Garden,* April, 1984, 204.
28. Rembert, *Mondrian,* 307. The Tremaines purchased *Composition 1863* by Davis.
29. Hoffmann, "Emily Tremaine and Friends," *The Hartford Courant Northeast Magazine,* 6 November 1988, 14.
30. Rembert, *Mondrian,* 85.
31. Ibid.
32. Ibid., 310.

CHAPTER 6: PAINTING TOWARD ARCHITECTURE

Unnumbered quote, Hitchcock, *Painting Toward Architecture,* 8.
1. Naylor, *Contemporary Artists,* 940.
2. *Art Digest,* 1 February 1948.
3. *Tremaine Collection,* 9.
4. In a letter to Hitchcock, January 23, 1948, Barr wrote that the collection "is weak in the Russians, too bad they couldn't get a Lissitzky anyway." The next year Emily took Barr's advice and purchased the series of lithographs titled *Victory Over the Sun.* In the *Tremaine Collection,* the purchase date is listed as 1944, but there is a receipt dated March 23, 1949 in the EHTF Archives. Barr papers, MoMA, available through AAA.
5. Louchheim, "Abstraction on the Assembly Line," 52.
6. Philip Johnson to Louise Johnson, 20 June 1930, as quoted in Schulze, *Philip Johnson,* 61.
7. *Art News,* 52.

8. Ibid., 25.

9. *Painting Toward Architecture*, 18.

10. Scully wrote to Barr on 16 June 1947 to ask his opinion about *Drawing 1916* and *Woman With a Fan*. Barr wrote back that he considered *Woman With a Fan* to be "bastard in style, a mixture of flat 'synthetic' areas with the stratified semi-impressionist hatching of the earlier areas, and altogether quite unpleasant." Barr Papers, MoMA.

11. "Art for Architecture's Sake," *Interiors*, February 1949, 3.

12. "Painting Toward Architecture," *Arts & Architecture*, June 1948, 24.

13. The correspondence between the Tremaines and Albers is in the archives of the Albers Foundation, Orange, Connecticut, and is reprinted with permission.

14. Louchheim, "Abstraction on the Assembly Line," 25.

15. Brach, "Toward Autonomy," 196–201.

16. David Gebhard traces the influence for the Riggs design to Wright's second Herbert Jacobs House in Middletown, Wisconsin. *Lutah Maria Riggs*, 31–32.

17. Weber, *Patron Saints*, 63.

18. Marks, *Dymaxion World*, 36–37. The letters from Emily to Fuller are in the archives of the Buckminster Fuller Institute, Santa Barbara, California, and are reprinted with permission.

19. "Produced Site Unseen," 98.

20. Gebhard, *Lutah Maria Riggs*, 31.

21. "Produced Site Unseen," 96.

22. *Art News*, 28.

23. The correspondence between Wright and the Tremaines is in the archives of the Frank Lloyd Wright Foundation, Taliesin West, Scottsdale, Arizona. It is used with permission.

24. *Painting Toward Architecture*, 42.

25. Schulze, *Philip Johnson*, 201.

26. Ibid., 222.

27. Smith, *A Tale of Two Families*, 121–123.

28. Interview, 1996, EHTF Archives.

29. Lecture by Johnson on 25 February 1984 on the opening of the Tremaine exhibition, WAA.

30. Tighe, "Art at its Best," 206.

31. Baro, "Decisive Art Collection," 150.

CHAPTER 7: IMPERFECTIONS OF THE HEART

Unnumbered quote, Eddy, *Science and Health*, 236.

1. Interview with Johns, 1997, EHTF Archives.

2. Interview with Patterson, 1996, EHTF Archives.

3. Interview with Gund, 1996, EHTF Archives.

4. Eddy, *Science and Health*, 61–62.

5. Interview with Glimcher, 1996, EHTF Archives.

CHAPTER 8: THE ABSTRACT EXPRESSIONISTS

Unnumbered quote, O'Neill, *Barnett Newman*, 173.

1. Interview with Leo Castelli by Paul Cummings, 14 May 1969, AAA, 72.

2. Louchheim, "Abstraction on the Assembly Line," 28.

3. Introduction to the Christie's auction catalog "Important Modern Paintings from the Tremaine Collection."

4. The term color field came to be applied to a different group of painters, which included Morris Louis, Kenneth Noland and Jules Olitski.

5. See Gruen, *Artist Observed*, 267.

6. *Tremaine Collection*, 12–13.

7. Interview, 1996, EHTF Archives.

8. Letter, EHTF Archives.

9. Tighe, "Art at its Best," 206.

10. According to Thomas B. Hess, *Tremaine Collection*, 18.

11. O'Neill, *Barnett Newman*, 255.

12. Telephone interview, 1996, EHTF archives.

13. Although in the *Tremaine Collection*, both *Outcry* and *The Moment II* are listed as having been acquired from Mrs. Newman, there is a note in the EHTF Archives indicating that instead of purchasing *The Moment II* outright, the Tremaines traded Jasper Johns's *Tango* for it through the dealer Harold Diamond, an even exchange valued at approximately $300,000.

14. Ferrier, *Art of Our Century*, 477.

15. For an analysis of the effect of the *Life* article on Pollock's career, see Naifeh and Smith, *Jackson Pollock*.

16. Interview, 1996, EHTF Archives. Naifeh and Smith state in their biography of Pollock that *Number 6* (1949) is one of the paintings in which Pollock had begun to explore "new directions, escape routes from what was often, even then, an exercise in composition and color. Rough biomorphic shapes, brushwork, and texture reappeared. But the *Life* article and the success that followed had cut off escape. Instead of moving on, he was drawn back into an easy style that increasingly threatened to turn into a rote exercise."

17. Naifeh, 607. A manuscript in which the sketchbook is discussed is in the EHTF Archives.

18. Lipsey, *An Art of Our Own*, 303.

19. Interview, 1996, EHTF Archives.

20. Lipsey, *An Art of Our Own*, 312.

21. On December 17, 1974, the Tremaines traded *Maroon and Blue* and a painting by Duchamp for works by Dorothea Rockburne, Dan Flavin, Carl Andre, Robert

Ryman, Jasper Johns (a flag print), Paul Mogenson, Agnes Martin, Robert Mangold, Michael Heizer, and Guy Dill. The transaction was worth over $100,000. In the *Tremaine Collection,* these works are listed as acquired from Sam Green.

22. Naylor, *Contemporary Artists,* 33.

23. EHTF Archives.

24. Ibid.

25. EHT, "A New York Collector Selects," 21 January 1965, EHTF Archives.

26. Ibid. It is not clear to which paintings Emily was referring. The first purchase of *Water Lilies* by MoMA was in April 1955, from Michael Monet, the artist's son. Funds for its purchase had come from Mrs. Simon Guggenheim. Barr saw others for sale in 1956 but had not purchased them. Tragically, the painting purchased in 1955 was destroyed in a fire at the museum on April 15, 1958. The following summer the museum purchased through art dealer Katia Granoff the triptych and the single-panel *Water Lilies.* Roob, "Fire and Water Lilies," 24–25.

27. *The International Council,* 19. Emily served as co-chair with Gund of the Australia/Asia Subcommittee.

28. EHTF Archives.

29. EHT, "A New York Collector Selects," EHTF Archives.

30. Interview, 1997, EHTF Archives.

31. Interview, 1997, EHTF Archives.

32. Naylor, *Contemporary Artists,* 462.

33. Interview, 1997, EHTF Archives.

34. EHT, "A New York Collector Selects," EHTF Archives.

CHAPTER 9: THE POP DECADE

Unnumbered quote, Warhol and Hackett, *POPism,* 16.

1. EHT, "A New York Collector Selects," EHTF Archives.

2. Quoted in the exhibition catalog for *The New Art,* 3. This exhibition was presented at Wesleyan University in 1964. The curator was Sam Green, who borrowed works by Lichtenstein, Warhol, Rosenquist, and Wesselmann from the Tremaines.

3. Ibid., 4.

4. Ibid.

5. Bonaffé as quoted by Rheims, *The Strange Life of Objects,* 7.

6. Interview with EHT by Fondlier, 4.

7. AAA, 21. Fondlier, 4.

8. Ibid., 4.

9. Hoffmann, "Emily Tremaine and Friends," 15.

10. Ibid., 14–15.

11. Fondlier, 1.

12. Emily told this to both Cummings and Fondlier, then edited it for inclusion in the *Tremaine Collection.*

13. Bourdon, *Warhol,* 126.
14. One of the more peculiar paintings by Dine that the Tremaines acquired was *An Animal* (1962), in which fur was attached to the canvas. It was sold to the National Gallery, Canberra, Australia.
15. Undated article with no byline or source in the EHTF Archives.
16. Hoffmann, "Emily Tremaine and Friends," 13.
17. Interview, 1996, EHTF Archives.
18. Green's parents were professors at Wesleyan University. In 1953, the Tremaines lent Calder's *Bougainvillea,* Marin's *A Street Seeing,* and Tobey's *Pattern of Conflict* for an exhibition at the Davison Art Center at Wesleyan.
19. Bockris, *Warhol,* 155.
20. EHT, "A New York Collector Selects," EHTF Archives.
21. Ibid.
22. Hoffmann, "Emily Tremaine and Friends," 13.
23. Tighe, "Art at its Best," 207.
24. Scott, "Artful Living," 28. The Tremaine family eventually returned the war god to the Zuni tribe.
25. Interview, 1996, EHTF Archives.

CHAPTER 10: DISEASE AND DISENCHANTMENT

Unnumbered quote, Rheims, *The Strange Life of Objects,* 7.
1. Christian Science Publishing Society, *Christian Science,* 221.
2. Eddy, *Science and Health,* 425.
3. Interview, 1996, EHTF Archives.
4. *Tremaine Collection,* 137.
5. Tighe, "Art at its Best," 206–207.
6. Scott, "Artful Living," 24.
7. Some earth works had to be viewed from an airplane to be appreciated. In this category was Michael Heizer's *Double Negative* completed in 1969, a 1,500 foot-long groove cut into a mesa in the Nevada desert.
8. In 1957 the Bar T Bar Ranch Company had created a separate corporation called Meteor Crater Enterprises, Inc., to which de Maria refers in his letter. Virginia Dwan became the owner of the *Lightning Field* concept. Later it was given to the DIA Arts Foundation and was constructed in New Mexico. EHTF Archives.
9. Smith, *A Tale of Two Families,* 128–129.
10. Interview, 1996, EHTF Archives.
11. Interview, 1995, EHTF Archives.
12. Hoffmann, "Emily Tremaine and Friends," 15.
13. Tighe, "Art at its Best," 207.
14. Geldzahler, "American Painting," 354.
15. Haden-Guest, *True Colors,* 10.
16. *Tremaine Collection,* 22.

17. Interview, 1996, EHTF Archives.
18. There may also have been friction over the fact that word had been leaked to the press that the National Gallery was negotiating for the entire Tremaine collection. An article appeared in the *Washington Post* on 1 September 1971.
19. Interview, 1996, EHTF Archives.
20. Ibid.
21. Norman, "Risk and Recession," 33.
22. Interview, 1996, EHTF Archives.

CHAPTER 11: THROUGH MONDRIAN'S WINDOW

Unnumbered quote, Lipsey, *An Art of Our Own*, 88.
1. All quotes from Glimcher are from the interview, 1996, EHTF Archives.
2. All quotes from Armstrong are from the interview, 1996, EHTF Archives.
3. Interview with Atkinson, 1996, EHTF Archives.
4. Interview with Johns, 1997, EHTF Archives.
5. Copy in EHTF Archives.
6. Emily's remarks are from her speech at the opening night dinner of the exhibition, EHTF Archives.
7. Letter from Weber to Tremaines, EHTF Archives.
8. Copy of resolution in EHTF Archives.
9. Interview, 1996, EHTF Archives.
10. Haden-Guest, *True Colors*, 169.
11. The invoice for *Venus* is dated 27 September 1984. The price paid was $22,000. EHTF Archives.
12. Other works sold by Gagosian were *Element I* by Marden, *Kinetic Seascape* and *Ceramic Head with Blue Shadows* by Lichtenstein, *Aluminum-Magnesium Plain* by Andre, *Julie* by Poons, *On a Clear Day, Untitled #6* and *Desert* by Martin, *Geometric Torn Paper* and *Human Lunar Spectral* by Arp, *Four Squares Within a Circle* by Mangold, *Pattern of Conflict* by Tobey, *A Beautiful Day* by Ernst, *Children at Play* by Tuttle, *La Femme au Chapeau* by Picasso, *Untitled* by Stankiewicz, *Splitting the Ergo* by Matta, *Windward* by Rauschenberg, *Parcours* by Dubuffet, *Farbgitter* by Moholy-Nagy, and *Crescent Wrench* by Jim Dine.

EPILOGUE: THE AUCTIONS

1. Press release from Christie's, 9 November 1988, 1.
2. Ibid., 3.
3. Haden-Guest is mistaken in his statement that the 1988 auction took place following the deaths of both Burton and Emily and, therefore, included the entire collection. *True Colors*, 173.

SELECTED BIBLIOGRAPHY

BOOKS

"Art Collection of the Late United States Senator William A. Clark," Sales
    catalog, Mr. O. Bernet and Mr. H.H. Parke. In the private collection of Erin
    Sigl, Butte, Montana.
Berman, Avis. *Rebels on Eighth Street: Juliana Force and the Whitney Museum of
    American Art.* New York: Atheneum, 1990.
Blotkamp, Carel. *Mondrian.* New York: Harry N. Abrams, 1994.
Bockris, Victor. *Warhol.* London: Frederick Muller, 1989.
Bourdon, David. *Warhol.* New York: Harry N. Abrams, 1989.
Butte Blue Book of 1901, Butte-Silver Bow Archives, Butte, Montana.
Christian Science: A Sourcebook of Contemporary Materials. Boston: Christian
    Science Publishing Society, 1990.
Crane, Diana. *The Transformation of the Avant-Garde: The New York Art World,
    1940–1985.* Chicago: University of Chicago Press, 1987.
Eddy, Mary Baker. *Science and Health with Key to the Scriptures.* Boston: The
    First Church of Christ, Scientist, 1875. Reprint 1971.
Ferrier, Jean-Louis, and Yonn Le Pichon. *Art of Our Century: The Chronicle of
    Western Art, 1900 to the Present.* New York: Prentice Hall, 1988.
Gebhard, David. *Lutah Maria Riggs, A Woman in Architecture.* Santa Barbara:
    Capra Press and Santa Barbara Museum of Art, 1992.
Geldzahler, Henry. *American Painting in the Twentieth Century.* New York:
    Metropolitan Museum of Art, 1965.
——*Making It New: Essays, Interviews, and Talks.* New York: Turtle Point, 1994.
Giedion-Welcker, Carola. *Constantin Brancusi, 1876–1957.* Neuchatel: Editions du
    Griffon, 1958.
Glasscock, C.B. *The War of the Copper Kings: Builders of Butte and Wolves of Wall
    Street.* New York: Grosset & Dunlap, 1935.

Goodrich, Lloyd. *Yasuo Kuniyoshi*. New York: Whitney Museum of American Art, 1948.

Gruen, John. *The Artist Observed: Twenty-eight Interviews With Contemporary Artists*. Pennington, New Jersey: a cappella, 1991.

Guggenheim, Peggy. *Out of This Century: Confessions of an Art Addict*. New York: Universe, 1979.

Haden-Guest, Anthony. *True Colors: The Real Life of the Art World*. New York: Atlantic Monthly Press, 1996.

Hedberg, Gregory, ed. *The Tremaine Collection: 20th Century Masters, The Spirit of Modernism*. Hartford: Wadsworth Atheneum, 1984.

Hess, Thomas B. *Barnett Newman*. New York: Walker, 1969.

History of Montana. N.P., 1899. Butte-Silver Bow Public Archives.

Hitchcock, Henry-Russell. *Painting Toward Architecture*. New York: Duell, Sloan and Pearce, 1948.

Holtzman, Harry, and Martin S. James, ed. and trans. *The New Art—The New Life: The Collected Writings of Piet Mondrian*. Boston: G. K. Hall, 1986.

Horne, Charles F. *Source Records of the Great War*, Vol. I. National Alumni, 1923.

Howard, Joseph Kinsey. *Montana: High, Wide, and Handsome*. New Haven: Yale University Press, 1943.

James, Don. *Butte's Memory Book*. Caldwell, Idaho: Caxton Printers, 1980.

Kasher, Steven. *The Art of Hitler*. Catalog produced for the exhibit "The Art of Hitler" at the Key Gallery, New York, Jan. 23–March 6, 1993.

Krauss, Rosalind E. *The Originality of the Avant-Garde, and Other Modernist Myths*. Cambridge: MIT Press, 1985.

Lane, John R., and Susan C. Larsen. *Abstract Painting and Sculpture in America, 1927–1944*. Pittsburgh: Museum of Art, Carnegie Institute and Harry N. Abrams, 1983.

Lindbergh, Charles A. *The Spirit of St. Louis*. New York: Charles Scribner's Sons, 1953.

Lipsey, Roger. *An Art of Our Own: The Spiritual in Twentieth Century Art*. Boston: Shambhala, 1997.

Lynes, Russell. *Good Old Modern: The Museum of Modern Art*. New York: Atheneum, 1973.

Marks, Robert W. *The Dymaxion World of Buckminster Fuller*. Garden City, NY: Anchor, 1973.

Marquis, Alice Goldfarb. *Alfred H. Barr, Jr.: Missionary for the Modern*. Chicago and New York: Contemporary, 1989.

Museum of Modern Art. *The International Council of the Museum of Modern Art: The First Forty Years*. New York: MoMA, 1993.

Myrick, David. *Montecito and Santa Barbara: The Days of the Great Estates*, Vol. II. Glendale: Trans-Anglo, 1991.

Naifeh, Steven, and Gregory White Smith. *Jackson Pollock: An American Saga*. New York: Clarkson N. Potter, 1989.

Naylor, Colin, ed. *Contemporary Artists*. Chicago: St James, 1989.

O'Neill, John P. ed. *Barnett Newman: Selected Writings and Interviews.* New York: Alfred A. Knopf, 1990.

Pruitt, Elizabeth, ed. *Tender Darkness: A Mary MacLane Anthology.* Belmont, Calif.: Abernathy & Brown, 1993.

Rheims, Maurice. *The Strange Life of Objects: Thirty-five Centuries of Art Collecting & Collectors.* New York: Atheneum Publishers, 1961.

Rosenthal, Mark. *Abstraction in the Twentieth Century: Total Risk, Freedom, Discipline.* New York: Guggenheim Museum Publications, 1996.

Rubinstein, Charlotte Streifer. *American Women Artists: From Early Indian Times to the Present.* Boston: G. K. Hall, 1982.

Saarinen, Aline B. *The Proud Possessors: The Lives, Times and Tastes of Some Adventurous American Art Collectors.* New York: Random House, 1958.

Scheips, Marguerite T. *The Miller Company: The First 150 Years.* Meriden: The Miller Company, 1995.

Schulze, Franz. *Philip Johnson: Life and Work.* New York: Alfred A. Knopf, 1994.

Seuphor, Michel. *Piet Mondrian: Life and Work.* New York: Harry N. Abrams, 1957.

Sims, Lowery Stokes. *Stuart Davis: American Painter.* New York: Metropolitan Museum of Art, 1991.

Smith, Dean. *A Tale of Two Families: The Tremaines and the Chilsons.* Flagstaff: Bar T Bar Ranch Company, Limited Partnership, 1994.

Turner, Jane, ed. *The Dictionary of Art,* Vol. 18 and 26. London: Macmillan, 1996.

Varnedoe, Kirk. *Jasper Johns: A Retrospective.* New York: Museum of Modern Art, 1996.

Wadsworth Atheneum. *A. Everett Austin, Jr.: A Director's Taste and Achievement.* Hartford: Wadsworth Atheneum, 1958.

Warhol, Andy, and Pat Hackett. *POPism: The Warhol '60s.* New York: Harcourt Brace Jovanovich, 1980.

Weber, Nicholas Fox. *Patron Saints: Five Rebels Who Opened America to a New Art, 1928–1943.* Paperback reprint, New Haven: Yale University Press, 1995.

Weld, Jacqueline Bograd. *Peggy: The Wayward Guggenheim.* New York: E. P. Dutton, 1986.

INTERVIEWS, SPEECHES, UNPUBLISHED
PAPERS, AND DISSERTATIONS

Alfred Barr, Papers. New York: Museum of Modern Art. Available through the Archives of American Art, Smithsonian Institute.

Rembert, Virginia Lee. "Mondrian, America and American Painting." Ph.D. Diss., Columbia University, 1970. Ann Arbor: University Microfilms, 1971.

Saalfield, Agnes, "Piet Mondrian's Victory Boogie-Woogie." Unpublished paper, December 4, 1978. Emily Hall Tremaine Foundation Archives.

Tremaine, Emily Hall. "A New York Collector Selects," speech before the Society

for the Encouragement of Contemporary Art (SECA), San Francisco Museum of Art, January 21, 1965. Emily Hall Tremaine Foundation Archives and Wadsworth Atheneum Archives.
— interview with Paul Cummings, January 24, 1973. Oral History Program, Archives of American Art, Smithsonian Institute.
— interview with Susan Fondlier, undated, Emily Hall Tremaine Foundation Archives.

PERIODICALS

"Art for Architecture's Sake." *Interiors*. February 1949, 3.
Baro, Gene. "Decisive Art Collection," *Vogue*. 15 February 1969, 132–141.
Brach, Paul. "Toward Autonomy," *Art in America*. April 1988, 196–201.
Bradley, Jay. "Piet Mondrian, 1872–1944: Greatest Dutch Painter of Our Time." *Knickerbocker Weekly,* 14 February 1944, 16–23.
Chermayeff, Serge. "Painting Toward Architecture," *Arts and Architecture*. June 1948: 24–31.
Christie's. *Auction Catalogs: The Tremaine Collection*. Nov. 1988, Nov. 1991.
Fraser, Andrea. "In and Out of Place," *Art in America,* June 1985, 124.
Hall, Joseph, ed. "Horace M. Hall's Letters from Gillespie County, Texas, 1871–1873," offprint from *The Southwestern Historical Quarterly*, 62:3, 1959.
Hoffmann, Joyce. "Emily Tremaine and Friends," *Northeast Magazine, The Hartford Courant*. 6 November 1988, 8–15.
Holtzman, Harry. "Piet Mondrian." *League Quarterly*. Spring 1947, 4.
Louchheim, Aline B. "Abstraction on the Assembly Line," *Art News,* December 1947, 25–27.
Norman, Geraldine. "Risk and Recession." *Art & Antiques,* November 1991, 33.
"Painting Toward Architecture." *Arts and Architecture,* June 1948, 24.
"Produced Site Unseen: Design for a Vacation House by Oscar Niemeyer," *Interiors,* April 1949, 96–106.
Roob, Rona. "Fire and Water Lilies." *MoMA Members Quarterly,* Spring 1991, 24–25.
Scott, Martha. "Artful Living," *Connecticut Home & Garden,* October 1985, 18–28.
Tighe, Mary Ann. "Art at its Best," *House & Garden,* April 1984, 146–155.

CROSS-REFERENCE OF ART WITH THE

1984 EXHIBITION CATALOG

The following works of art appear in the exhibition catalog *The Tremaine Collection: Twentieth Century Masters, The Spirit of Modernism*. The asterisk indicates that the work is mentioned in this biography. Because the exhibition catalog is not indexed, page numbers are included for cross-reference.

INDEX

Seawright, James, 138
Secrets of the Sun (Erskine), 187
Segal, George, 174–5
Seitz, William, 175
Seuphor, Michel, 148, 150–1
7 Cent Air Mail (Warhol), 168
7-UP (Oldenburg) 1, 166
70 S & H Green Stamps (Warhol), 168
Sheeler, Charles, 94, 99, 174, 189
Signal (Takis), 153, 184
Silver and Black (Pollock), 147
Sinclair (Chamberlain), 169
Sinjerli Variation I (Stella), 207
Sleeping Girl (Taubes), 57
Small Black Screwdriver (Dine), 168
Small Blue Flowers (Warhol), 168
Small Landscape (Lichtenstein), 184
Smith, Beauchamp, 12
Smith, Stephen Morgan, 12–3
Soby, James Thrall, 98
Society for the Encouragement of Contemporary Art, 152, 174
Sonnabend, Ileana, 139
Sotheby's, 217
Soto, Jésus Raphael, 138, 149, 153, 184
Space-Time Construction No. III (Van Doesburg), 87, 98
Spanish Elegy Number 17 (Motherwell), 153, 184
Splitting the Ergo (Matta), 93
Spoon Woman (Giacometti), 137, 174, 189, 210
Spreckels, Adolph, 3, 46–52
Spring (Amino), 99
Stability Animated (Kandinsky), 71, 120
Stack (Noland), 188
Stanley, Janet Tremaine, 119, 121–2, 124, 129, 131
Stations of the Cross (Newman), 143, 208
Stella, Frank, 2, 120, 153, 182, 207
Still Life (Le Corbusier), 98
Still Life (Nicholson), 98
Still Life with Bird (Taubes), 56

Still-Life with Pears (Gris), 94
Street Head I (Oldenburg), 164
Strider, Marjorie, 172
Strong Arm (Oldenburg), 210
Swamp Pepperwood (Hague), 151
Sweeney, James J., 78, 164

Takis, Vassilakis, 138, 148–9, 153, 184
Tam-Tam, 148, 172–3
Tamayo, Rufino, 69, 259
Tango (Johns), 155, 189
Tate Gallery, 200
Taubes, Frederic, 56
Thompson, Bradbury, 98
Three Flags (Johns), 5, 104, 155–6, 200–4
Tinguely, Jean, 138, 148, 153
Tobey, Mark, 94–5
Transcendental Meditation, 181
Transfluent Lines (Pereira), 138
Tremaine, Alan, 106
Tremaine, Bertine, 106
Tremaine, Burton Gad (Lucky BG), 56, 106
Tremaine, Jr., Burton Gad, 114–5, 119, 130–5, 145, 193, 195, 219
Tremaine, Sr., Burton Gad, childhood, 53; death, 212; dispute with Wright, 111; first major art purchase, 141; marriage to Emily, 55; the Miller Co., 3, 53, 95–7
Tremaine, III, Burton Gad (Tony), 83, 119, 122
Tremaine, Carl, 106
Tremaine, Catherine, 133–4
Tremaine, Emily Hall, art director the Miller Co., 95; birth, 15; childhood, 15–23; courtship with Von Romberg, 22–3; courtship with Tremaine, 53–5; death, 212; death of Von Romberg, 44–5; divorce from Spreckels, 52; editor *Apéritif,* 33; marriage to Spreckels, 46; marriage to Tremaine, 55; marriage to Von Romberg, 26

PERMISSION ACKNOWLEDGMENTS

Correspondence from Frank Lloyd Wright to the Tremaines ©The Frank Lloyd Wright Foundation, Scottsdale, AZ, 85261.

PHOTOGRAPHIC CREDITS

The photographs of the Tremaine house in Madison, Connecticut, and the New York apartment were taken by Adam Bartos for *House and Garden,* April 1984, and are reprinted with his permission.

Tremaine with Laursen, from *The International Council of The Museum of Modern Art, The First Forty Years.* Tony Record and Gene Gordon, Telegram Photos. Courtesy of The International Council.

Board of Directors, The Emily Hall Tremaine Foundation, Lucien Capehart Photography Inc.